THE HIGH TIDE OF
AMERICAN CONSERVATISM

THE HIGH TIDE OF
AMERICAN CONSERVATISM

DAVIS, COOLIDGE, AND THE 1924 ELECTION

GARLAND S. TUCKER, III

EMERALD
BOOK CO.

Published by Emerald Book Company
Austin, TX
www.emeraldbookcompany.com

Distributed by Emerald Book Company

For ordering information or special discounts for bulk purchases, please contact Emerald Book Company at PO Box 91869, Austin, TX 78709, 512.891.6100.

Design and composition by Greenleaf Book Group LLC
Cover design by Greenleaf Book Group LLC

Publisher's Cataloging-In-Publication Data
(Prepared by The Donohue Group, Inc.)
Tucker, Garland S.
    The high tide of American conservatism : Davis, Coolidge, and the 1924 election / Garland S. Tucker, III. -- 1st ed.
      p. : ill. ; cm.
    ISBN: 978-1-934572-50-4

    1. Presidents--United States--Election--1924. 2. United States--Politics and government--1923-1929. 3. Conservatism--United States--History--20th century. 4. Davis, John W. (John William), 1873-1955. 5. Coolidge, Calvin, 1872-1933. 6. Presidential candidates--United States--Biography. I. Title.
JK526 1924 .T83 2010
324.973/0915   2010930972

Part of the Tree Neutral™ program, which offsets the number of trees consumed in the production and printing of this book by taking proactive steps, such as planting trees in direct proportion to the number of trees used: www.treeneutral.com

Printed in the United States of America on acid-free paper

10 11 12 13 14   10 9 8 7 6 5 4 3 2 1

First Edition

*This work is dedicated
to my wife, Greyson,
without whose encouragement I would have
neither started nor completed this book,*

and

*to the memory of my great friend Frank J. Gilliam,
who was a friend of John W. Davis and who
first introduced me to the Davis half of this story.*

TABLE OF CONTENTS

FOREWORD

When Ronald Reagan took down the portrait of Harry Truman in the Cabinet Room at the White House and replaced it with one of Calvin Coolidge, the press treated it as an act of meaningless eccentricity. It wasn't. Reagan had been an admirer of Coolidge for many years. For him, the change of portraits had real meaning. Their experiences, their values, even the issues that most engaged them were the same for Reagan and Coolidge.

It was in 1919 when Coolidge, then governor of Massachusetts, was catapulted onto the national stage by a single incident: his crackdown on the Boston police strike. "There is no right to strike against the public safety by anybody, anytime, anywhere," Coolidge declared. A similar moment occurred for Reagan in 1981, his first year as president. He fired striking air-traffic controllers and summoned the military to operate America's airports. Both Coolidge and Reagan acted against the advice of their closest advisers. In both cases, the decision to move boldly to preserve public order showed them to be no-nonsense leaders who would not be intimidated or trifled with.

I mention the similarity between Coolidge and Reagan because it touches on one of the central points of Garland

Tucker's riveting account of the 1924 presidential election that pitted Coolidge, the Republican incumbent, against Democrat John W. Davis. The consensus of historians is that the race was utterly conventional and uninteresting, the candidates dull and unimportant. Tucker shows the opposite is true. The election, with Robert La Follette running as a third-party Progressive, focused on issues that would rise again and again in American politics, notably in Reagan's time and more recently in the Barack Obama era. The 1924 race also foreshadowed the political struggle between an increasingly conservative Republican party and an unflinchingly liberal Democratic party that has endured ever since.

That historians (with a few exceptions like Robert Sobel) have largely failed to understand the significance of that election points to what Tucker has accomplished as a nonhistorian. His revisionist account not only upgrades the election in historical terms, but it also casts a fresh light on Coolidge and Davis. Tucker, an investment banker in Raleigh, North Carolina, with an MBA from Harvard Business School, is a pure amateur.

The contest between Coolidge and Davis was unique. It was the last time Republicans and Democrats chose conservatives as presidential candidates to run against each other. Tucker is justified, I think, in calling the election "the high tide of American conservatism." Both candidates favored limited government—minimalist in Coolidge's case—individual freedom, and low taxes, and the election took place in the middle of the politically conservative 1920s. Coolidge and Davis got 83 percent of the vote, the lone liberal, Robert La Follette, a meager 17 percent.

La Follette was old hat, a battler for progressivism for forty years. Compared to him, Coolidge and Davis were newcomers.

Based on his popularity for having broken the police strike, Coolidge was picked as Warren Harding's vice presidential running mate in 1920. When Harding died in 1923, Coolidge became president. Davis was a Wall Street lawyer who had served in Woodrow Wilson's administration as solicitor general and ambassador to Great Britain. It took 103 ballots at the Democratic convention before he won the nomination, still a record.

There was something more to Coolidge and Davis, something special, and Tucker captures it brilliantly. They grew up in small towns—Coolidge in Vermont, Davis in West Virginia—and were gentlemen admired for their personal integrity and unblemished morality. Coolidge was famous for being terse. Davis was noted for his graciousness. They were neither mean-spirited nor power hungry. I can't recall a presidential race in modern times between two such honorable men.

The nomination of Davis proved to be the last hurrah of Democratic conservatives. Never again would the party nominate a conservative as its presidential candidate. The 1924 election realigned the parties, though few other than Tucker have noted this. The Progressive Party collapsed afterward, and its supporters joined liberal Republicans in flocking to the Democratic Party. And the party lines that were set in stone—conservative Republicans versus liberal Democrats—have remained until now.

The Coolidge legacy is important. But, again, few historians have acknowledged it. Coolidge and Treasury Secretary Andrew Mellon fashioned an economic policy that emphasized across-the-board tax cuts, including a drop in the top rate on individual income that had risen to 77 percent during World War I. "I am convinced that the larger income of the country would actually yield more revenue to the government if the basis of taxation were scientifically revised downward," Coolidge said in his speech to Congress in December 1924. Two years later, the Revenue Act reduced the top rate to 25 percent. The result: higher tax revenues and what became known as the Coolidge Prosperity.

In the 1970s, a handful of free-market economists, several politicians, editorial writers for *The Wall Street Journal*, and syndicated columnist Robert Novak rediscovered the Coolidge economic formula. "The Coolidge boom," Novak wrote, "was built, not on stock speculation, but on his tax cuts." The born-again Coolidgites recruited Ronald Reagan, who was considering a bid for the 1980 Republican presidential nomination. Reagan, soon a true believer, persuaded Congress to cut individual tax rates by 25 percent in 1981.

In 1985, just after Reagan's second inauguration, he received a copy of Coolidge's Christmas greeting of 1927 from a man in Vermont named James M. Huntley. "I'm delighted to have it," Reagan wrote back to Huntley. "I happen to be an admirer of 'Silent Cal' and believe he has been badly treated by history. I've done considerable reading and researching of his presidency. He served this country very well and accomplished much before speaking the words, 'I do not choose to run.'" (That was Coolidge's concise statement that he wouldn't seek reelection in 1928.) I suspect Reagan would have liked Tucker's book enormously because it does what Reagan himself did in hanging Coolidge's portrait in the White House. It elevates Coolidge to a place of honor and respect among presidents.

—Fred Barnes, executive editor, *The Weekly Standard*

PREFACE

*The truth is the twenties was the most
fortunate decade in American history.*
—Paul Johnson

This book is first and foremost the story of two remarkable men,
John W. Davis and Calvin Coolidge. Modern historians have
consistently and regrettably ignored or belittled them. While
Coolidge has been summarily dismissed as an accidental president
who did nothing and thought nothing, Davis has faded quietly
into obscurity. It was through years of reading about these two
men that I developed a deep respect for them and decided to
write this book.

Calvin Coolidge was—in Paul Johnson's words—"the most
internally consistent and single-minded of American presidents."[1]
He was a successful and able politician who, despite his sobriquet
"Silent Cal," has left an articulate record of his conservative creed.
He was repeatedly elected to office by the people of Massachusetts,
finally serving as governor. In 1920, he was elected vice president
under President Harding and stepped into the presidency upon

Harding's death in 1923. With the gradual revelation of Harding administration scandals, it was a tribute to Coolidge's integrity that no scandal touched him. Not only did he articulate a coherent, thoughtful strand of conservatism, but he also came—quite accurately—to be seen as an icon for those solid American values of honesty, hard work, self-reliance, and thrift. In an age of sound bites, political spin, image handlers, and the like, it is refreshing to discover a president who was in every sense himself. Calvin Coolidge was the real thing—like him or not, you knew what he was.

The Democratic nominee in 1924, John W. Davis, was a man of unimpeachable integrity, immense personal charm, and extraordinary legal ability. He emerged from the House of Representatives to serve under Wilson, with widely recognized distinction, as solicitor general and as ambassador to Great Britain. He headed a major Wall Street firm, serving as counsel to J. P. Morgan & Co. and many other major corporations, and was president of the American Bar Association. By the end of his career, he had argued more cases before the Supreme Court, 140 in all, than anyone since Daniel Webster and was hailed among his profession as truly a lawyer's lawyer. Davis was an articulate champion of conservatism as a candidate in 1924, as a major opponent of the New Deal, and as a brilliant advocate before the Supreme Court. Although it is difficult for the modern reader to imagine, there appears never to have been even a trace of self-promotion in Davis's long career; he was always put forward for office by friends who knew him well. As Walter Lippmann observed of Davis, "I have seen a good many men under the awful temptation of the presidency. I have never seen another who had such absolute respect."[2]

Although Coolidge and Davis had very different personalities, there were interesting similarities in their political lives. Both were successful politicians, both emerged politically in the early Progressive era, both became increasingly conservative, both exemplified great integrity and personal ethics, and both reflected the best qualities of their respective regions. Davis was a Democrat dedicated to small government, states' rights, individual freedom, and free trade in the tradition of Jefferson, Madison, Cleveland, and Parker. Coolidge was a conservative Republican in the tradition of Lincoln, McKinley, and Harding. Both revered Jefferson's philosophy of limited government and individual freedom; and, coincidentally, Davis was born on Jefferson's birthday, and Coolidge was born on the Fourth of July. The old progressive warhorse William Jennings Bryan observed at the Democratic convention in July 1924 that Davis was a man of fine character; but he added with disgust, "So is Mr. Coolidge. There is no difference between them."[3]

Indeed, the 1920s—the setting for this story—is a decade long dismissed as a time of ephemeral prosperity, totally overshadowed and discredited by the events of the Great Depression and what was seen as the ensuing, final triumph of New Deal progressivism. The majority of American historians have viewed this decade as a temporary interruption in the rise of progressivism, sandwiched between Woodrow Wilson and Franklin D. Roosevelt. As Coolidge biographer Robert Sobel noted,

> Few presidents in all American history had as many acolytes among intellectuals as did Woodrow Wilson. Arthur M. Schlesinger, Jr., was an ardent

admirer of Wilson, whom he saw as the president who played John the Baptist for Franklin D. Roosevelt. Schlesinger was one of those who helped fashion this legend. In *The Age of Roosevelt*, in which Schlesinger presented this thesis, he discussed "the coming of the Republicans as though they were barbarians sacking Rome."[4]

Schlesinger was not alone in his partisan depiction of the Republican-dominated 1920s. In the widely acclaimed *A Pocket History of the United States*, Allan Nevins and Henry Steele Commager claimed, "The idealism of the Wilson era was in the past, the Rooseveltian passion for humanitarianism was in the future. The decade of the twenties was dull, bourgeois, and ruthless."[5] Two generations of American historians have now viewed the 1920s through the Schlesinger/Nevins/Commager prism. It is no wonder that the prevalent popular view of this era is in need of some historical balance. As economist Paul Rubin has written recently, "We now know that FDR's policies likely prolonged the Great Depression because the economy never fully recovered in the 1930s, and actually got worse in the latter half of the decade."[6]

With the advent of Ronald Reagan and the resurgence of American conservatism, the twentieth century can now be viewed in the context of a long-term, continuing national struggle between conservatism and liberalism. As modern historian Paul Johnson has concluded, "Coolidge Prosperity was huge, real, widespread," and it "showed that the concept of a property-owning democracy could be realized."[7] When viewed instead through this prism, the

1920s can be recognized as a period of remarkable economic growth, affirmation of basic conservative values, and emphasis on individual freedom and responsibility. It was quite a shock to most Americans in 1981—especially historians—when Ronald Reagan retrieved the portrait of Calvin Coolidge from storage and symbolically installed it in the White House Cabinet Room.

Buried within this decade of the 1920s, the 1924 presidential campaign lies largely forgotten. Much as the far more heralded election of 1912 represented the high tide of Progressivism, the election of 1924 can convincingly be viewed as the high tide of American conservatism. Of the twentieth-century presidents, Calvin Coolidge was the most Jeffersonian in philosophy and practice; and John W. Davis was the last nominee from the conservative, Jeffersonian wing of the Democratic Party. It is remarkable that both political parties nominated a bona fide conservative; and, in some ways, this election was a defining moment in American presidential election history.

Senator Robert La Follette and his short-lived resurrection of the Progressive Party in 1924 kept the progressive ideals before the public and ultimately provided a useful stopping point for progressive Republicans who eventually joined the Democratic Party. Since 1924, the Republican Party has generally been the conservative party, while the Democratic Party has not even seriously considered nominating a conservative candidate. Franklin Roosevelt commented shortly after Election Day, 1924, that it was useless for the Democrats to "wear the livery of the conservative"—a lesson the Democrats have not yet forgotten.[8]

The story of this election includes the astounding account of the 1924 Democratic convention. For two sweltering weeks and

103 ballots the Democrats tore themselves to shreds in the longest, most divisive convention in American history. In stark contrast, the Republican convention was touted as the most harmonious— and the dullest—convention on record. The ensuing campaign was valiantly, but hopelessly, waged by Davis and the Democrats, while Calvin Coolidge and the Republicans ran one of the most masterful campaigns ever.

As the country continues the historic debate over the proper role of government in a free society, Americans should reconsider the significance of the twenties, the 1924 election, and, most importantly, these conservative titans—John W. Davis and Calvin Coolidge.

Part One

THE SETTING: 1920–24

Chapter One

THE COUNTRY TURNS RIGHT

*The radicalism which had tinged our whole political and
economic life from soon after 1900 to the World War period
was passed. Its power had gone. The country had little interest
in mere destructive criticism. It wanted the progress that alone
comes from constructive policies.*
—Calvin Coolidge

As the presidential train lumbered across the Alps on January
6, 1919, returning from Italy to the Paris peace conference, an
aide handed President Woodrow Wilson a telegram. Wilson's old
political adversary and fellow progressive, Theodore Roosevelt,
was dead at age sixty. It was fewer than seven years since the
election of 1912, what has come to be viewed as the "high tide of
progressivism," and things were beginning to change.[1] Roosevelt
had dominated the Republican Party for two decades, constantly
pushing—sometimes bullying—the party into a leftward direction.
There was no progressive heir apparent within the party, and
conservative Republicans were sensing a change in the mood of
the country. At this moment, Woodrow Wilson stood upon the

pinnacle of popularity as the savior of Europe and architect of peace. However, within a mere eighteen months Wilson would fall victim to his own political ineptitude, a stroke, and the increasingly conservative mood of the country.

Progressivism had burst onto the American presidential scene in 1896 with William Jennings Bryan's galvanizing "cross of gold" speech to the Democratic convention. Bryan was catapulted forward as the party's nominee in 1896 and again in 1900 and yet again in 1908. In the first two elections, Bryan was squared off against Republican conservatism under William McKinley and soundly defeated twice. Progressivism then surfaced in the Republican Party under the dynamic Theodore Roosevelt. Roosevelt relished the exercise of power and executive action, believing the Constitution is not a straightjacket but rather a tool to be used by honest politicians for the betterment of the nation. Through the sheer force of his personality, Roosevelt was able to pull the Republican Party in a leftward direction. His handpicked successor, William Howard Taft, remained faithful to Roosevelt's progressive agenda but lacked the personality and drive to expand it.

The election of 1912 saw progressivism in full flower. Roosevelt challenged Taft for the Republican nomination and charged him with abandoning his progressive agenda. A tenacious battle ensued between Roosevelt, as the leader of the diehard progressives, and Taft, as the leader of moderate progressives and conservatives. When Taft was narrowly nominated, Roosevelt bolted the party and formed the Progressive (or Bull Moose) Party. Sensing the ascendant, progressive mood of the country, the Democrats nominated the reform-minded governor of New Jersey,

Woodrow Wilson. The great debate of 1912 was not whether to pursue a progressive agenda but rather at what speed. Taft was not for rolling back the recently enacted regulatory reforms, but Wilson and Roosevelt "embraced change, recognizing that their own careers could not flourish if they were to hold back the tide of reform. Neither leader believed that repose was essential to the happiness of mankind."[2] Wilson won the electoral vote handily, while securing only a minority of the popular vote; however, Wilson's and Roosevelt's combined popular vote represented a thumping endorsement for progressivism.

(COURTESY LIBRARY OF CONGRESS)

The election of 1912 marked the "high tide of progressivism." Here, Taft and his elephant and Wilson and his donkey are being attacked from the rear by Theodore Roosevelt on his bull moose.

Exactly what was the genesis of this progressive movement and what were its basic tenets? Some of the progressive tenets can be traced back to Jefferson. His vision of an agrarian democracy with power residing in the people and his distrust of Hamiltonian commercial interests became deeply embedded in nineteenth-century American thought, especially in the Democratic Party. These Jeffersonian principles were behind the postwar emergence of the Populist movement in the South and Midwest, which produced William Jennings Bryan.

It was under Bryan at the turn of the century that old-line Jeffersonian, small-government Democrats began to view the government not with Jeffersonian suspicion but rather as an ally and a necessary countervailing balance to protect individuals against what they saw as a dangerous concentration of economic power in American business. A fierce struggle raged within the Democratic Party in the last half of the nineteenth century between the economically conservative, "gold standard" faction personified by President Grover Cleveland and the Populist, "free silver" faction personified ultimately by Bryan. Because of his Populist roots, "weak currency" policies, and overheated rhetoric, Bryan was never able to capture the full support of the conservative wing of the Democratic Party.

The Republican Party experienced a similar struggle. In response to the post–Civil War emergence of a stronger, centralized Federal government, the rapid industrialization of America with significant concentration of wealth and power, and the corruption scandals resulting from a long period of Republican Party dominance, there emerged a Reform wing of the Republican Party. This Reform wing did not have Populist origins as in the Democratic Party, nor did it have a Jeffersonian distrust of government, but rather it focused on rooting out corruption and counterbalancing the perceived excesses of laissez-faire capitalism. Instead of the Populist, egalitarian, antibusiness views of the Democratic Progressives, there was more a sense of noblesse oblige in the Republican reformers. They tended to be at the very heart of the "eastern establishment," and it was from this background that Theodore Roosevelt emerged.

Roosevelt and the Republican reformers were presented their opportunity to govern with the assassination of William McKinley, who represented the conservative, "sound money," minimalist government, laissez-faire wing of the GOP. With his dynamic personality and boundless energy, Roosevelt became the dominant figure both within the Republican Party and on the national stage from his ascendancy to the presidency in 1901 until his death in 1919, despite the fact that he never fully won over the conservative, pro-business Republican base.

By the election of 1920, the country had experienced nineteen years of progressivism under Roosevelt's Square Deal, Taft's conscientious enforcement of Roosevelt's reforms, and Wilson's New Freedom. In addition to the domestic reforms, the massive effort required to wage World War I resulted in centralizing, interventionist policies. The advent of the United States as a world power brought the high-flown idealism of Wilson's Fourteen Points and the great fight over the League of Nations. The country was understandably tired from the war effort, but it also seemed exhausted by the exhortations of Roosevelt and Wilson for activism, reform, and government intervention.

The Democrats faced the 1920 election with President Wilson sequestered in a White House bedroom as an invalid, guarded from the public by his wife. The party turned aside President Wilson's pathetic overtures for a third term and nominated the businessman-editor governor of Ohio, James M. Cox after forty-four exhausting ballots. Cox was an effective, business-oriented Democrat in a Republican state. He was a popular governor and the first Democrat elected three times governor in Ohio as a moderate progressive. Cox declared, "I sympathize with Jefferson's view that that is the best government that governs least—but in this age, I consider also the best government is the one that concerns itself most with the betterment of its people."[3] In gaining the nomination, Cox defeated seventeen potential candidates, including William G. McAdoo, Wilson's son-in-law; A. Mitchell Palmer, Wilson's red-baiting attorney general; and Al Smith of New York. Cox proved to be the right Democratic candidate to unite the disparate elements of the party: Wilson progressives, southern conservatives, wets, drys, labor, and business. The vice presidential nomination went to Franklin D. Roosevelt, former assistant secretary of the Navy, in the hope of transferring some luster to the ticket from a famous name. Cox and Roosevelt, somewhat halfheartedly, picked up the Wilsonian mantle, supported the League of Nations, and spoke vaguely of continued domestic reform.

After their bruising convention, Democrats tried to rally around Cox, but it was clear to most observers that the tide was running strongly against them. Cox and Roosevelt made a sober pilgrimage to obtain Wilson's blessing and then campaigned on the old Progressive platform. On the stump, Cox told voters, "I have no doubt that the thought of the country is predominantly and decisively progressive. The prevailing feeling of the country is progressive."[4] Cox and Roosevelt conducted a high-level campaign that focused on the issues, but they "misjudged the mind of the people. The people were tired: tired from war, tired from the suffering and bloodshed, tired from hysteria, tired from the vast expenditures of money and morale and manpower, tired from eight years of idealism."[5] Frederick Lewis Allen further explained the national mood in *Only Yesterday*: "The nation was spiritually tired. Wearied by the excitements of the war and the nervous tension of the Big Red Scare, they hoped for quiet and healing. Sick of Wilson and his talk of America's duty to humanity, callous to political idealism, they hoped for a chance to pursue their private affairs without governmental interference and to forget about public affairs."[6]

The Republicans correctly sensed the conservative swing in popular sentiment. After a bruising, indecisive contest among General Leonard Wood, Senator Hiram Johnson of California, and Illinois Governor Frank Lowden, Ohio Senator Warren Harding emerged as the nominee. The war-weary country was leery of the old Rough Rider, General Wood. The party regulars had never forgiven Senator Johnson for his role in Charles Evans Hughes's failure to carry California in 1916, which consequently reelected Wilson. Governor Lowden, the son-in-law of millionaire George Pullman, was viewed as too conservative by the progressives. As stalemate settled over the convention, the party bosses convened in a proverbially smoked-filled hotel room and settled on Warren Harding. He was a McKinley/Hanna conservative and represented "the 'old America' before the Wilson watershed."[7] Warren Harding was a small-town Ohio newspaper editor with just the sort of image and values the American people were looking for in 1920. He was congenial but dignified, conservative but not reactionary, formidable but not intimidating. He seemed just the right sort of man to return the country to "normalcy." As Allen noted, "There might be no such word in the dictionary as *normalcy*, but normalcy was what they (the American people) wanted."[8] Even the progressives saw something appealing in Harding: *The New Republic* wrote, "Harding stands for a kind of candid and unpretentious reaction that anyone can respect, and that a great many people momentarily desire."[9]

In a development that was *not* orchestrated by the Republican Party bosses and was to prove historically significant, the convention delegates rejected the bosses' choice, Senator Irvine Lenroot, for the vice presidential nomination and resoundingly nominated Massachusetts Governor Calvin Coolidge by a wide margin. This groundswell of delegate support for Coolidge was an important indicator of the mood of the people. Calvin Coolidge had served the people of Massachusetts in a series of offices before his election as governor in 1918. He had developed a consistent image as a hardworking, honest, conservative politician, whose trademark was brevity—universally acknowledged to be a most unusual trademark in his profession.

Coolidge was thrust onto the national stage in the summer of 1919 with the Boston police strike. This strike was set against the backdrop of the first Red Scare. The American public recoiled from the excesses of the Russian revolution and fear of spreading bolshevism and anarchy. In addition, the labor reforms of the past twenty years were encouraging millions of Americans to strike in the postwar period. This strike burst upon the national scene and received widespread national press coverage. The leading labor organizer of the day, Samuel Gompers, was soon involved and opposing lines were quickly drawn.

Governor Coolidge responded slowly but with skill and deliberation to defuse the potentially explosive situation. There were intense negotiations between the police commissioner and Gompers, and Governor Coolidge sought to find a peaceful, nonconfrontational solution. At the critical moment, as negotiations began clearly to fail, the governor issued the dramatic, yet terse, statement, "There is no right to strike against the public safety by anybody, anywhere, anytime."[10] When the union blinked and violent action was averted, Coolidge became a national celebrity: "The pithy announcement was classic Coolidge, neatly articulating what struck many as commonplace wisdom with a tautness that made it ripe for repetition in newspapers, newsreels, and conversation."[11]

The sound bite struck a responsive cord in the American public; but more significantly, this episode foreshadowed how Coolidge was to govern as president. He tended to work intensely, but quietly, on a problem until he became convinced of the correct plan of action and that the time for action was at hand. Then he acted decisively. Ironically, he was arguably better at carrying out Roosevelt's admonition, "Speak softly and carry a big stick," than Roosevelt himself.

Nominee Harding announced a McKinleyesque front-porch campaign, pointedly harkening back to the pre-Roosevelt era. GOP progressives made several halfhearted attempts to revive the Bull Moose Party, but there emerged no third party challenge in 1920. The Republican progressives perceived the rightward shift and anticipated that a Harding administration would reflect the cautious, conservative record of the senator's legislative career. While Coolidge campaigned leisurely in New England and the South, Harding issued a series of statements from his front porch in Marion, Ohio. Both men supported the League of Nations—of course, with the Lodge reservations—and both men spoke often in favor of lower taxes and reduced government expenditures and intervention. It was clear the spirit of Mark Hanna had prevailed over that of Roosevelt, and the GOP was tacking to the right.

The Republican delegates in Chicago accurately read the times in nominating Harding and Coolidge. The Republican ticket was elected in a landslide: over 60 percent of the popular vote and 404 of the 531 electoral votes. The Republicans swept the congressional races: the GOP senate margin rose from two to twenty, while Republicans in the House of Representatives rose from 233 to 289. The Democrats held on to the South but little else. Coolidge declared years later in his autobiography that this progressivism, which had "tinged our whole political and economic life" for the first two decades of the twentieth century was now repudiated. The election of 1920 ended an era that had "seemed to substitute words for things."[12]

Chapter Two

COOLIDGE'S AMERICA:
ARCADIA OR BABYLON?

*If Harding loved America as Arcadia, Coolidge was best
equipped to preserve it as such. No public man carried
into modern times more comprehensively the founding
principles of Americanism.*
—Paul Johnson

With the election of Harding and Coolidge in 1920, the country
took a decided turn to the right. Harding's campaign prescription
was, "America's present need is not heroes but healing; not
nostrums but normalcy; not revolution but restoration . . . not
surgery but serenity."[1] This return to normalcy struck a responsive
chord with a public that was exhausted and disillusioned by a
world war, fearful of the Red Scare, suspicious of the League
of Nations, and grappling with one of the sharpest recessions in
U. S. history. The civilian as well as the military bureaucracy had
ballooned rapidly over the war years, and the country now faced
the imminent need to absorb these civilian and military wartime
workers back into the American economy.

With the October 1917 revolution in Russia, the threat and fear of communist upheaval spread through western Europe and to the United States. As Frederick Lewis Allen noted, "If the American people turned a deaf ear to Woodrow Wilson's plea for the League of Nations during the early years of the post war decade, it was not simply because they were too weary of foreign entanglements and noble efforts to heed him. They were listening to something else. They were listening to ugly rumors of a huge radical conspiracy against the government and institutions of the United States."[2] While Wilson was largely removed from governmental affairs by his illness, his attorney general, A. Mitchell Palmer, mounted a highly publicized response to the Red Scare. In public statements, Palmer warned the American public that Red plots were a real threat, and the public responded with hysteria. There was widespread suspicion and intolerance, and a concurrent development was the resurgence of the Ku Klux Klan as a political power well outside the South.

The League of Nations, which had begun as a loosely defined bipartisan call to achieve the peace that had been promised by the "war to end all wars," had sunk into the quagmire of international wrangling at the Versailles conference and partisan sniping in the United States Senate. Incapacitated by illness, Wilson became adamant in his refusal to accept any reservations or changes to the treaty. Senator Henry Cabot Lodge and the Republicans generally favored the treaty but insisted on a number of reservations. After an exhausting struggle in the Senate, the treaty was finally defeated. A separate resolution for peace with Germany was passed by both houses but vetoed by Wilson. The country remained technically still at war, while as Frederick Lewis Allen noted, "President Wilson's last hope was that the election of 1920 would serve as a 'great and solemn referendum' in which the masses of the people—those masses who, he had always claimed, were on his side—would rise to vindicate him and the country."[3]

Against this backdrop of postwar dislocation and mild unrest, the country entered a very sharp recession in early 1919. Unemployment ultimately soared to 20 percent and GNP plunged by a whopping 17 percent. Bankruptcies hit an all-time high of more than thirty thousand in 1920, and there were some half million farm foreclosures. As Robert Sobel observed, "Economic fears now compounded the disillusion with the war."[4]

In accepting the vice presidential nomination in 1920, Coolidge had laid out the Republicans' rightward vision with clarity: "In a free republic, a great government is the product of a great people. They will look to themselves rather than government for success. The destiny, the greatness of America lies around the hearthstone. If thrift and industry are taught there, and the example of self-sacrifice oft appears, if honor abide there, and high ideals, if there the building of fortune be subordinate to the building of character, America will live in security, rejoicing in an abundant prosperity and good government at home and in peace, respect, and confidence abroad."[5]

As president-elect, Harding assembled a cabinet that included some first-rate leaders: Charles Evans Hughes at State, Andrew Mellon at Treasury, and Herbert Hoover at Commerce. Hughes was former governor of New York, Supreme Court justice, and GOP presidential nominee, and he was widely regarded as one of the foremost statesmen of the era. Andrew Mellon was probably the second-richest man in the country, after John D. Rockefeller. And he had built a banking and industrial empire with unquestioned personal integrity. He was a regular financial backer of the GOP but was generally believed to be above partisan politics. Herbert Hoover was widely revered as an humanitarian hero of the war in recognition of his postwar efforts to feed a starving Europe.

(COURTESY OF LIBRARY CONGRESS)

This 1921 photo captures President Harding and his cabinet assembling on the White House grounds.

Unfortunately, Harding was less careful in selecting friends and colleagues to fill other slots, especially Harry Daugherty as attorney general and Albert Fall as secretary of the interior. Daugherty was a political confidant of Harding's and his campaign manager in the landslide 1920 victory. Daugherty assured Harding, "I know who the crooks are, and I want to stand between Harding and them."[6] Regrettably, Daugherty failed to deliver on his pledge.

Fall was a generally well-regarded senator from New Mexico. He enjoyed the support of Hughes, but would soon prove unworthy of the trust Hughes, Harding, and others placed in him. As details of the infamous Teapot Dome scandal surfaced, Fall resigned in disgrace in March 1923, after Harding summoned him to the White House and blasted him with "You double-crossing bastard."[7]

Harding exercised his electoral mandate by cutting government expenditures an amazing 40 percent from Wilson's postwar levels, decreasing taxes, promoting an environment conducive to economic expansion, and pursuing a mildly internationalist foreign policy. On the domestic front, Harding successfully dealt with the severe recession by lowering government spending, cutting taxes, allowing wages to fall, and encouraging business investment to return. By late 1921, the recession was over, and the economy was booming. As Paul Johnson has written, this was "the last time a major industrial power treated a recession by classic laissez-faire methods, allowing wages to fall to their natural level."[8]

It has been difficult for historians who are sympathetic to Wilson's and FDR's progressivism to appreciate—or even to understand—Harding's governing philosophy. He viewed government's primary role as providing a stable, hospitable environment that encouraged capital investment and individual initiative. Secretary Mellon articulated administration economic policy, and he firmly believed that "reducing taxation on business earnings would enable more of the profits to be plowed back in for expansion and growth, thereby creating new jobs and promoting economic recovery."[9] Revealingly, Allan Nevins has written of

Harding's administration, "As Wilson's towering vision crashed into the dust, Harding, Coolidge, and Mellon opened an era of selfish materialism."[10] Similarly, "In Schlesinger's view, which is quite typical of critics of the Republican 1920s, the period is a dismal valley between reformist Wilsonian New Freedom and the Rooseveltian New Deal. Wilson appears on the scene and clearly is a hero, but then he is followed by the foolish and short-sighted trios of Harding-Coolidge-Hoover, and they in turn are succeeded by a reincarnation of Wilson in the form of Franklin D. Roosevelt."[11]

In foreign policy, Harding was not an isolationist. Significant foreign policy achievements included a peace treaty with the Central Powers, the Washington Naval Conference of 1921, and the end of the Red Scare. Hughes and Mellon adroitly negotiated with the European nations on war debt and reparations issues. While Mellon noted, "We ended the war with everyone owing us and our owing no one,"[12] he was realistic about the need for payment flexibility and recognition of the economic problems facing postwar Europe. Mellon exerted firm leadership in these matters throughout the 1920s and established strong ties of credibility between Europe and the United States, which proved significant in the years leading up to World War II.

Harding continued to enjoy tremendous popularity with the American public during his three-year presidency, despite several scandals surfacing during his last months in office. He had dealt with Secretary Fall, would have probably dealt successfully with Daugherty had he lived, and "his own hands were completely clean, so far as the latest historical research has been able to establish."[13] As Harding headed west in mid-1923, he was beginning to worry about the misdeeds of his weaker appointments, but the country gave every indication of approval of their president.

In the months following Harding's death on August 2, 1923, details of these scandals were fully aired. Although no direct link to Harding himself was ever proven, the scandals stained his historical record. More significantly, a majority of historians began a relentless deconstruction of the Harding record and, in its place, have left a widely held view that Harding was himself a crook, a philanderer, and a political lightweight. In the years after his death, a stream of historians, including Frederick Lewis Allen, Allan Nevins, Arthur Schlesinger, Jr., and others, consistently denigrated Harding along with Coolidge and Hoover, and, by the 1960s, a poll of America's leading historians ranked Harding as one of the least-effective presidents. It is quite surprising to most twenty-first-century Americans to learn that upon Harding's death, his body lay in state in the Capitol rotunda, the country was plunged into heartfelt mourning, and "the name of Lincoln continued to be heard incessantly."[14]

As the country absorbed the news of Harding's sudden death and genuinely mourned his passing, the picture of Calvin Coolidge taking the oath of office became indelibly stamped on the country's collective consciousness. Coolidge was vacationing at his father's farm in Vermont when word came by telegraph of Harding's death. He took the oath of office from his father, Colonel John Coolidge, a notary, in the small family living room by the light of a kerosene lamp. It is impossible to imagine a more appropriate backdrop for Coolidge's rise to the presidency. He was the product of rural America—a man totally without pretense—straightforward, frugal, and honest. Upon being told by his father that he had become president, Coolidge dressed, knelt by his bed to offer a short prayer, and then proceeded downstairs, thinking (as he later recalled) "I believe I can swing it."[15] This was the first picture Americans got of their new president, and they liked what they saw. It is true that all presidents enter the office with a honeymoon period of goodwill, and this was certainly the case as Coolidge succeeded the popular Harding. However, Coolidge was to prove a master at retaining the public's affection throughout his tenure as president and, indeed, throughout his life.

(BY PERMISSION DIVISION FOR HISTORIC PRESERVATION, STATE OF VERMONT.)

The swearing in of Calvin Coolidge as president by his father in the family's modest Vermont living room by lamplight provided the perfect launching pad for Coolidge's 1924 reelection campaign.

The country was about to discover that Calvin Coolidge was totally unlike any national politician it had encountered. He seemed consistently to eschew the conventional political necessities of warmth and congeniality; and even more surprising, he was truly a man of very few words. He was at once both, in William Allen

White's words, a "throwback to the more primitive days of the Republic" and also a highly successful modern politician, who was the first president to use radio, photography, and public relations adroitly. It was remarkable that this physically unimpressive, undramatic, reticent New Englander could have so dominated his era, elicited the affections of the public, and modeled the virtues that gave it substance. For an America that was experiencing postwar disillusionment and a bewildering modern secularism, Coolidge offered faith in a mythic America of honesty, hard work, thrift, and religion. As William Allen White concluded, Coolidge was, in fact, a political genius, but this genius was surprisingly— fascinatingly—unconventional in every way.[16]

(COURTESY OF THE "DING" DARLING WILDLIFE SOCIETY)

This 1923 cartoon shows the ghost of Warren Harding placing a pen in Coolidge's hand as he begins to write the history of his own administration.

Coolidge was comfortable with the conservative philosophy of Warren Harding, but he brought a more systematic and focused philosophy of government to the office than did Harding. He was dedicated first and foremost to the rule of law. Coolidge began his political career in the waning days of Lord Salisbury's career in England and developed a very similar philosophy of government. Salisbury often compared the English nation to a boat being carried down river, with the function of a wise government being "merely to put out an oar when there is any danger of its drifting into the bank."[17] Paul Johnson has noted that Coolidge's philosophy of government was more a "state of mind" rather than a philosophy. Much like Queen Elizabeth I, Coolidge consistently practiced a policy of "masterly inaction."[18] As Walter Lippmann wrote perceptively during Coolidge's presidency, "Mr. Coolidge's genius for inactivity is developed to a very high point. It is far from being an indolent activity. It is a grim, determined, alert inactivity which keeps Mr. Coolidge occupied constantly."[19] A key to understanding Coolidge's philosophy of intentional inaction is in the advice he once gave to Herbert Hoover: "If you see ten troubles coming down the road, you can be sure that nine will run into the ditch before they reach you, and you have to battle with only one of them."[20] Coolidge was consistently a minimalist. Twentieth-century historians have tended to lionize activist presidents and, hence, have not been sympathetic to Coolidge.

Coolidge retained Harding's cabinet as he settled into the presidency. He held an interesting view concerning presidential delegation, which was no doubt informed by his experience as Harding's vice president. He believed a president should delegate a great deal of authority to cabinet members, explaining, "The

This photo captures the face of the Republican Party in the 1920s: President Calvin Coolidge, Secretary of Treasury Andrew Mellon, and Secretary of Commerce Herbert Hoover.

president shouldn't do too much, and he shouldn't *know* too much. The president can't resign. If a member of the cabinet makes a mistake and destroys his standing with the country, he can get out, or the president can ask him to get out. But if he has involved the president in the mistake, the president has to stay there to the end of his term."[21]

Coolidge's most trusted advisor became Treasury Secretary Andrew Mellon with whom he developed and implemented the economic framework for the great economic expansion of the 1920s. A modern historian has written, "Between Coolidge and

Mellon there was also a personal bond. Later it would be said of them that they conversed entirely in pauses."[22] Theirs was a shared faith in minimal government, individual responsibility, and free markets. Coolidge developed a more strained relationship with Commerce Secretary Herbert Hoover. Because of Hoover's propensity to attack economic problems with governmental action, Coolidge called Hoover "Wonder Boy" and once commented of Hoover, "That man has given me nothing but advice, and all of it bad."[23]

(COURTESY FORBES LIBRARY, NORTHAMPTON, MA)

The Coolidge cabinet, 1925. To the president's left, Secretary Mellon, Attorney General Sargent, and Secretaries Wilbur, Jardine, and Davis. Front: Secretaries Kellogg, Weeks, New, Woods, and Hoover.

In addition to retaining Harding's cabinet, Coolidge carefully retained Harding's agenda at the outset of his presidency. He saw his first objective as to handle expeditiously the scandals he inherited from Harding and to gain the public's respect. In this he was extremely successful. He dealt with the Teapot Dome Affair, Secretary Fall, and Attorney General Daugherty without sustaining any allegation of impropriety on his part. Similarly, his first State of the Union message was cautiously launched from Harding's agenda. The *Cincinnati Enquirer* reported, "No one can read the [State of the Union] message of President Coolidge without appreciating how fully he is in sympathy and accord with every vital policy of the Harding administration. Comprehensive in scope, frank and clear in all suggestions and recommendations, dealing plainly with the most controversial issues, it is a message to

(COURTESY OF THE "DING" DARLING WILDLIFE SOCIETY)

Coolidge heads into his own presidency burdened with numerous troubles inherited from his predecessor.

all the people as well as to the Congress."[24] Coolidge was the last American president to write his own speeches, and he proved to be a master of communicating with the American public. Consistently he emphasized brevity, but he developed a real rapport with the people who came to believe in his candor and honesty.

In his first year as president, Coolidge spoke often about the need for cutting taxes. The federal income tax was only ten years old, but it had been expanded greatly during the war. Despite peace, the top bracket in 1920 stood at an oppressive 73 percent, and there was a general outcry for tax reduction. Coolidge and Mellon strongly urged Congress to return rates to their prewar levels, and they finally compromised with the passage of the Simmons-Longworth Bill in 1923, which reduced the top rate to 40 percent. Tax reductions were to become the centerpiece of Coolidge-Mellon economic policy both in the 1924 election and in Coolidge's elected term as president.

Secretary Mellon's rationale for tax cuts was laid out in his book, *Taxation: the People's Business.* His claim was simple: tax rates affect the behavior of business and investors, lower tax rates will produce general economic growth and also higher revenues for government. The heart of Mellon's tax policy was "Any man of energy and initiative in this country can get what he wants out of life. But when initiative is crippled by legislation or by a tax system which denies him the right to receive a reasonable share of his earnings, then he will no longer exert himself and the country will be deprived of the energy on which its continued greatness depends."[25] Coolidge stoutly endorsed Mellon's views, saying, "the wise and correct course to follow in taxation and all other economic legislation is not to destroy those who have already secured success but to create conditions under which every one will have a better chance to be successful."[26] Early in his presidency, tax reform became a Coolidge issue, resounding positively with the public, as the election of 1924 would soon indicate.

Historians continue to debate the 1920s. Was the America of this decade the biblical Whore of Babylon, prostituting herself for materialism? Nevins and Commager decried the decade as "dull, bourgeois, and ruthless";[27] and William Allen White forever identified Coolidge as the "Puritan in Babylon." Effete intellectuals belittled the 1920s in such phrases as Edmund Wilson's "a drunken fiesta" and F. Scott Fitzgerald's "the greatest, gaudiest spree in history." They saw the great "Coolidge Prosperity" as ephemeral and were repulsed by what they saw as intellectual shallowness.

In stark contrast, other historians, such as Paul Johnson, have hailed the decade as the "Last Arcadia"—"What the twenties demonstrates was the relative speed with which industrial productivity could transform luxuries into necessities and spread them down the class pyramid."[28] Economic facts indicate that prosperity was indeed more widespread—and more widely distributed—than at any time in American history up to this point. Millions of Americans for the first time acquired a home, a car, and labor-saving appliances—many of the middle-class advantages that had hitherto been beyond their reach. "Coolidge Prosperity" was indeed real, but it was not permanent. "What prosperity ever is? But it is foolish and unhistorical to judge it insubstantial because of what we now know followed later."[29]

Part Two

THE PARTIES

Chapter Three

THE DEMOCRATS

Historically, the Democratic Party has been a product
of discordant elements and discordant ideas.
—Henry L. Stimson

From its inception until the early decades of the twentieth century, the Democratic Party was commonly observed to be not so much a unified political party with a cohesive philosophy but rather a loose coalition of disparate groups held together primarily by the hope of winning national elections. Party roots could be traced back to Jefferson, who formed a national anti-Federalist party based on limited government and individual rights. The party was further defined by Andrew Jackson, who successfully defeated the Whigs and the Bank of the United States. The antebellum Democratic Party had a strongly proslavery faction in the South, while northern Democrats were unionists but not abolitionists. In the watershed election of 1860, the Democrats split, with John Breckinridge leading the southern wing and Stephen A. Douglas leading the "national" Democrats. With this split, the Democrats handed the election to Lincoln and the newly emerged Republican Party.

After the Civil War and the end of Reconstruction, the Democratic Party was essentially the sole political party in what became known as "the solid South." Southern Democrats espoused generally Jeffersonian ideals, especially states' rights, free trade, and white supremacy. The Republican Party reveled in its history as the party of Lincoln, became known as "the Grand Old Party" that saved the Republic, advocated high tariffs to protect American business, and was the dominant party from New England across the Midwest to the West Coast. The Democrats surfaced outside the South after the Civil War as a competitive force, especially in urban centers with heavy immigrant populations such as New York, Philadelphia, and Chicago. These national Democrats tended to support free trade and, in general, less federal government intervention. From 1868 until 1932, the country's partisan division remained relatively unchanged. The South was solidly Democratic, while New England and the rural Midwest were largely Republican. The challenge for the Democrats was always to nominate a presidential candidate who could hold the South while appealing to enough northern and midwestern Independent and Republican voters to win an electoral majority. Between 1860 and 1912, Grover Cleveland, the popular conservative governor of New York, was the only Democrat to cobble together a national victory. As long as the Republicans were united, they tended to be the dominant party.

With the advent of William Jennings Bryan and his populist message in the late 1890s, the Democrats began moving toward a more national philosophy. Bryan's populism appealed to the South, midwestern farmers, and the labor/immigrant population in urban America. However, Bryan's economic policies split the Democrats into "Cleveland Democrats," who supported "sound money" and retention of the gold standard, and Bryanites, who supported "free silver" and abandonment of the gold standard. It was from this populist, Bryan base that Woodrow Wilson was able to defeat a divided Republican Party in 1912 and, more impressively, to secure narrowly his reelection over a united Republican Party in 1916. With his boldly progressive domestic agenda and especially with the requirements of wartime governance, Wilson introduced America and the Democratic Party to a greatly expanded federal government. With Wilson, the Democratic Party moved away from its Jeffersonian roots of limited government. Paul Johnson observed that the Democratic Party gradually "began to see a strong federal government, with wide powers of intervention, as the defender of the ordinary man and woman against the excesses of corporate power."[1]

(LIBRARY OF CONGRESS)
Woodrow Wilson won the election of 1912, riding the
"high tide of progressivism" into the White House.

After campaigning on a decidedly antiwar platform in 1916, a reelected Wilson soon found himself leading a somewhat reluctant, somewhat isolationist America into a World War of unprecedented proportions. The resources required to wage this war resulted in enormous pressure to centralize the American federal system. Democrats, who had heretofore espoused Jefferson's tenets of small government, now found themselves presiding over a rapidly expanding and increasingly interventionist government. Wilson's administration was indeed a watershed event for the Democratic Party as well as the nation. The shadow of Woodrow Wilson loomed large over his party in the 1920s. As the nation shifted to the right in the election of 1920, would the Democrats abandon Bryan/Wilson progressivism and revert to their Jeffersonian roots? The party hedged in nominating Ohio Governor James M. Cox as a compromise candidate, appealing to both Wilson progressives as well as the more conservative Democrats. The result was a stinging defeat with each side blaming the other. As the Democrats approached the 1924 election, they were very much a split party with many still defining themselves as Jeffersonian, small-government Democrats.

Reeling from the drubbing in 1920, the Democrats scored something of a rebound in the off-year elections in 1922, although the GOP retained control of both houses of Congress. With the death of Harding in 1923, the as yet unproven abilities of Calvin Coolidge, and the emergence of the Harding scandals, the Democrats began to sense at least the possibility of victory in 1924.

Several front-runners emerged. Woodrow Wilson's son-in-law, William G. McAdoo, was without question the best-known candidate nationally. He had served quite ably as secretary of the treasury and was in many ways the father of the modern Federal Reserve System, and he personified a number of the core Democratic constituencies. He was a southerner who had become a successful businessman in New York City and who had broad appeal to the significant Prohibitionist and Ku Klux Klan factions in the party. He was an important figure in this era, who, as one historian noted, "never quite got his deserts [sic] in the political arena at the time, or has received the historic accolade he earned."[2] Despite these attributes and accomplishments, McAdoo had throughout his career also developed a reputation for being too ambitious. Newton Baker, Wilson's secretary of war, remarked, "McAdoo had the greatest lust for power I ever saw."[3] Though McAdoo had been a serious candidate in 1920, he failed to carry the convention. He entered the 1924 convention with approximately half the delegate votes, but the required two-thirds majority was well beyond his reach.

The second front-runner, Governor Al Smith of New York, was one of the most colorful characters in American politics. Hailing from the Lower East Side of New York City and with the rasping accent to prove it, Al Smith was both beloved and widely caricatured. "The Happy Warrior," as he was known, combined a number of seemingly contradictory elements of the party. He was urban, devoutly Catholic, and fiercely wet, but he also advocated a return to states' rights. While a liberal on civil liberties and an overall supporter of Wilsonian progressivism, he sounded like an old-line southern Democrat on states' rights when he frequently blasted Washington for meddlesome interference and stoutly defended "the old-time Democratic theory of the rights of the states."[4]

Far behind these two front-runners were Senator Oscar Underwood of Alabama, Senator Carter Glass of Virginia, Governor Samuel Ralston of Indiana, and John W. Davis of New York via West Virginia. This was an interesting group of dark horses. Underwood was, surprisingly, an outspoken critic of the Ku Klux Klan; and, as a result, he had little southern support outside his native Alabama. He was widely admired as a capable legislator and a sound conservative, but he did not have a solid base of delegate support from which to launch a successful convention effort. He was, however, the second choice of many delegates.

Senator Carter Glass was the favorite son candidate of Virginia. An old-line southern aristocrat, Glass was conservative, able, and somewhat abrasive personally. He followed McAdoo as secretary of the Treasury under Wilson, became the Democrats' Senate spokesman on fiscal policy in the 1920s, and was widely respected both in the South and in the major financial centers of the country. Significantly, he managed to maintain good relations with both the McAdoo and Smith forces, which would prove crucial at the convention; however, he was never a serious contender.

Governor Ralston of Indiana was a dark horse from central casting. He was governor of a midwestern swing state who enjoyed wide support from wets, drys, Catholics, the KKK, progressives, and conservatives. His Indiana constituents reported that he had very few enemies or opponents—perhaps because he "said little."[5] He was certainly a possible choice if the convention deadlocked. In today's television-driven political era, it may surprise readers to know that Governor Ralston weighed some three hundred pounds, but in the pretelevision 1920s this apparently was not considered an image problem. The memory of the avuncular William Howard Taft was no doubt still fresh in the delegates' minds.

The fourth dark horse was John W. Davis, former solicitor general of the United States, ambassador to the Court of St. James's, and prominent Wall Street lawyer. Davis had received seventy-six votes on the fortieth ballot at the 1920 convention, but he had been little more than a favorite son candidate from his native West Virginia. He enjoyed a national reputation as a result of having served with distinction as Wilson's solicitor general and later as ambassador to London and was seen as having an acceptable tie back to Wilsonian progressivism. As early as May 23, 1920, the *New York Times* in an editorial entitled "A Great Democrat" recognized Davis's qualities: "We urge the Democrats to consider . . . [Davis] as a candidate sure to command great strength, and as a man who, if elected, would bring to the executive office high qualifications of character, learning, cultivation, long experience in public affairs, full knowledge of the processes of the Government and personal qualities that have won for him the friendship, confidence and admiration of all with whom he has been associated."[6]

While Davis had widespread respect as a brilliant lawyer and advocate and was an attractive and personable candidate, a serious question about his candidacy arose in early 1924. Davis's New York firm and Davis himself regularly represented J. P. Morgan & Co., and the House of Morgan was anathema to the old Bryan populists in the Democratic Party. Davis's friends wrote to him that he should abandon his Wall Street practice and return to West Virginia in order to mount a serious bid for the presidency. Davis reflected on this advice and, on March 4, 1924, wrote a letter in which he concluded that he could not in good conscience follow such a course. After explaining that he had over his career as a lawyer represented many clients and never "confined my services to a single client," he wrote, "No one in all this list of clients has ever controlled or even fancied that he could control my personal or my political conscience. I am vain enough to imagine that no one ever will." He concluded by forcefully refusing to accede to what he viewed as political expediency.[7]

With this letter, Davis appeared to have ended his candidacy. However, the letter was subsequently sent by a Davis supporter to the editor of the *Pittsburgh Post*, who first published it. Finally, the letter was published by the *New York Times*, *New York Tribune*, *Baltimore Sun*, and many other newspapers around the country, and then followed by many laudatory editorials. Both media and popular reaction to this letter were favorable; and, thereafter, the taint of Morgan and Wall Street did not seem to be a serious issue for Davis. His West Virginia supporters moved ahead to advance his candidacy with little direct support from the candidate himself.

In addition to killing the "Morgan question," the letter was also important in revealing Davis's character, which was arguably his greatest asset. Throughout his career, Davis had an impressive ability to engender trust and respect from whomever he engaged. His rapid political advancement had always been the result of friends' putting him forward, very unlike McAdoo's transparent self-promotion. Clem Shaver, Davis's childhood friend and campaign manager, commented to his political associates, "John Davis will be President of the United States if people ever get to know him."[8]

These were the Democrats' possible candidates as they approached the June 1924 convention in New York City, but what were the party's prospects for victory? As Harding and the Republicans swept to a huge victory in 1920, the country was facing a severe recession. By 1921, unemployment was over 20 percent, and GNP had fallen sharply. In those days, the government was expected to do little to reverse a recession, and Harding responded primarily by advocating a strongly pro-business, lower taxation policy, which encouraged capital investment. The economic response was quick and positive. By mid-1921, the economy was clearly in recovery.

In the off-year election of 1922, the Democrats were able to pick up seats, but the Republicans still maintained majorities in both houses of Congress. Aside from some lingering debate over the League of Nations, the major economic issue facing the Democrats was how to respond to the Republican administration's Mellon Tax Plan. Secretary of the Treasury Andrew Mellon was rapidly becoming the central figure in the Harding/Coolidge administration with his consistent advocacy of lower taxes. While Harding admired Mellon, Coolidge developed an extremely close working relationship with his multimillionaire secretary. The two men were temperamentally very similar and shared the same economic philosophy. Republicans were generally united behind Mellon, and the economy was responding to the prospect of lower taxes, but this issue sharply divided the Democrats along the old Cleveland/Bryan fault line. Progressives in the Bryan and Wilson tradition were generally not in support of tax reduction, though conservative Democrats in the Cleveland/Parker tradition supported tax reduction. As Davis, a member of the latter group, wrote in December 1923, that the traditional Democratic position was to "out-Mellon Mellon."[9]

As the 1924 convention approached, two social issues were proving divisive for the Democrats: Prohibition and the Ku Klux Klan. With the passage of the Volstead Act and the requisite constitutional amendment in 1919, America embraced one of the great twentieth-century experiments in social engineering. The country was far from united, and hypocrisy was rife when it came to compliance and enforcement. As Paul Johnson has noted, "Socially, the experience was a catastrophe for the United States."[10] Coolidge had simply stated that Congress had passed it and he would support it, while adding "Any law that inspires disrespect for other laws—the good laws—is a bad law."[11] But the Democrats were engaged in a heated struggle over Prohibition. McAdoo was adamantly for Prohibition, while Smith was adamantly wet, and there was no middle ground.

The KKK had been revived in 1915 as a more national organization that demanded "100 percent Americanism." In addition to anti-black, anti-Catholic, anti-Semitic, anti-immigrant positions, the resurgent Klan was aggressively promoting the "supremacy of the white race." This xenophobic message was taking hold well beyond the South. McAdoo enjoyed strong Klan support, while Smith, a Catholic immigrant, was anathema to the Protestant KKK. Again, there was no middle ground.

As the Democrats headed into their 1924 convention, the divisions were deep and involved both race and religion. The party had a long history of acrimony and infighting, and it was still saddled with a great procedural liability—the nominee was required to secure a two-thirds majority. A perfect political storm was brewing.

Chapter Four

THE REPUBLICANS

*The Republican Party was, of course, the party of Lincoln,
which had emancipated the slaves and won the Civil War.
It had also been the party of Theodore Roosevelt and
progressive capital. But it was, at the same time, the party of
social conservatism and free market economics. In the 1920s
its mastery was overwhelming.*
—Paul Johnson

The Republican Party can trace its roots back to the beginning
of the republic, although perhaps not quite so directly as the
Democrats. Alexander Hamilton is generally considered the
ideological father of the Republicans. In general, Hamilton and
his Federalist Party were pro-republic, but antidemocratic. A strong
central government was viewed as necessary to promote safety,
stability, and economic growth, while states' rights and expansion
of the voting franchise were viewed with apprehension. Property
rights were seen as synonymous with individual rights. Federalists
were generally the party of the well-to-do, propertied class while
Jefferson's Democrats carried more than a whiff of radicalism and
even a hint of anarchy.

As the Jeffersonians evolved into the Democratic Party under Andrew Jackson, the old Federalist Party largely faded away, and a successor party, the Whigs, emerged. Old Jeffersonians who could not quite stomach the frontier democracy of Jackson and the remnants of the Federalist Party joined together as Whigs. They advocated a distinct Hamiltonian philosophy from the outset—protective tariffs for American industry, internal improvements financed by a strong central government, and a central bank to promote economic growth. Interestingly, the three great congressional leaders of the pre–Civil War era were all Whigs: Henry Clay of Kentucky, Daniel Webster of Massachusetts, and John C. Calhoun of South Carolina. Clay promoted the "American System" about which Calhoun wrote, "We are greatly and rapidly—I was about to say fearfully—growing. This is our pride and our danger; our weakness and our strength . . . Let us, then, bind the Republic together with a perfect system of roads and canals. Protection would make the parts adhere more closely . . . It would form a new and most powerful cement."[1] Despite this plethora of able leaders and a unifying, national platform, the Whig Party split over slavery in 1848, twelve years before the Democrats.

As the Whig Party began to disintegrate in 1848, two separate groups emerged and began to organize as political parties. Those Whigs who embraced the old Hamiltonian ideas of a limited franchise and a republic ruled by the propertied class were becoming greatly disturbed by Jacksonian democracy and especially by the influx of immigrants. Xenophobic fears were rising particularly against Catholic immigrants from Ireland and Germany. By 1856 the anti-immigrant group had formed the Native American Party, which became widely known as the Know

Nothing Party. When questioned about their xenophobic beliefs, party candidates were instructed to respond, "I know nothing." The Know Nothings captured Massachusetts and were strong in a number of other states, including New York. In 1856, the Know Nothings nominated ex-President Millard Fillmore, who proved a weak candidate, receiving only eight electoral votes.

As the issue of slavery came more and more to the forefront of American political debate, northern antislavery Whigs began to organize an avowedly antislavery party. By 1856, these Whigs had formed the Republican Party, which held its first national nominating convention in Philadelphia. The dashing "Pathfinder of the West," John C. Frémont, was nominated amidst a great outpouring of enthusiasm and moralism. The platform dedicated the Republicans "to prohibit in the territories those twin relics of barbarism, polygamy and slavery."[2] Frémont established the viability of the new party by carrying 114 electoral votes, while James Buchanan held together a fractured Democratic Party to win the election decisively.

It was the final split of the Democratic Party over slavery that led to the ascendancy of the Republicans in 1860. The Republicans turned to an Illinois Whig, Abraham Lincoln, who was strongly antislavery but not yet abolitionist. Along with his antislavery views, Lincoln brought a traditional Whig philosophy of strong central government, tariff protection, and internal improvements. With the Democrats nominating a northern candidate, Stephen A. Douglas, and a southern candidate, John C. Breckinridge, and a few diehard southern Whigs supporting John Bell as a Unionist, the field was open for Republicans to sweep the New England, mid-Atlantic, and midwestern states. Lincoln was able to turn a

40 percent popular vote plurality into a 180-vote mandate in the electoral college.

It is a truism of American history that the Civil War was *the* defining event in the development of the United States, and the same is equally true for the Republican Party. Lincoln's Hamiltonian/Whig philosophy of government was a perfect match for the challenges of 1860 and the war that followed. To wage a war on this scale required a strong, central government, and Lincoln oversaw a massive expansion of government activity. The ensuing surge in industrialization to meet the war needs accelerated the U. S. transition from an agrarian economy. In addition to waging the war, Lincoln and the Republicans initiated construction of the transcontinental railroad, which was at that time the largest, most costly public works project ever attempted—in the world.

With the war won, slavery ended, the transcontinental railroad moving to completion, the industrial base of America booming, and Lincoln lionized as a martyr, the Republican Party stood astride an ascendant nation as the majority party, indeed, now the Grand Old Party. From 1860 to 1912, Republicans held the White House for forty-four of the fifty-two years. They were able repeatedly to label the Democrats as the "party of Rum, Romanism, and Rebellion"—not so subtly playing to the fears of their Protestant, Caucasian, unionist voter base. Only twice were the Democrats able to wrest the presidency away from the Republicans with the victory of a conservative New York Democrat, governor Grover Cleveland.

These years saw transforming economic growth, political stability, the emergence of big business and Wall Street, and the entry of the United States on the world scene as a power to be reckoned with. These were not only formative years for the nation, but also for the Republican Party. The party began to see itself as the voice of political stability, American business, and strength at home and abroad. By 1896, the Democrats had become disillusioned after succeeding only in electing *one* president, Cleveland, who was economically as conservative as the Republicans; and, in an effort to differentiate themselves from the GOP, they stampeded enthusiastically to the charismatic William Jennings Bryan and his free silver, populist, anti–Wall Street message.

An inevitable result of these long years of Republican electoral success and power was corruption and cronyism; and, as the country neared the end of the nineteenth century, a reform movement was developing within the party. The Mugwumps, as the reformers were called, had opposed Speaker of the House James G. Blaine, the quintessential Republican insider, as early as 1884. Reform within the GOP was not so much ideologically as ethically driven. There was no populist or antibusiness thrust to the reform movement; rather these reformers were generally upper-class, ethical politicians dedicated to stamping out corruption. It was from this high-minded group of reformers that Theodore Roosevelt emerged to dominate the political stage between 1900 and 1919.

William McKinley had soundly defeated Bryan in 1896, proven to be a popular and able leader of a conservative administration, and successfully won the "splendid little war" with Spain in Cuba, when the Republicans nominated Theodore Roosevelt as vice president in 1900. Few thought at the time that McKinley or the

Republicans needed any help from the reform-minded governor of New York in order to win the election of 1900. And, in fact, McKinley and his patron, advisor, and campaign manager, Mark Hanna, decisively defeated Bryan a second time. When McKinley was assassinated in September 1901, he was genuinely mourned as a great American president. Concurrently, Roosevelt's ascension to the presidency was viewed with alarm in some Republican quarters. On hearing of McKinley's death, Mark Hanna gasped, "Now that damned cowboy is president!"[3]

(COURTESY LIBRARY OF CONGRESS)
The dynamic Theodore Roosevelt addresses a crowd in Asheville, North Carolina, in 1902, with typical fervor.

With his succession of McKinley, Roosevelt began an eighteen-year love-hate relationship with the Republican Party. From 1901 to 1908, he was a wildly popular president and could undoubtedly have been elected for a second full term. In 1912, he split the party, abandoned the GOP, formed the Progressive (Bull Moose) Party, and delivered the White House to Woodrow Wilson. By the time of his death in 1919, he was once again back in the fold and considered the front-runner for the GOP nomination in 1920. During his presidency, he had led the GOP—and the nation—toward a more activist, interventionist government. During his Bull Moose run for the presidency in 1912, he veered sharply left and became decidedly more antibusiness, pro-government expansion than he had been as president. Following the 1912 election, he reverted toward the more moderate philosophy of his presidential years; and, by his death, he was generally well received—and forgiven—by the GOP.

This Progressive Era, 1900–1920, was a period of substantial realignment for both the Democrats and the Republicans. After Bryan's failure to win the presidency against McKinley in 1896 and again in 1900, Roosevelt became the first national figure to campaign and win on a progressive platform in 1904. The Democrats veered right, nominated the colorless but competent Alton B. Parker, and received a thorough electoral drubbing by Roosevelt and Republicans. It appeared that Roosevelt had successfully foisted his progressive agenda onto a reluctant GOP and left the Democrats floundering without a coherent philosophy. In 1908, the Democrats turned back to Bryan, but the old magic of the "Boy Orator of the Plains" had worn thin, and the Democrats were again soundly defeated. The Republicans now appeared to be the party of progressivism, as pundit Finley Peter Dunne's "Mr. Dooley" observed of Roosevelt, "He's a gr'-reat man, an th' thing

I like best about him is that in th' dark ye can hardly tell him fr'm a Dimmycrat."[4]

The election of 1912 brought about a clearer definition in the parties. Roosevelt was only fifty years old when he turned the presidency over to his good friend and political heir, Will Taft, in 1908. He could have easily won a full second term had he decided to run. It was not long before boredom brought him back to the arena. He restlessly watched from the sidelines for three years as Taft sought conscientiously to implement Roosevelt's progressive agenda. Finally, Roosevelt threw himself into the race in 1912. He laid out a more radically progressive platform and very nearly wrested the nomination from Taft. However, in the end, the conservative elements in the party prevailed, and Taft was renominated. Roosevelt, in a fit of pique, bolted the GOP and accepted the nomination of the newly formed Progressive Party. In typical fashion, he announced himself "fit as a bull moose," and suddenly the Progressive Party was thenceforth the Bull Moose Party.

The GOP split provided the Democrats a tremendous opportunity, and Woodrow Wilson exploited it adroitly. Although he had been elected governor of New Jersey with the support of the conservative state party bosses, Wilson, once elected, had embraced a progressive agenda. At the Democratic convention of 1912, he was nominated with the support of the Bryan progressives and mounted a national campaign to reclaim the progressive mantle for the Democrats. In this election and the ensuing eight-year Wilson administration, the Democrats skillfully blended Bryan's populist, pro-farmer, free-silver philosophy with the basic tenets of Roosevelt's Square Deal—pro-labor, trust-busting, conservationist policies. The Republicans were never again to challenge the Democrats as the party of progressivism.

Roosevelt's death in 1919 was well timed to accommodate the conservative wing's reclamation of the party. The mood of the country was clearly swinging away from Wilsonian progressivism; and, with Roosevelt's unexpected death, the conservative Republicans, or Stalwarts as they were known, were unchallenged in realigning the GOP in a more McKinleyesque direction.

The old Rough Rider, General Leonard Wood, made a run at the nomination in 1920, but he was more a sentimental candidate, evoking memories of Roosevelt's big-stick diplomacy, rather than a serious ideological progressive. When General Wood and conservative Illinois Governor Frank Lowden deadlocked after ten ballots, the GOP bosses adjourned to the famous thirteenth floor of the Blackstone Hotel to complete the conservative takeover of the party in the proverbial "smoked filled room." The solidly conservative, handsome, extroverted Senator Warren Harding emerged as the candidate to lead the party back to the halcyon days of McKinley. If ever there was a man for the mood of the hour it was Harding. As the country staggered out of its war years, exhausted by the divisive League of Nations debate, and tumbled headlong into a sobering recession, people longed for reassurance and stability, and Harding was the right candidate.

In a little noticed, but ultimately significant action, the convention bucked the will of the party bosses and nominated Governor Calvin Coolidge of Massachusetts for vice president. Famous for his peaceful but forceful settlement of the 1919 Boston police strike and author of a widely admired book, *Law and Order*, on the nation's hottest issue, Coolidge was the perfect complement for Harding. While the campaign managers stationed Harding nostalgically on his front porch in Marion, Ohio, in an obvious attempt to evoke the memory of William McKinley's "front porch" campaigns, Coolidge stumped the country offering solid Republican ideals. On the postwar challenges, he declared, "The lessons of the war are plain. Can we carry them into peace? Can we still act on the principle that there is no sacrifice too great to maintain the right? Shall we continue to advocate and practice thrift and industry? Shall we require unswerving loyalty to our country? These are the foundations of greatness" and added the caution, "What the public has, the public must pay for. From this there is no escape."[5]

The 1920 election was a landslide of historic proportions with the Republicans receiving more than 60 percent of the popular vote and a three-to-one electoral college victory. Harding and the Republicans saw this victory as a mandate to move the country to the right, and they did. While Secretary of State Charles Evans Hughes kept the country on an internationalist course and resisted a retreat into postwar isolationism, Treasury Secretary Andrew Mellon's policies of tax reduction and reduced government expenditures became the administration's centerpiece. The administration saw the economy through the 1919–1920 recession, and the country was soon moving into a robust recovery. The Republicans had provided a program supportive of business expansion and capital investment, business was booming, and Secretary Mellon was being hailed as "the greatest treasury secretary since Alexander Hamilton."[6] In addition, Harding's congenial personality served him well. He exuded confidence and good will, and people genuinely liked him.

Harding's sudden death in 1923 was a shock to the public and was followed by an impressive outpouring of public mourning. A reporter for the *New York Times* wrote, "It is believed to be the most remarkable demonstration in American history of affection, respect, and reverence."[7] After lying in state in Washington, Harding's body was taken to Marion, Ohio, for burial. Flags across the nation flew at half-staff, businesses closed, religious services were held in every quarter. Bishop Manning, in New York's Cathedral of St. John the Devine, spoke for the nation, "May God ever give to our country leaders as faithful, as wise, as noble in spirit, as the one whom we now mourn."[8]

(COURTESY OF THE "DING" DARLING WILDLIFE SOCIETY)

California Governor Hiram Johnson, a progressive Republican, and his supporter, media mogul William Randolph Hearst, halt a timid Calvin Coolidge at the 1924 schoolhouse door.

As Calvin Coolidge took the reins of government in 1923, his future was in no way certain. While he enjoyed a groundswell of public approval and goodwill—more than the typical "honeymoon season"—and economic conditions were improving, scandals were beginning to surface in the Harding administration, remnants of the progressive wing were restless, and his leadership was untested. Coolidge navigated the transition period with a steady hand and established an enduring rapport with the American public. Impressively, he was able to clean up Harding scandals in such a way that he was in no way implicated in any wrongdoing. Coolidge solidified his base within the Republican Party, while successfully minimalizing the old Roosevelt Progressives. Senator Robert La Follette correctly recognized that the GOP had abandoned progressivism and began efforts to revive the Progressive Party. Only California Governor Hiram Johnson stood as a progressive candidate against Coolidge, and he was eliminated when Coolidge won the California Republican primary. As 1924 approached, the country, still saddened by Harding's death, was growing comfortable with President Coolidge and developing a genuine respect for his lack of pretension, his brevity, his New England values, and, more importantly, his solid conservative ideology.

Part Three

THE CONVENTIONS

Chapter Five

THE PUBLIC AUDITORIUM: CLEVELAND

I've been longin' to attend a convention and see the excitement and hear the shouts. Now, when I do get a chance, I draw this one.
—Will Rogers

Cleveland was in every way an appropriate host city for the GOP convention in 1924. Since Lincoln's presidency, Ohio had been arguably *the* key state in Republican presidential strategy. In the fourteen elections from 1868 to 1920, the Republicans turned to an Ohioan as its standard bearer *nine* times. Geographically, Ohio bridged the traditional New England and eastern GOP strongholds with the industrialized upper Midwest and western states. Cleveland was an industrial boomtown—the result of Republican prosperity. The city's population had more than doubled from 1900 to 1920, and it exemplified the power, scope, and success of American manufacturing.

Cleveland in many ways symbolized the great industrialization of America that had occurred from 1880 to 1920, and in particular the city's growth was largely driven by the rise of the automobile. From 1910 to 1925, U.S. production of automobiles soared from slightly over 500,000 per year to more than 5,000,000 per year. In 1924, European car production totaled only 11 percent of the U.S. output, and almost one in five Americans owned a car.[1] While Detroit was the automobile capital of the United States, many of the parts for those cars were produced in Cleveland. The mansions in Shaker Heights were in every way comparable to those in Grosse Point, and the GOP was seen as synonymous with Ohio industry and general economic prosperity. With the national electoral landslide of 1920 still fresh in their minds, the memory of Warren Harding still largely unsullied, and the "Mellon economy" humming promisingly, Republicans prepared to gather in a self-congratulatory and optimistic mood.

By June, as the delegates began to converge on Cleveland's shiny new 12,000-seat Public Auditorium, it was apparent to all that Calvin Coolidge would be the nominee. When Warren Harding suddenly died in San Francisco on August 2, 1923, the American public was not well acquainted with his vice president. After years of steady political success and solid public service in Massachusetts, the newly elected Governor Coolidge emerged on the national scene in 1919 with his handling of the Boston police strike. From the successful settlement of the strike, he was moved forward as Massachusetts's favorite-son presidential candidate at the 1920 convention. Although his presidential candidacy attracted little support outside his native state, the convention enthusiastically nominated Coolidge as Warren Harding's running mate.

After a cautious and somewhat sedate campaign, the GOP ticket was elected in a landslide and the Coolidges settled into Washington. Although his relationship with Harding was cordial— which was true of almost everyone's relationship with Harding— Coolidge was never an administration insider. He presided conscientiously over the Senate, performed the usual ceremonial roles of a vice president, and lived quietly and modestly at the Willard Hotel. There was some talk in 1923 that Harding might replace Coolidge as his running mate in 1924, but little evidence exists that this would have happened.[2] In general, Coolidge seemed a good match with the popular, outgoing Harding. They were politically compatible, and Coolidge was never seen to upstage his senior partner.

Even though reports of impropriety were beginning to circulate in 1923, the public's image of Warren Harding remained extremely positive. He had restored postwar order and stability, while moving the country into economic prosperity; and, in addition, he was a very likeable, attractive man. The public expressed genuine, widespread grief at his sudden death, and Coolidge was accorded a honeymoon period of public goodwill. At this point, the leading pundits of the day and a number of senior GOP leaders underestimated and "belittled Coolidge. They described him as inveterately lucky, somehow always at the right place at the right time. Even people who knew him well and admired him didn't necessarily think him presidential material."[3]

As he carefully endorsed Harding's basic agenda and took over the reins of government, Coolidge moved uncharacteristically quickly to indicate he would seek the nomination in 1924. In less than a year Coolidge had successfully silenced his critics and skeptics. He was aided by the fact that many of the old Republican leaders, who were influential at the 1920 convention, had either died or slipped into retirement, such as Leonard Wood, Frank Lowden, and Henry Cabot Lodge. Even though the Republicans had suffered losses in the 1922 off-year election, they still controlled both houses, and Coolidge was able to push through much of Mellon's economic policy, which was the framework for what was to become known as the Coolidge Prosperity. Equally significant, Coolidge was able to contain the political damage from the Harding scandals. William Allen White's immortalization of Coolidge as "the Puritan in Babylon" resonated with the public, as "this cautious, unassuming Vermonter would come to embody the virtues of probity and moderation, dutifulness and thrift."[4]

Coming off the congressional gains in the 1922 elections, the Democrats entered 1924 with hope that they could retake the White House. In March, the Kiplinger *Washington Letter* predicted, "We think the Republican Party will not be kept in power." The following month, *New Republic* suggested, "The outlook for the Democratic Party is more cheerful than that for the Republicans."[5] Initially after Harding's death, Coolidge had the confidence of neither the Old Guard conservative Republicans nor the progressive Republicans; however, by the spring of 1924, Coolidge had successfully solidified his conservative Republican base, and his only opposition within the party was the progressive wing. This remnant of the old Roosevelt wing of the party was now largely made up of westerners such as William Borah, Robert La Follette, Hiram Johnson, and George Norris and a few easterners such as Gifford Pinchot of Pennsylvania.

While this remnant was not dominant, these progressives held important congressional posts and were still formidable opponents. The successive blows of Wilson's presidency, Roosevelt's sudden death in 1919, and then Harding's electoral triumph in 1920 had left them seriously overshadowed by the Old Guard conservative Republicans. By 1924, "Fighting Bob" La Follette had decided he had best fight outside the GOP and moved to revive the old Progressive Party for a third party campaign. Coolidge had successfully courted a number of the more moderate Republican progressives, especially Senator Borah, and convinced them to stay within the GOP, hence adroitly isolating the more radical La Follette.

Surprisingly, Coolidge found an unlikely ally in public relations. It is ironic that a man so often caricatured as "Silent Cal" or "the Sphinx" would prove a master of public relations. He understood the function of the modern press and cultivated his relationship with it, meeting regularly with the White House reporters twice each week. He also was the first president to use radio, and he proved very effective at going straight to the American people through this new medium. As the *Detroit News* noted, "He avoided every appearance of publicity seeking, but he probably was the most photographed man who ever occupied the White House."[6] While Coolidge was regularly belittled by H. L. Mencken, Lincoln Steffens, and other ideological critics, he generally received sympathetic treatment in the general press.

In formulating his economic policy in 1924, Coolidge addressed the public directly. He presented a 1924 budget that was considerably smaller than any since the start of the war and reduced spending in virtually all areas. Before a GOP gathering in February he laid out in considerable detail his fiscal philosophy, especially with regard to taxation, and it was pure Andrew Mellon: "I agree perfectly with those who wish to relieve the small taxpayer by getting the largest possible contribution form the people with large incomes. But if the rates on large incomes are so high that they disappear, the small taxpayer will be left to bear the entire burden."[7] Coolidge and Mellon proposed an across the board 25 percent cut in income taxes, and Coolidge proved highly effective in presenting the rationale to the American public, hammering it home in succinct, commonsense language the American public could understand.

This May 1, 1924, cartoon by Clifford Berryman prophetically contrasted the upcoming conventions of the hapless, contentious Democrats with the well-orchestrated GOP.

While Coolidge was successfully solidifying his base, the Democrats' situation worsened. Their leading candidate, William Gibbs McAdoo, was linked to serious oil scandals, and the backing of the Ku Klux Klan was making him unacceptable to eastern Democrats. By the spring of 1924, the pundits saw Coolidge's nomination as assured. The GOP was planning what William Allen White called a "meeting of chambers of commerce and bankers and Rotarians of which Coolidge was the captain."[8] Only two questions remained for the convention: the platform and a running mate. Coolidge and the party leaders dictated that the platform be brief, in keeping with Coolidge's well-advertised commitment to brevity, and bland in avoiding controversy at all costs. The GOP wisely sought to minimize their intraparty differences and to skirt the most inflammatory issues of the day—Prohibition, the Klan, and the League.

The selection of Coolidge's running mate required more serious attention. In the past twenty years, two vice presidents, Theodore Roosevelt and Calvin Coolidge, had ascended to the presidency, creating a strong general awareness of the potential significance of the vice presidential selection. In addition, the nomination was the only chance for excitement in an otherwise scripted and boring convention. "Except for some anticipation about a fight for the vice presidential nomination," the Raleigh *News & Observer* summarized, "the preparation for this convention as a whole went ahead with almost as much quiet and decorum as a New England town meeting."[9]

The opening session began with a stirring tribute to the fallen Warren Harding and then moved on to Ohio Representative

Theodore Burton's key-note address. The attendance was "one of the scantiest ever seen at the opening of a national convention; the keynote speech was addressed to some 8,000 spectators and 4,000 empty seats."[10] Coolidge was lauded predictably as a most worthy successor to Harding: "There is none who can surpass Calvin Coolidge in honesty, in courage, or in high devotion to his country."[11] There was obviously no drama here; for, although Coolidge would not be formally nominated until Thursday, the convention on opening day announced the ten-member delegation that would officially notify him of his nomination. The New York *Herald Tribune* headline ran, "Convention Runs as Smoothly as Machine That Makes Nails." The reporter noted

This preconvention cartoon shows Coolidge as the master chef cooking the platform stew to suit the various GOP constituencies.

that the convention "was generally viewed as a cold, cautious, programmed, standardized and lugubrious affair . . . Superficially it is as methodical as a machine that makes wire nails."[12] Apparently the manufacturing of wire nails was a Cleveland specialty. Things got so dull that Will Rogers advised Cleveland to open up its churches "to liven things up a bit."[13]

By Wednesday, June 11, the work of the Platform Committee was complete, and the draft was presented to the convention. The *New York Times* facetiously challenged the GOP to go for the ultimate in a short platform: "Coolidge, that's all."[14] Instead, the committee produced a lengthy document that was quintessential Republican orthodoxy. The La Follette forces, largely comprised of the Wisconsin delegation, mounted a pitifully weak challenge, and their substitute planks were resoundingly defeated on the convention floor. The adoption of the platform was immediately followed by a well-orchestrated floor demonstration for Coolidge. It was widely reported around the convention floor that President Coolidge was listening in approvingly on his radio at the White House.

The 1924 Republican Platform commenced solemnly: "We the delegates of the Republican Party in national convention assembled bow our heads in reverent memory of Warren G. Harding." After praising the fallen Harding, the platform laid claim to the impressive economic improvement achieved since the 1920 election. While the tariff, foreign affairs, labor, education, and agriculture were all addressed, the platform focused on the central importance of taxation and economic policy for the 1924 campaign. The reduction of both taxes and expenditures under

Harding and Coolidge were trumpeted as the administration's major achievements, and the platform clearly promised more of the same. As the La Follete planks were shouted down on the floor of the convention, Secretary Mellon from his seat in the Pennsylvania delegation was observed to be smiling broadly—with uncharacteristic warmth and enthusiasm. The party had sounded its theme for 1924.

The convention organizers left nothing to chance. There was to be only one name placed in nomination before the balloting began. A close friend of President Coolidge, Dr. Marion Burton, former president of Smith College and current president of the University of Michigan, delivered a lengthy nominating address. Predictably the speech built upon the achievements of the past four years and reached its climax in presenting "the staunch American—the real human being—Calvin Coolidge!" A series of nine seconding speeches followed before the convention chairman swiftly closed the nominations and began the balloting. One of the seconders captured the sense of the convention as he thundered, "Coolidge never wasted any time, never wasted any words, and never wasted any public money."[15] A smattering of votes—only thirty-four—went to either Johnson or La Follette, while the remainder went to Coolidge, enabling the chairman to proclaim, "With the exception of a very few voices the nomination of Calvin Coolidge for president of the United States is made unanimous."[16]

Ever vigilant for an opportunity to undergird the president's homespun image, the Coolidge managers had ensured that the press was covering Col. John Coolidge up in Vermont. Earlier that week, headlines announced, "Crops Keep Coolidge's Father From

(COURTESY OF THE "DING" DARLING WILDLIFE SOCIETY)

A confidence-inspiring Calvin Coolidge wraps one arm around the central issues of the day while wrapping his other arm around the GOP nomination.

Cleveland." Old Colonel Coolidge had turned down the invitation of the Republican National Committee to attend the convention because his spring planting was "a little later than normal this year," but the party had installed a new radio in the same, simple living room where son Calvin had taken the oath of office the preceding year. *New York Times* June 13 headlines proclaimed, "Colonel Coolidge In Tears Hears Son Nominated," and the article reported, "As the cheers which greeted the President's name came to him through the air, the old man's eyes watered, but his nerves were steady and he calmly took out his watch and timed each long round of applause."[17] That picture was worth a thousand pages of newsprint. The public was convinced that Calvin Coolidge was indeed the real thing—an unassuming, honest, hardworking, and thrifty New England patriot.

At this point Coolidge's managers somehow lost control of the convention, and it veered briefly off the prescribed script. As the convention moved quickly on to the vice presidential nomination, a groundswell of sentiment surfaced for Governor Frank Lowden of Illinois. Lowden, who was a presidential contender in 1920 and was very popular with the Republican rank and file, had publicly indicated he would not accept the nomination, but the convention threw his name into nomination and then proceeded to nominate him on the second ballot. Immediately, Lowden dispatched a representative to decline the nomination, and the convention was left in an awkward moment. Since becoming president in 1923, Coolidge had assiduously courted Senator William Borah of Idaho in an attempt to keep the progressives within the GOP and now let it be known that he would welcome Borah on the ticket; but Borah quickly declined for health reasons. This left Charles Dawes and Herbert Hoover as the remaining candidates.

Herbert Hoover was commerce secretary in Harding's—and now Coolidge's—administration. He was a world-renowned engineer and humanitarian, responsible for massive postwar relief programs in Europe. Although Harding had been an ardent booster of Hoover, Coolidge was not much of a Hoover fan, believing Hoover was too much of a governmental interventionist and jokingly calling him "Wonder Boy."[18] In addition, the popular Hoover was already in Coolidge's cabinet, and his nomination as vice president would bring little new popular appeal to the ticket. Coolidge's managers quietly discouraged Hoover's efforts for the nomination and spoke approvingly of Dawes.

(COURTESY OF THE FORBES LIBRARY, NORTHAMPTON, MA)
The Republican nominees, Coolidge and Dawes, confer on the front porch of the Coolidge homestead in Plymouth Notch.

Charles Dawes was an interesting and unconventional candidate. A talented business executive, he had successfully alternated between industry and public service for many years. He was comptroller of the currency under McKinley before becoming a successful banker and utility executive. In World War I Dawes served as head of the General Purchasing Board, where he was responsible for provisioning the army and was ultimately appointed brigadier general. Dawes was fifty-nine years old—seven years Coolidge's senior—and widely known as a man who spoke his mind. He was something of a maverick. On some issues, such as labor and right-to-work, he was staunchly conservative, while on other issues he could be unpredictably progressive. Somewhat like Coolidge, he was seen as a nonpolitician, a man of honesty and integrity; and while Coolidge disliked campaigning, Dawes relished it.

After Lowden's swift refusal, the convention voted overwhelmingly to nominate Dawes—682 votes to Hoover's 234. Popular reaction was generally favorable. Business was heartened by the addition of Dawes to the ticket, primarily because of his strong right-to-work stance. Progressives were encouraged by his internationalism. Coolidge wired his congratulations, and Dawes expressed his desire to hit the campaign hard. The Republicans believed they had nominated a cohesive, articulate, and appealing ticket. Their belief was confirmed when Democratic congressional leaders immediately blasted the ticket and the platform as "one of the most reactionary in the history of this country."[19]

Chapter Six

MADISON SQUARE GARDEN

The dimmycratic party ain't on speakin' terms with itself.
—Finley Peter Dunne ("Mr. Dooley")

Since the Civil War, New York had been *the* key state in Democratic Party presidential political strategy. To win the White House, Democrats had to win enough northern electoral votes to add to their solid southern base, and New York was always their best bet, as well as the largest state. In the fourteen elections from 1868 to 1920, the Democrats nominated a New Yorker *eight* times. In 1884 and 1892, Cleveland carried New York and won the election, though in 1888 he lost New York and the election. In 1924, New York had a popular Democrat in the governor's office, Alfred E. Smith, and a thoroughly Democratic municipal administration in New York City. Hence, it was natural for the Democrats to convene their convention in New York City in June 1924. In addition, Madison Square Garden offered the world's largest convention hall with permanent seating for more than eight thousand and floor seating for thousands more. Standing at Madison Avenue and

26th Street, this cavernous hall measured 200 x 350 feet and was New York's second tallest building.

(COLLECTION OF NEW-YORK HISTORICAL SOCIETY, NEGATIVE #69265)
Stanford White's landmark building, Madison Square Garden, is here decked in bunting for the 1924 Democratic convention.

As delegates converged on New York City in late June, the Democratic Party, never known for being a cohesive or well-disciplined group, was more deeply divided than usual. The tradition of Wilson's (and Bryan's) progressivism had seemingly been repudiated by voters in 1920, and the party was thrown back into its pre-Wilson internal struggle between its progressive and conservative wings. In addition, the continuing debate over the League of Nations, the resurgence of the Ku Klux Klan, the adoption of prohibition, and the growing unrest of midwestern farm interests were divisive issues for the Democrats. And to make electoral prospects still worse, the economy was improving, and Calvin Coolidge had emerged amazingly unscathed by the revelations of the Harding scandals. It was hardly an encouraging backdrop for the convention.

In the months of preconvention maneuvering, two dominant factors hung over the party. William Gibbs McAdoo, Wilson's son-in-law and the acknowledged front-runner, claimed the support of approximately one half the delegates, while his rival, Governor Al Smith, held some one quarter of the total. These two men were deeply divided on the main issues of the day: the Ku Klux Klan, Prohibition, progressivism, and farming issues, and there was no apparent ground for compromise. As the McAdoo-Smith rivalry became more intense, the party was increasingly faced with an unsolvable dilemma. To nominate McAdoo, and reject

(U.S. SENATE COLLECTION/CENTER FOR LEGISLATIVE ARCHIVES)

In June 1924, the Democratic race was becoming seriously overcrowded as the low-profile Senator Jim Reed joins seven other candidates.

Smith, would alienate American Catholics, who constituted some 16 percent of the popular vote, and who generally voted the Democratic ticket. To nominate Smith and reject McAdoo would solidify anti-Catholic feeling and alienate the otherwise solid South. Whichever direction was chosen would significantly affect the future of the Democratic Party.

Compounding this ideological standoff was the antiquated party rule requiring a two-thirds majority to secure the nomination. Going into the convention, McAdoo had a virtual veto on the nomination but little prospect of gaining enough support to put him over the two-thirds requirement. McAdoo finally advocated abandoning the two-thirds rule, but his Protestant supporters wanted to retain their veto over a Catholic nominee. In addition, the South saw the two-thirds rule as a protection of their sectional interests. In late June 1924, a record summer heat wave moved over New York City. Soon the temperature inside the Garden would far exceed the oppressive heat outside.

It had become evident to political pundits, if not to McAdoo or Smith, that the Democrats' only hope was to nominate a compromise candidate as quickly as possible before the party tore itself to shreds. As the *Washington Post* wrote on June 25, "John W. Davis, of West Virginia, is the most-talked-of second choice."[1] Because of his genuine ambivalence about entering the race, Davis had not campaigned actively and had generally avoided taking positions on the most divisive issues—thereby strengthening his chances for the nomination. Progressives took comfort in his service as Wilson's solicitor general where he was progressivism's voice before the Supreme Court, while conservatives saw his current Wall Street connections as most reassuring and more indicative

(COURTESY LIBRARY OF CONGRESS)

New York governor, Al Smith, addresses supporters in his ever-present derby.

of Davis's conservative personal convictions. Southerners saw him as a favorite son of West Virginia, though at the time he resided in New York City. Die-hard proponents of the League believed Davis still stood with them, but he had not been involved in the bitter congressional battle.

Davis's name had first been thrust into presidential politics in 1920 when some of his oldest friends in West Virginia organized a favorite son initiative on his behalf. Davis was still ambassador to Great Britain at the time and gave no public support to the effort. His candidacy did receive notice nationally when the *New York Times* endorsed Davis on May 23, 1920, as "A Great Democrat," and urged the upcoming convention to nominate him.[2] There was some feeling in 1920 that, had the convention stalemate continued, Davis may well have emerged as the compromise candidate. With the nomination of Cox, Davis dismissed all thought of presidential politics, served out his appointment as Ambassador, and returned to the United States to establish an immensely distinguished and profitable legal practice on Wall Street. However, his name remained somewhat in the public eye with his election as president of the American Bar Association in 1922.

In late 1923, the same group of West Virginia friends, led by John Huntley and Clem Shaver, approached Davis about the possibility of becoming a candidate in 1924. Davis responded that he would not be an active candidate. Despite his lack of enthusiasm, the West Virginians moved ahead and soon Davis-for-president offices were opening in West Virginia—and beyond. On a visit back to Clarksburg in early spring 1924, Davis told Clem Shaver, "I feel obliged to protest against your activities" to which Shaver retorted, "You're not responsible for what your fool friends do." Years later, Davis further described his feelings: "I didn't want to be nominated. I had just this feeling about it: 'If I run away, the rest of my life I'll be wondering if at that particular moment I didn't show the white feather. I don't want to live with a white feather. If Fate is headed toward me, I must stand in the middle of the road and see whether she comes on or whether she doesn't.'"[3]

As the grassroots Davis campaign gathered steam, his friends saw only one serious impediment to securing the nomination—Davis's current ties to Wall Street. John Huntley wrote earnestly to his friend urging him to remove the "taint of Wall Street" by leaving his New York practice, returning to West Virginia, and seeking the nomination. Davis brushed off Huntley's request by humorously asking if it was not Mark Twain who quipped that all Wall Street money had a "double taint—'taint yours, 'taint mine." Huntley refused to take no for an answer and wrote again. This time Davis responded at length. He articulately explained why he could not in good conscience abandon his reputable clients and loyal associates. In conclusion, Davis responded with force and apparent finality.[4]

The door seemed shut, but Huntley did not give up. As he reread Davis's letter, he recognized the character and integrity of the man he so admired, and he reasoned, "If it [the letter] could reach the public it would wipe out the 'Wall Street taint.'"[5] So, again, Huntley wrote Davis, this time seeking his permission to publish his letter. Davis responded by giving his permission with the provision that the letter only be published in its entirety. This was the opening Huntley sought. He immediately sent the letter to a friend, the publisher of *The Pittsburgh Post*, who published it on March 30. As Huntley wrote later, "The reaction was instantaneous. A flood of editorial comment resulted, for the most part favorable." Davis quickly became a leading dark horse candidate, and the Wall Street issue faded.[6] From this point until the convention, the Davis campaign gathered momentum, and his "fool friends" converged on the Garden with high hopes.

One of history's minor, but interesting, side notes occurred in May 1924. Davis's alma mater, Washington and Lee University in Lexington, Virginia, had originated a quite distinctive student activity—the quadrennial mock convention in which the collegians put forward a nominee for president for the political party out of power. This activity dated back to a 1908 campus visit from William Jennings Bryan, who was then seeking his third Democratic nomination. By 1924 the mock convention was a serious part of student life at Washington and Lee, and the students were developing a record for accuracy in predicting the eventual actual nominee. As a Virginia reporter observed, "It was not lacking in a single detail when compared to the real convention."[7]

The W&L fireworks started with a bitter—and prophetic—platform fight over Prohibition. Rousing speeches from the wets and the drys followed. Toward the end of the speeches, a student rushed to the podium to read an urgent telegram from the Plumbers' Union of Bangor, Maine, urging the convention "to take action toward modification of the Bone Dry Law." It was not reported exactly why the Bangor plumbers' input was offered, but their input was apparently not decisive, as the convention narrowly passed—no doubt above the students' own better judgment—a strong Prohibition platform. As the wet forces protested, the student chairman, Randolph "Booze" Whittle, declared the issue settled and the platform ratified.

Next the students turned their attention to the central business of nominating a candidate, and again they proved amazingly prophetic. The mock convention endured twenty-two ballots during which McAdoo and Smith waxed and waned, while the favorite son candidates refused to release their delegates. The mock convention was operating under the same two-thirds rule as the Democratic Party, and it became apparent that deadlock had set in.

At the conclusion of the twenty-second ballot, the convention chairman made an impassioned plea for party unity, which was followed by the mysterious "withdrawal from the convention of the Texas, Ohio, and Connecticut delegations." This withdrawal threw the convention into an uproar as rumors circulated of a "back room deal." After struggling to regain order and securing the return of the three missing delegations, the chairman began the twenty-third ballot. These three delegations threw their support to W&L's favorite son, and there followed a mad stampede to Davis. After much hoopla, the students adjourned for a raucous post-convention celebration—presumably not in conformity with their dry platform. When the almost identical scene was reenacted at Madison Square Garden two months later—albeit with many more ballots, the reputation of the W&L Mock Convention was forever established and has continued to the current day as a nationally publicized event every four years.[8]

As the New York temperatures were hitting record highs, delegates convened on June 24 while the nation listened in by radio for the first time in history. It was announced that AT&T and RCA had secured arrangements to make the proceedings available to half the country through a link up with stations as far west as Kansas City. Newspaper reports talked of the "furnace-like air in the draped hall that kept fans and straw hats waving vigorously."[9] As the party platform committee began its work, headlines already talked ominously of "ticklish problems" likely to produce fights over the platform. Sides were quickly forming within the platform committee over what the party should say about the League, the Klan, and Prohibition, leading one observer to note, "The

Democratic convention did its best to lose the election before it had nominated a candidate."[10] Indeed they did.

At the convention outset, the party seemed briefly unified in support of Senator Pat Harrison's keynote address in which he blistered the GOP as "the Grand *Oil* Party." As Harrison nostalgically longed "for one in the White House whose heart might be melted and courage aroused to sympathize and fight"—"not a sphinx," the crowd roared its approval, while back in Washington President Coolidge listened in on the White House radio in the solitude of his White House study.[11]

This display of unity lasted no longer than Harrison's keynote speech. Dissension over the Klan issue boiled up from the Resolutions Committee hearings and soon spilled onto the convention floor. Headlines on the June 26 *Washington Post* were ominous: "Delegates in Fist Fights On Floor Over Klan."[12] After an hour-long demonstration following the nominating speech for McAdoo, the nominating speech for Senator Underwood ignited the Klan issue and triggered a succession of fistfights around the convention floor. Photographs gave the public an all too memorable picture of the Democrats' disarray.

A high point of the nominating speeches was Franklin Roosevelt's speech nominating Alfred E. Smith. It immortalized Smith as "The Happy Warrior" and marked the return of FDR to public life following his debilitating bout with polio. Syndicated columnist Mark Sullivan issued this report from the convention floor: "When you heard Franklin D. Roosevelt's speech, you almost wished you could sandbag your knowledge of practical politics for an hour and permit yourself to think that Smith's chances are in

(COLLECTION OF NEW-YORK HISTORICAL SOCIETY, NEGATIVE #83269D)

Front-runner William Gibbs McAdoo addresses a crowd of supporters in front of New York's Vanderbilt Hotel on June 24, 1924.

proportion to the enthusiasm of his supporters. It was one of the very best nominating speeches this writer has ever heard—and he has heard, Oh Lord, how many!"

It was Roosevelt's speech that pulled the trigger to ignite the "hometown advantage" for Smith. A convention demonstration unparalleled in intensity, volume, and length erupted on the floor. Newspapers wrote of the "terrifying pandemonium." Delegates "howled, yelled, screamed, and sang from densely crowded galleries." They flooded the aisles—abetted by sympathetic New York police officers—and carried the demonstration out into the streets surrounding the Garden. Senator Walsh, the convention chairman, banged his gavel furiously and threatened, "If we cannot transact our business here, I shall move that we go to some other city."[13]

(COURTESY AP/WIDE WORLD PHOTOS)

As Franklin Roosevelt entered Al Smith's name in nomination, the most chaotic demonstration in American political history erupted on the convention floor. The "hometown advantage" was obvious as the Garden was jammed with thousands of screaming Smith supporters, who wreaked bedlam on the convention for well over an hour.

When Judge John Holt of Huntington placed Davis's name in nomination it was 3 a.m. on the morning of June 27. Holt challenged the delegates to remember they had come not just to nominate a candidate but also to elect a president, and they should consider character above all else. "Give us a man who will rescue the Department of Justice from the scorn of an indignant people, protect the public domain with the flaming sword of common honesty, relieve the people from unnecessary taxation—and in Heaven's name—simplify the machinery by which these taxes are levied . . . I nominate a man who would become a platform within himself during the campaign and, after the election—a chief executive of whom every American could be proud—John

W. Davis of West Virginia!"[14] Despite the late hour, the exhausted delegates responded with a respectable demonstration that was considerably shorter and more subdued than Governor Smith's.

As the nominating speeches concluded, speculation increased that Davis would be the compromise choice, resulting in rumors that "William Jennings Bryan intends to attack Davis on the floor of the convention and point out where, in his estimation, the distinguished West Virginian falls short of meeting the requirements for Democratic success."[15] It was reported during the convention that Davis had represented Standard Oil Company. This revived the issue of Davis's Wall Street connections, causing the "Great Commoner" great consternation.

Former secretary of the Navy and veteran Democratic warhorse Josephus Daniels wrote from the convention to the folks back home in North Carolina not "to mistake the side show for the big event." As amusing as the speeches, floor fights, and name-calling were to the public, he urged voters not to be diverted from the important issues before the Democratic Party—to win back the White House, "to clean up Washington, and to take a seat in the world council." Daniels also observed that the convention was "chock full of religion. It eats religion, dreams it and smokes it." One delegate confided to Daniels that he came to New York thinking he was to attend a political convention but instead he had found a religious convocation. Daniels warned, "The convention has left the denunciation of Republicans for religious warfare among themselves."[16]

Before the voting could begin, however, the Party had to adopt a platform, and here it was all out warfare. A motion to condemn the Klan was defeated by one vote, and a compromise measure proposed by Bryan was rejected also. The Texas delegation attempted briefly to light a cross in front of Madison Square Garden and was deterred by the New York police. In one of the most dramatic scenes of the convention, Miss Marion Colley, a delegate from Washington, Georgia, was recognized by the chairman as the vote on the Klan plank concluded and announced she was changing her vote to no. A staunch opponent of the Klan, Miss Colley initially supported the substitute plank, which condemned the Klan by name; but, in the name of party unity, she reversed her vote and thereby secured the defeat of the plank. Immediately, she was "surrounded by howling, threatening, and pleading men in the Georgia delegation."[17] Her faint voice was not audible above the din of the crowd as she tearfully tried to explain her vote. Headlines the next morning, "Georgia Woman Becomes Famous," brought to light the growing role of women in the political process.

Former Secretary of War Newton D. Baker made an impassioned, heartrending plea for all-out support of the League, but this was defeated, and instead the convention backed Bryan's compromise call for a national referendum. The McAdoo people attacked Smith's Catholic religion and his opposition to Prohibition, while the Smith supporters tied McAdoo to the Teapot Dome oil scandal. Finally, at 2 a.m. on June 29, the party adopted a platform about which, the *Washington Post* claimed, "It will go to the country in November, containing pussyfooting compromises on two great issues which have all but rent it asunder—the League of Nations and the Ku Klux Klan."[18] After these disruptive proceedings, there were calls to reconvene the convention in a more remote, "neutral" location, perhaps Kansas City, while others proposed closing the convention to radio coverage. Unfortunately for the party, the damage was already done.

As finally adopted, the 1924 Democratic platform began by "paying homage to the memory of Woodrow Wilson, whose spirit and influence will live on through the ages." It made a gracious acknowledgement of Harding in stating, "Our party stands uncovered at the bier of Warren G. Harding," substituting "grave" for "bier" at the pious suggestion of Bryan to placate the Prohibitionists.[19] The platform continued on to contrast a Democratic Party that "believes in equal rights for all and special privileges to none" as opposed to a Republican Party, which "holds that special privileges are essential to national prosperity. It believes that national prosperity must originate with the special interests and seep down to the wage earners. It has enthroned privilege and nurtured selfishness." And in an effort to reignite the party's old progressive spirit, the platform preamble concluded, "The Democratic Party stands for progress. The Republican Party stands still."

Predictably, the platform hit Republicans hard on the Harding scandals, the protective tariff, and states' rights—all unifying issues for the Democrats. But on the three most divisive issues of the convention—the League, the KKK, and Prohibition—the platform was largely noncommittal. While sanctimoniously opposing the "wholesale slaughter of human beings on the battlefield," the platform sidestepped the League issue by advocating a national referendum. The platform charged the Republicans with "trafficking in liquor permits" and "protecting the violators of the law," but it said nothing of how the Democrats would enforce Prohibition. And, finally, the Klan was not mentioned at all.

Now the primary task of nominating a candidate finally began. The first ballot showed the following division: McAdoo 431; Smith 241; Underwood 43; and Davis 31.

By July 1, the convention had labored through fifteen ballots with hardly any movement among the leading candidates: McAdoo 479; Smith 305; Underwood 39; and Davis 61.

By July 2, reporters saw Davis's strength rising. David Lawrence's syndicated column ranked "the compromise candidates in the order of their chances to win appear tonight as follows: John W. Davis of West Virginia, Senator Carter Glass of Virginia, and James M. Cox of Ohio."[20] Bryan issued a statement saying he would not support a Davis candidacy, noting he admired Davis personally but felt he was too much like Coolidge. Still McAdoo and Smith refused to withdraw, and the *Washington Post* was ominously referring to Madison Square Garden as the "burial ground of the Democratic Party."[21] On July 3, Bryan addressed the convention to propose compromise candidates but was perceived as favoring McAdoo. The delegates responded by roundly booing their three-time standard bearer, and the mayhem rolled on. By July 4 reports were flying that many delegates were "weary and broke."[22]

After sailing past the old Democratic Party record of fifty-seven ballots, which had been set at the 1860 convention in Charleston, the seventieth ballot showed no material change: McAdoo 415; Smith 323; and Davis 76.

The acrimony was pervasive. In historian David Burner's words, "The deadlock that developed might as well have been between the Pope and Imperial Wizard of the KKK, so solidly did the Catholic delegates support Smith and the Klan delegates support McAdoo."[23] The Smith supporters talked openly of prolonging the convention in order to bankrupt the McAdoo forces. The McAdoo forces responded, "We've ordered our winter clothes and will stay till Christmas if necessary." Liquor flowed freely even among the Prohibition forces. McAdoo complained, "Some of my best men have been hopelessly drunk ever since they landed in New York."[24] "How long can you Western delegates stay here?" asked a New Yorker of an Oregon delegate. "Until you Smith men lose your voices" was the response. One South Carolinian was heard to complain, "The only trouble with staying here all summer is that the price of hog jowl and turnip greens in New York City is too damn high."[25]

Davis remained detached on the sidelines, declining to comment on the issues and meeting sporadically with reporters to urge party unity. After the sixtieth ballot, he considered with-drawing but was dissuaded by his law partner Frank Polk. McAdoo devised a plan to scuttle the two-thirds majority requirement but could not muster the necessary support to enact the change. The favorite son–dark horse candidates held firm, reluctant to release their votes so long as the convention remained closely divided. David Lawrence's dispatch in the July 6 newspapers concluded that "out of the deadlock, the name of John W. Davis of West Virginia appears tonight to stand out as the compromise candidate."[26]

Josephus Daniels was again updating the folks back home in North Carolina with his latest musing from New York: "Are national conventions a thing of the past? The cold-storage performance in Cleveland (the GOP convention) and the fervid one here at New York cause any thoughtful person to wonder if some better plan could not be devised."[27]

On July 8, the convention was accorded a brief respite as tragedy struck the Coolidge family. The president's son, Calvin, Jr., died as the result of blood poisoning, and the convention adjourned out of respect. Sometime on July 9, Davis met with Senator Glass, and they agreed that Glass would temporarily release half of Virginia's delegates. If the next round of balloting did not produce victory for Davis, then Davis would withdraw and support Glass. Concurrent with this discussion, Governor Cox, the 1920 nominee, endorsed Davis. And most importantly, after the ninety-sixth ballot, McAdoo and Smith finally released their delegates on July 9, but even here the party missed a chance to redeem some hope of unity. McAdoo withdrew so reluctantly and ambivalently—without any trace of graciousness—that there seemed no hope the Democrats would come together.

Davis's support now swelled quickly, as the Texas delegation announced their forty votes were moving to that "great outstanding liberal" Democrat John W. Davis. That was news to many of the Davis supporters who knew he was a conservative Democrat; but at this stage, who could refuse forty votes! Finally, Davis was nominated on the one-hundred-third ballot when Franklin Roosevelt dramatically struggled to his feet, clutching his crutches, and cast sixty of New York's votes for Davis. The convention moved to make Davis's nomination unanimous by acclamation, and the traditional floor demonstration began with the West Virginia delegation claiming its place in the sun. Flamboyantly waiving her scarf at the head of the procession was Izetta Jewel

Brown, who had seconded Davis's nomination in a memorable speech lauding Davis as "a woman's ideal man for President."[28] The convention then recessed after nine days of balloting and a total of fifteen days in session before reassembling to nominate a vice presidential candidate.

The Last Ballots of the Convention

Ballot	McAdoo	Smith	Underwood	Davis	Meredith	Walsh
100th	190	351	41	203	75	52
101st	52	121	229	316	13	98
102nd	21	44	307	415	66	123
103rd	Davis by acclamation					

In order to leave the Garden with any semblance of unity, Davis and his supporters believed they must select a progressive as vice president. Senator Walsh of Montana, the popular convention chairman, was their first choice, but Walsh declined. He remained loyal to the party and would support Davis, but thought his nomination had been "a tragic mistake."[29] Similarly, former Agriculture Secretary Edward Meredith of Iowa declined. Davis's close friend and fellow Washington and Lee graduate, former Secretary of War Newton D. Baker, was considered, but backed away because of health reasons before being asked. Finally, consensus formed around Nebraska Governor Charles Bryan, the younger brother of William Jennings Bryan.

"Brother Charlie" brought a well-known name to the ticket, but he did little to bring the desperately needed unity. His selection was seen as "window dressing," which neither suited nor fooled either faction of the party. Josephus Daniels called the ticket an odd attempt to "mix oil and water."[30] Carter Glass bitterly complained that Bryan "is not worth a bauble." He believed Bryan would weaken the ticket in the east where Davis had to draw traditional Democrats if he was to be elected.[31] Glass correctly foresaw that Bryan would not pull in the progressive voters in the Midwest, while his very presence on the ticket ensured no Independent or Republican voters would swing to Davis.

The final chapter of this interminably long convention was the obligatory effort to rally around the candidate at the conclusion. In a precedent-shattering gesture, Davis entered the Garden and addressed the delegates in person. He appropriately and mercifully addressed the convention for a total of only eight minutes. He did all he could to assuage the divisions of the party, and he was enthusiastically received as he called for an end to religious and sectional differences.

At the close, there was a rush of support from both wings of the party. Progressives and conservatives both hailed Davis as one of their own, but conservatives knew they had won the day. In summation, Walter Lippmann wrote, "Davis' nomination was the result of confidence in his character rather than of studied agreement with his views."[32] Indeed, after the most divisive convention in American history, the Democratic Party had turned in utter exhaustion to a man of unquestioned ability and integrity who had at least not been an active participant in the intraparty fratricide.

Part Four

THE CANDIDATES

Chapter Seven

THE MOST PERFECT GENTLEMAN

John W. Davis was the most perfect
gentleman I have ever met.
—King George V

As the exhausted delegates headed home from Madison Square
Garden on July 11, 1924, there remained much uncertainty
about just what kind of candidate they had nominated. Liberals
and conservatives alike were claiming victory, while both sides
agreed that Davis was a man of great ability, broad experience,
and winsome charm. As the liberal Democrat Jonathan Daniels
wrote from New York on July 12 for the Raleigh *News & Observer*,
"Davis is the sort of man it will be mighty easy to get extravagant
about before this campaign is over. He is what is called a magnetic
personality. People turn to him instinctively."[1]

Daniels' portrayal explained, in part, Davis's final triumph
at the convention as a compromise candidate. The decision to
nominate Davis was more a tribute to his ability and personal
characteristics than any kind of ideological victory. Throughout

his public career, he had been put forth for office by his friends; and, without exception, he had performed with great distinction in each position in which he had served. In 1924, there was never any serious question as to whether he was qualified to serve as president. As Walter Lippmann wrote,

> They acted on an intuition that told them that in an extreme crisis only the ablest man is good enough. That is how a disorderly convention came to select a man with a deep sense of order; how a convention boiling with passion selected a man of serene temper; how a convention charged with ignorance and prejudice selected a man of lucid and judicious intelligence; how a convention filled with crusaders in which two factions utterly distrusted each other united at last on a man who gives at once a sense of assurance. In this case men who had looked into a witches' cauldron of hatred and disunion yielded to a half-conscious judgment which was far more reliable than their common sense. For they turned to the one candidate who embodied preeminently those very qualities for lack of which the party had almost destroyed itself.[2]

In selecting Davis, the Democrats had not only chosen an attractive, experienced, and competent candidate, but they had also turned—albeit in search of compromise—to the conservative wing of their party. John W. Davis was above all a Jeffersonian

Democrat—a believer in limited government, states' rights, and free trade. He traced his conservative Democratic political lineage back through Alton Parker, Grover Cleveland, Samuel Tilden, and Horatio Seymour. While he had served under Woodrow Wilson, he was not a Wilson-Bryan progressive—save in foreign affairs where he was a Wilsonian internationalist. In retrospect, it is clear that Davis's nomination in 1924 was indeed the high-water mark of the conservative wing of the Democratic Party, for the party has never again turned to a conservative candidate. Davis was the last in a long line of Jeffersonian Democrats to lead his party.

Although the party nominated a Wall Street lawyer and former ambassador to the Court of St. James's, their nominee was very much a product of his native region—the South. His grandfather, John Davis, had moved from eastern Virginia to Clarksburg in 1820; and his father, John J. Davis, was a Unionist active in the formation of West Virginia, which separated from Virginia in 1863, and served two terms in the U. S. Congress from 1871 to 75. The father became a prominent lawyer with a statewide practice and was ever a loyal Democrat, who idolized Thomas Jefferson and was known for his unswerving devotion to Democratic principles. As Davis reminisced in later life, "All his life my father was a pronounced individualist. I have never known any man who was more insistent on making up his own mind and really less inclined to yield to the opinions of others."[3]

Davis's mother was Anna Kennedy, who was reared and educated in Baltimore and brought both an active mind and a forceful personality to her marriage with John J. Davis. Anna was a lifelong reader of the classics and, with her husband, an equally devoted disciple of Thomas Jefferson. Davis remembered her as "the most commanding person I ever knew."[4] After the birth of five daughters, the Davis's sixth child was a boy, who was born on April 13, 1873, not insignificantly, Thomas Jefferson's birthday. Family folklore chronicled that Anna Davis was characteristically engrossed in trying to finish the final volume of Gibbon's monumental *The Decline and Fall of the Roman Empire* late on the evening of April 13, 1873, when she laid aside her reading in order to ensure that her son would be born on Jefferson's birthday.[5]

(WEST VIRGINIA AND REGIONAL HISTORY COLLECTION, WEST VIRGINIA UNIVERSITY LIBRARIES)
John W. Davis's father, John J. Davis, was a lifelong Jeffersonian Democrat whose reputation in West Virginia for both legal ability and moral rectitude was unsurpassed.

It was into this family of a prominent father, a strong-willed mother, and five adoring older sisters that John W. Davis was born and securely nurtured. The family home in Clarksburg was a large, three-story Victorian house on Lee Street, and it was here that Davis received his first ten years of formal education at the hands of his mother. As one of Davis's sisters wrote of their mother, "Study was her life,"[6] and Anna Kennedy Davis was determined to inculcate this love of learning in her six children. Anna was fluent in French and German and had a working knowledge of Greek and Latin. She was a painter, poet, and pianist; and she poured her enthusiasm for learning into the education of her children.

Davis was learning Latin at the age of eight and writing essays at the age of ten. One of her cardinal rules of composition was to serve Davis well in his career before the bar. She demanded that he, "Condense, condense, condense! I want to make him positive, brief, concise."[7] She was always demanding. As Davis wrote in later life, "I *knew* I must be attentive. I *knew* I must follow what she said. I *knew* that it wasn't worthwhile to file a petition for a rehearing. That case was closed."[8] As Anna oversaw these early

(WEST VIRGINIA AND REGIONAL HISTORY COLLECTION, WEST VIRGINIA UNIVERSITY LIBRARIES)

This substantial Victorian house was the Davis home on Lee Street in Clarksburg, West Virginia. It was here that Davis and his sisters received their early education from their mother.

years of education for her son, she concluded, "I do not think John is brilliant, but I am sure he will work as hard as any man alive."[9]

At age twelve, Davis was enrolled along with several other boys in the only local preparatory school, Clarksburg Female Seminary, where he studied for the next three years with some sixty-five female fellow students; and in 1887, he was sent to Pantops Academy, a boys' preparatory school near Charlottesville, Virginia. In addition to finishing his college preparatory work over the next two years, Davis acquired the nickname "Bones," reflecting his lanky stature, and also first encountered his political hero, Thomas Jefferson. From nearby Pantops, Davis and a friend hiked up the hill to Monticello and persuaded the caretaker to let them walk the grounds, including a long-remembered visit to Jefferson's grave.[10]

(THE WEST VIRGINIA AND REGIONAL HISTORY COLLECTION, WEST VIRGINIA UNIVERSITY LIBRARIES)

Left: This photograph of a young John W. Davis was taken about the time he enrolled in Pantops Academy in Charlottesville, Virginia, in 1887.
Right: Young Davis on horseback in Clarksburg. Even as a teenager, Davis appeared always to be meticulous and dapper in his attire.

In 1889, Anna and John J. Davis made a decision that would have a lifelong impact on their son. They decided he would attend Washington and Lee University. Princeton, University of Virginia, and Hampden-Sydney had all been considered, but the decision for Washington and Lee was the result of both John J. Davis's friendship with Judge John W. Brockenbrough, who was long associated with Washington and Lee, and the Davis family's reverence for General Robert E. Lee, who had served as college president after the Civil War. As Davis entered W&L, the college was still very much in the shadow of General Lee. From Lee's death in 1870 until 1897, Lee's son Custis served as president and continued largely on the path set by his father. General Lee had presided over a five-year postwar renaissance of the college, followed by some contraction in enrollment and financial strains in the later years of Custis Lee's long tenure.[11]

(WASHINGTON AND LEE UNIVERSITY)
The historic colonnade at Washington and Lee University
appears today as it did in Davis's student days.

(WASHINGTON AND LEE UNIVERSITY)

(Left) General Robert E. Lee's presidency of Washington College ended with his
death in 1870, but his presence was still keenly felt during Davis's student days there.
(Right) General Lee's son G. W. Custis Lee succeeded his father and was president
during Davis's tenure.

Davis completed his undergraduate requirements at W&L in
three years with academic achievement in Latin, English, history,
and geology. In logic and rhetoric, he was stimulated and challenged
by Professor James Quarles, whom Davis later credited with
providing "the basis of most of my work at the bar."[12] He pledged
Phi Kappa Psi, the largest fraternity on campus; and at various
times, he played tennis and football and boxed. His classmates were
to remember him later as "popular and industrious—and one
whose frolics did not run to license."[13] Years later Davis reflected
back on his years at Washington and Lee, "Of what I carried away,
the personality of the old faculty is of greater value than any book
learning they were able to drill into me."[14]

At the end of his undergraduate years Davis made two
important decisions. He committed himself to the study of law,

and he accepted a position as tutor to the nine children and six nephews and nieces of Major Edward McDonald of Charles Town, West Virginia. He would have entered law school in 1892 but the family funds for his continued education were depleted. The tutoring position was for nine months, and the salary was $300 with board included. Davis's students ranged from ages six to twenty, and the routine was five hours of grueling classroom work every morning, labor on the farm in the afternoons, followed by evenings of preparation. Davis's letters to his family that fall found him weary and depressed, but by spring he had fallen in love with Major McDonald's second daughter, Julia. She was nineteen, and Davis was only twenty. They reached an understanding that they would become engaged when Davis had begun to establish himself.[15]

(WEST VIRGINIA AND REGIONAL HISTORY COLLECTION)

Davis's experience at Washington and Lee University was to have a lifelong impact on him. Here the nineteen-year-old Davis was photographed as he entered W&L in 1892.

Davis returned home to Clarksburg in June 1893, to face an uncertain future. The country was gripped by a financial panic, and his father did not have the resources to send him to law school. In order to pursue his hope for a legal career, Davis agreed to clerk for his father for the next year. During this fourteen-month period, he read Blackstone and closely observed his father's practice. In the fall of 1894, Davis entered the Washington and Lee School of Law, along with fifty fellow students under the two-man faculty of Dean John Randolph Tucker and Professor Charles A. Graves.

These two men had a reputation for excellence that was quite remarkable. Tucker was a former president of the American Bar Association and former congressman, and, a commanding figure. As Davis later reflected, Tucker's eloquent lectures "filled the dullest student with a perception of the majesty of the law."[16] Tucker was a passionate disciple of Jefferson and Calhoun and a devoted proponent of states' rights. He stood with Grover Cleveland against all forms of expanded government and for a stable, sound currency. These tenets of conservative Jeffersonian thought took seed in young John Davis.

Professor Graves was in Davis's opinion, "an educational genius." Much more professorial in style than Tucker, Graves taught Common and Statute Law and was credited with grounding a generation of Washington and Lee students in the basics of common law. Davis always held Graves in reverential affection and concluded, "I owe to him a debt beyond my power to repay."[17] It was to Tucker whom Davis owed his love of constitutional law, and it was to Graves to whom he attributed his interest in real property.[18]

These two professors instilled in young Davis a respect for the law and a conservative worldview that would serve as his political and legal bedrock for his entire career. In later life, Davis approvingly recalled his legal training, "The professors were not so concerned with teaching us to criticize. They were more concerned that you should learn what the law *was*, than that you should be invited to speculate on what the law *ought* to be. I don't believe in educating the law student to be first a critic and afterwards a student. In law school, I don't think we students sat in judgment of the law."[19]

(WASHINGTON AND LEE UNIVERSITY)

(Left) John Randolph Tucker was Dean of the Washington and Lee Law School and exerted a lasting influence on Davis's constitutional philosophy.
(Right) Davis held law professor Charles A. Graves in reverential regard.

After completing his law school training in half the normal two-year period, Davis joined his father for a year in establishing the Davis & Davis firm in Clarksburg. The following year he accepted a one-year assistant professorship at the Washington and Lee Law School, which Davis later claimed gave him "under pressure, the best legal education possible," and then he returned to Clarksburg to resume partnership with his father in 1897.[20]

It was in Clarksburg that Davis learned what it meant to be, in his words, a "country lawyer." After losing his first three cases, a dejected Davis sought out his father, who was reading by the fireside in his library, and stated, "I'm going to quit this business. I don't like it. I want to be in some business that isn't a fight all the time." Davis reported his father's response as immediate and forceful, "He stood me with my back to that coal fire and gave me the damndest lecture, winding up that he never expected to hear anything like that from me again, and I went up to bed."[21]

Davis never specialized in any particular area of the law but rather represented individuals in small matters as well as corporations in major cases. As West Virginia's economy grew around its natural resources, he took on both management and labor clients involved in the coal, oil, and gas industries; and, by 1906, at the age of thirty-three, he was elected president of the West Virginia Bar Association. Davis was always to speak nostalgically of these years as a country lawyer, "I wouldn't take a fortune for having been through it. It does teach you to fear God and take your own part. There you stand. Your client's behind you, true, but the fight is yours."[22]

As he steadily established himself as a lawyer, Davis continued his pursuit of Julia McDonald, and after six years of courtship they were married on June 20, 1899, at Media, the McDonald family farm. After a honeymoon trip to Washington, they settled in Clarksburg in the Lee Street home of Davis's parents, where "Julia's warmth and enthusiasm brought gaiety and spontaneity into the Davis household."[23] In the fall of their first year of marriage, Julia became pregnant. When she went into labor several weeks late in mid-July, the family doctor was ill and unable to attend her. The substitute physician arrived half drunk, accomplished the delivery, but failed to sterilize his instruments. The baby daughter, named Anna Kennedy, was fine, but Julia developed puerperal fever and died in Davis's arms a month later.

The loss was devastating for Davis. He renamed his daughter Julia, gave over her upbringing to his mother and sisters, and threw himself headlong into his profession. Long after, Julia described their relationship: "His hours grew longer, his trips more frequent, his return to the office after dinner invariable. He was always kindly, often abstracted, but I knew then, and I know still, that looking at me hurt his heart."[24] Sadly, what Julia wanted was his time, but he was not able to offer it.

While Davis was developing his legal practice, he found himself quite naturally drawn into politics. His father was still active in the Democratic Party, and Davis inherited from him a residue of goodwill and a network of political friends. In 1898, he was thrust onto the state political stage by the Democrats of Harrison County. Republicans had represented the county for the last twenty years, and the Democrats sensed a change of fortunes in 1898. Responding to rumors that he might be nominated, Davis announced before the state convention convened that he was not a candidate, but his Democratic friends were not to be denied. As Davis told the story years later, Colonel James Allen "popped up and nominated me for the legislature. I arose and said I didn't desire the nomination. There were cries of 'Sit down!' I was about to rise again, but Squire Camp sitting on one side and somebody else . . . grabbed my coat and held me in my seat, and before I knew it I was nominated."[25] He went on to win the election and entered the House of Delegates in January 1899.

In a pattern that was to be repeated throughout his career, Davis's cohorts quickly recognized his leadership abilities and elected him Democratic leader and chairman of the Judiciary Committee. After Julia's death, he declined to run for reelection to a second term but remained active as chairman of the Harrison County Democratic Committee and was chosen as a delegate to the 1904 national convention. At this convention he got his first taste of national politics and approvingly saw the nomination of the conservative Alton B. Parker for president. During the first decade of the new century, Davis turned away several opportunities to run for congress and for governor, always explaining that the demands of his growing practice prevented it.

For the preceding ten years, no Democrat had been elected to Congress from West Virginia, but by 1910 there seemed to be a growing dissatisfaction with President Taft and the Republicans. The Democratic state leaders sent forth the word, "Name your strongest men. If necessary, draft them,"[26] and Clem Shaver, a leading Democrat from neighboring Marion County, approached Davis about running from the first congressional district. Davis flatly refused, unwilling to leave his burgeoning law practice; and his refusal was strongly bolstered by his father's opposition.

Upon arriving at the party state convention, Davis issued a statement restating his refusal, but his "fool friends," as he called them, "got hold of the newspaper boys and got them so drunk they couldn't hand in their reports," while the convention proceeded to nominate Davis over his protests. He reluctantly agreed to "take his medicine" and accepted the nomination.

Weeks later one of his close friends somewhat sheepishly handed Davis two telegrams sent by John J. Davis to his son during the Wheeling convention. The first urged, "Do not yield to solicitations. Stand Firm on declination." The second, wired on the day of the nomination, demanded, "Say no and be firm."[27] Knowing the reverence Davis had for his father, the friend elected to pocket both telegrams until after Davis was safely nominated. In the general election, the party bosses were proven right. Davis attracted significant Republican support, despite his constant attacks on the Republican tariff policies, and carried the district by 20,370 votes to 16,962. As Davis headed for Washington in early 1911, he could not have known that he was at a pivotal point in his career and would never again reside in his beloved West Virginia.

The off-year congressional elections of 1910 returned a whopping gain of 58 seats to the Democrats, giving them a margin of 230 seats to 162 for the GOP. The congressional vote clearly showed growing dissatisfaction with President Taft and a developing split between Republican conservatives and progressives. Davis, along with the Democrats nationally, had relentlessly attacked the Republican tariff, charging that the GOP policy benefitted "the few at the expense of the many, and had enhanced the swollen profits of those already rich, beyond the dreams of avarice." While it was indeed a Democratic year, Davis's character and stature played a crucial role in wresting the formerly safe seat from the GOP, and his Republican opponent, Charles E. Carrigan, stated, "It is no disgrace to be beaten by a man like John W. Davis."[28]

The first order of business for the newly empowered Democratic majority, in which Davis participated enthusiastically, was the election of Missourian Champ Clark as Speaker. As the House Democrats moved quickly to organize themselves, it was clear that Davis's reputation as an able lawyer had preceded him. He was assigned to the prestigious Judiciary Committee, as Chairman Henry Clayton was in need of an able draftsman. Davis was instrumental in drafting, presenting, and passing a substantial reform of the use of injunctions in labor cases, which was finally passed as the Clayton Antitrust Act. Davis's speech on behalf of the legislation was, according to Felix Frankfurter, the "ablest" of the debate and drew wide attention as the bill passed by a large bipartisan margin. As Speaker Clark observed by the end of the term, he could not recall a freshman congressman who had earned so much respect as Davis.[29]

As the country entered the election of 1912, the tide of progressivism was running strong. Theodore Roosevelt could contain himself no longer on the sidelines and plunged into the race to challenge his erstwhile friend and anointed successor, William Howard Taft. Roosevelt embraced a boldly progressive agenda that set him at clear odds with the more middle-of-the-road Taft. Meanwhile the Democrats sensed the same public opinion currents, and nominated the scholarly progressive governor of New Jersey, Woodrow Wilson. Although Davis had been elected to Congress in 1910 as a classic Jeffersonian Democrat, he enthusiastically supported Wilson. The Republicans attacked Davis's anti-tariff record vigorously, linking it to economic problems in West Virginia; and, even more significantly, Theodore Roosevelt's Progressive Party opted not to field a congressional candidate but rather endorsed Davis's Republican opponent.

Again, character—not Davis's lack of progressivism—proved decisive, although the margin of his reelection was a very slim 248 votes. At this point, the Republicans called for a recount and somewhat suspiciously reported an additional 100 votes for Davis's opponent, reducing Davis's margin to 148 votes. As Davis recalled years later, "Then, in the chief Democratic county, where they'd demanded a recount, they went to my friend Cal Conaway, who was head of the returning board. They said, 'Cal, when are you going to count these Marion County votes?' He said, 'Just as soon as we find out how many votes John Davis needs'. Thereupon the Republicans threw up their hands and abandoned the recount."[30]

It was during this term in Congress that Davis remarried. He had grown up with Ellen Graham Bassell, "Nell" as she was called, and her five sisters in Clarksburg, about whom Davis once wrote, "They aspire to lead the fast set here." Nell's father was a leading lawyer and frequently opposed Davis's father in court. One of Davis's lifelong friends wrote, "It was a common saying in the old days that when two disputants would decide to go into court, and wanted the best lawyer obtainable, one would get John Bassell and the other would get John Davis."[31]

Nell had been married to a Clarksburg man who reportedly had become an adulterer and drug addict, and only shortly before his death, she had secured a divorce. Even under these unfortunate circumstances, divorce was not lightly sanctioned, and Davis's family was greatly concerned when he became seriously interested in Nell in 1907. After an off-and-on again courtship over the next three years, Davis concluded by 1910 that he wanted to marry Nell and began to try to overcome his family's objections. He wrote to his mother, "You think that if I marry Nell Bassett I shall be unhappy. You may be right. I know that if I do not I shall be of all men most miserable."[32]

Finally, without the support of his family, Davis concluded the decision was his alone and married Nell in the rectory of the Episcopal Church in Clarksburg in a quiet, private ceremony on January 2, 1912. Davis's decision was soon vindicated, as Nell Bassell proved to be both a loving wife and a considerable asset to his career. Although her formal education was prematurely terminated when she contracted a severe case of scarlet fever in her early teens, she was an imposing woman, an accomplished hostess and conversationalist, a shrewd judge of character, and a devoted wife. Shortly after their marriage, Nell confided to her sister that Davis would have been hopelessly mired in the legal profession "if he had married a woman as timid as he is." As it became evident that Nell was indeed a good mate for Davis, she gradually won over his family, and even old John J. told Nell shortly before his death what "a noble woman you are."[33]

It was early in Davis's second congressional term that two unusual events catapulted him into the national spotlight: the impeachment trial of Federal Judge Robert W. Archibald of Pennsylvania and the contempt action against Charles C. Glover, an influential Washington banker. On July 11, 1912, Judge Archibald was impeached for using his position for personal gain. Davis was chosen as one of the managers for the trial, and, after losing confidence in the ability of Representative Clayton to lead the trial, Davis filed his argument in the *Congressional Record*, where it received bipartisan acclaim. Davis's summation was widely quoted, "This confidence of the people in the integrity of their officers is the foundation stone, the prop, the support of all free governments."[34] Only five federal judges had been impeached in the history of the Republic, and progressives were advocating the recall of judges as the only effective means of holding the judiciary accountable. Davis and other conservatives strongly opposed recall as unwise and unconstitutional, and the Archibald case was an important deterrent to the recall movement. Archibald was convicted on January 13, 1913.

The Glover incident was a media sensation. Late in the sixty-second Congress, Representative Thetus W. Sims of Tennessee attacked a pending bill that authorized the purchase of a large tract of land owned by Glover. Some weeks later after angrily brooding over Sims's attack, Glover accosted Sims in Faragut Square in Washington, called him a "contemptible liar," and slammed his fist into Sims's jaw. Speaker Clark promptly appointed Davis chairman of a five-man investigative committee.

There were no questions of fact since Glover and Sims agreed on what had happened, but there was an important question of the law. Did congressional immunity apply? If so, what would be the method of trial and what could be the punishment? As the newspapers grabbed the story, Davis was squarely in the national spotlight. On April 26, 1913, Davis returned to the House his clear assertion that a congressman's freedom of speech is inviolable, which renders him immune from challenge in any other place for a speech made in Congress. The House overwhelmingly approved the report, ordered the arrest of Glover, and summoned him to the well of the House where he was rebuked by Speaker Clark.

Davis's evenhanded, decisive, and articulate handling of the Archibald and Glover cases proved very quickly to be pivotal to his career. As the cases unfolded, President Wilson and his attorney general, James C. McReynolds, were pondering the selection of a solicitor general, and they concluded Davis was their man. McReynolds had some months earlier considered nominating Davis for a federal judgeship. For the only time in his career, Davis had actively sought an appointment. It appeared he would be selected as recommendations began to flow into McReynolds's office. "If the Almighty ever created a finer man than John W. Davis, I never knew him," wrote James M. Cox, the 1920 presidential nominee and then colleague of Davis's in the House.[35] The House Judiciary Committee unanimously endorsed him.

As McReynolds prepared to recommend Davis for the judgeship, President Wilson informed McReynolds that he felt obligated to nominate Justice Charles Woods of South Carolina. Although Davis admitted he was "hell-bent in those days to go on the bench" and was disappointed, he later saw this as a "great personal service—it cured me" of desiring to serve on the bench. In less than two months, President Wilson nominated Davis solicitor general of the United States, a position Davis called "the most attractive office within the gift of the government for the man who loves the practice of law."[36]

For Davis, the government was now his client, and he was the government's chief advocate. He assumed this role at a critical time, and much of the progressive legislation passed under Roosevelt, Taft, and Wilson was ultimately challenged during Davis's tenure as solicitor general. He was often called upon to defend

(WEST VIRGINIA AND REGIONAL HISTORY COLLECTION, WEST VIRGINIA UNIVERSITY LIBRARIES)
Davis as President Wilson's solicitor general in 1917.

the extension of governmental power, and he never allowed his personal, Jeffersonian reservations to affect his service. He firmly believed the solicitor general served one purpose alone and that was to represent his client—the government—as effectively as possible. During his five-year tenure, Davis established a record, never equaled before or since, of personally arguing sixty-seven cases before the Court.

Among the more famous cases were the Pipe Line cases in which he successfully defended the Hepburn Act of 1906; two civil rights cases, *Guinn v. United States* and *United States v. Mosley*, in which he defended federal authority over the states; the defense of conservation policy and executive authority in *United States v. Midwest Oil*; several cases arising under the Interstate Commerce Act; and the test case for the Selective Service Act. Much of Davis's last years as solicitor general dealt with problems arising from America's emergence as a world power in World War I. He successfully argued that "laws which had been adequate under normal circumstances must be supplemented and enlarged to meet unforeseen situations, and with the coming of war itself increasing drafts upon the reservoir of governmental power became necessary."[37]

Within months of his arrival at the Court, Attorney General McReynolds reported that every member of the Court had expressed pleasure with Davis's performance. His arguments were noted for their brevity, wit, and clarity. Justice Joseph Lamar admitted, "John W. Davis has such a perfect flow of language that we don't ask questions when we should."[38] Observing Davis's impact on the court, one commentator compared the justices to "doting grandfathers enjoying the performance of a precocious and favorite grandson. The Court fairly hovered over Mr. Davis in its solicitude, particularly Chief Justice White. The Court can be most unapproachable and aloof in its demeanor toward the bar . . . But it never heckled its fair-haired boy: John W. Davis."[39]

The generally chilly Justice Charles Evans Hughes admitted it was "an intellectual treat" to hear Davis present an argument. Chief Justice White, once remarked admiringly, "Of course, no one has due process of law when Mr. Davis is on the other side." Even the Court pages spoke admiringly of Davis's dignity, kindness, and graciousness. One page noted, "Everyone was rooting for Mr. Davis."[40] Two successive chief justices, White and Taft, expressed their hope that Davis would be appointed their successor.[41] On January 5, 1920, Davis made a revealing entry in his diary: "Sent off new year letter to Chief Justice White. I shall always think that the greatest direct compliment I ever received was his statement when I went to say goodbye to him in Washington in December, 1918, that he had hoped that I might succeed him as Chief Justice. No man wants the bed in which he has slept narrowed to fit his successor."[42]

Those men whom Davis gathered around him as associates in those years came to view him with a certain amount of reverence. Huston Thompson observed, "He never made an enemy I know of. I never heard him criticize a man." Robert Szold wrote, "Nobody could have treated me better. He was witty, pleasant, and unfailingly courteous. He always had time for small, kindly things." Above all else, said John Lord O'Brian, "John W. Davis had the gift of graciousness." They were agreed in their respect for Davis's grasp of the law and the power of his reasoning. "Everything was on a high level—his preparation, his oral argument, his personal relations. The whole atmosphere," said Szold, "was of lofty dedication to the public welfare."[43]

Davis brought to the solicitor generalship a conviction that the proper role of the state is limited narrowly to the maintenance of order and national security and protection of private property and personal liberty. He said, "Human rights and rights of property are not different or antagonistic but parts of one and the same thing going to make up the bundle of rights which constitute American liberty. History furnishes no instance where the right of man to acquire and hold property has been taken away without the complete destruction of liberty in all its forms."[44] He further defined the government's role as ensuring that no group received preferential treatment, hence his views on the tariff and antitrust.

There is no evidence that Davis's conservative political views changed during this period; and, for a Jeffersonian Democrat, it was sometimes personally difficult for Davis to argue for his client. However, these years as solicitor general afforded Davis an unparalleled opportunity to test and hone his political views and enabled him to move forward in his career with an even more clearly defined and articulated conservatism. Also, during this period Davis established his reputation, especially among the nation's lawyers and among the Democratic Party leaders, many of whom were also lawyers.

As solicitor general during the World War, Davis was called upon to argue the government's position in a number of war-related cases including the draft and the president's ability to send American soldiers overseas. During the war years, he began to speak out on foreign affairs for the first time in his career, and he also became a close friend of Secretary of State Robert Lansing. Near the end of the war, Secretary Lansing and President Wilson selected Davis to serve on a five-man commission to negotiate with the Imperial Government of Germany on exchange of war criminals, and in September 1918, Davis crossed the Atlantic to attend the conference to be held in Switzerland.

While Davis was en route to Europe, U. S. Ambassador to Great Britain Walter Hines Page tendered his resignation because of ill health. Lansing and Wilson reviewed the list of potential replacements, and Lansing recommended Davis with Wilson's quick concurrence. Word of Davis's selection had leaked out in Washington, but Davis knew nothing of it when he landed in England to spend several days before continuing on to Switzerland.

He had reached Claridge's Hotel in London and was standing on the lobby stairway chatting with young Christian

Herter, a U. S. foreign service officer who later became Secretary of State under President Eisenhower, when he was handed two telegrams. He opened the first, which was from Nell, and was perplexed about "the offer," which she urged him to accept. He then turned to the second, which was the formal notification from Lansing of his nomination to represent the United States at the Court of St. James's. As Davis noted in his diary, "If the dome of St. Paul's had suddenly fallen on my head I could have been little more surprised."[45]

The ambassadorship to Great Britain had always been the premier diplomatic post in the U. S. Foreign Service, and a long line of outstanding men had served in the post over the years. Most often they had not only been men of achievement but also men of substantial personal wealth, as the United States did not provide an embassy and the expenses for entertaining and staffing were only partially covered by Congress. Davis was by no means a man of personal wealth, and he immediately wired Lansing that "financial reasons alone would seem to be prohibitive. My resources are meager as you know." Lansing responded, "Your eminent fitness beyond question. Understand that financial demand is between thirty and thirty-five thousand per annum. I know that it would be a great sacrifice but unhesitatingly say that I feel it your duty to accept. I have discussed this feature with your wife who agrees absolutely that you ought to accept in spite of financial sacrifice." Finally a week later on September 18, after another telegram from Nell again strongly urging his acceptance, Davis wired Lansing, "You may say to President accordingly that I will accept. I trust I fully appreciate both the great honor and the corresponding obligations, and shall do my best to vindicate my selection."[46]

While Davis was in no way a seasoned diplomat, his appointment was met with strong approval. House Republican Leader Gillette of Massachusetts spoke warmly of Davis: "We all admire him and trust him as a man of sound judgment, of broad culture and learning, of high character and of most charming personality."[47] The *Washington Post* reported,

> President Wilson in appointing John W. Davis, the Solicitor General, to succeed Walter Hines Page as Ambassador to the Court of St. James's, has not only selected the right man for the right place but has placed at the head of America's diplomatic service a man who is truly representative of America's firm resolve to crush German military power.
>
> Spontaneous approval went up at once when the appointment became known.[48]

Davis himself described the challenge, "I do not intend to pretend to be anything other than I am—an American citizen of modest means—living like a gentleman—doing his best to bear himself with the dignity befitting his office, but on no 'side'—not taking himself too seriously, but realizing that he has a tremendous job on his hands and giving it all the steam in the boiler."[49]

Davis had thus accepted the most formidable challenge of his career to this point. With no diplomatic training or experience, he was about to become the senior U. S. diplomat in Europe in a turbulent postwar period when America had just entered the world stage as a major player. It was indeed a test of his ability, his character, and his charm. This appointment was a turning point in Davis's career, for it provided him the platform for the development of his foreign policy views and left him with a lifelong love and admiration for England and the English people.

The role of the American ambassador to London had always been a dual one—both social and substantive. Despite their "meager means," the Davises established residence in a fashionable area of London staffed by the necessary household servants. Davis was to conclude at the end of his tenure in London, that he had to come out of pocket some $20,000 per year to cover the embassy's operating expenses. Nell was never of greater assistance to him, as she quickly grew into her role of diplomatic hostess. She loved the constant round of social activities and often provided Davis with helpful perspective. An example of her effectiveness was reported by Davis's grateful embassy staff. At a diplomatic dinner, an English general turned to Nell and demanded to know her views on President Wilson's interpretation of "freedom of the seas." At that time, the English perceived the "freedom of the seas" issue as a threat to their naval supremacy, and it was at the heart of tension between England and the U.S. Nell, with shrewd demureness and feigned innocence, answered that she really didn't know much about it but thought it "had something to do with mixed bathing, hadn't it?"[50]

The Davises were soon sought-after guests for London dinners and weekend house parties. Davis developed close and valuable friendships with Lord Reading, Lloyd George, Winston Churchill, Herbert Asquith, Lord Robert Cecil, Lord Halifax, and other leading English statesmen. His self-deprecating humor, unfailing courtesy, and quiet dignity elicited a response of universal

(WEST VIRGINIA AND REGIONAL HISTORY COLLECTION, WEST VIRGINIA UNIVERSITY LIBRARIES)

Winston Churchill was flanked here by Ambassador and Mrs. Davis at the annual Washington's birthday dinner in London, February 22, 1919.

approval from his English hosts. They were quick to give him their friendship and to share with him their private views on the important issues confronting the postwar period. It was no small compliment indeed when King George V said, "John W. Davis was the most perfect gentleman I have ever met."[51] Not surprisingly, Davis reciprocated with an unstinting admiration for the British people and the British Empire as forces for stability and civility in the world.

During his service as ambassador Davis dealt with a number of serious Anglo-American issues. The Paris Peace Conference and the ensuing fight over the League of Nations was an issue throughout his time in London. Davis accompanied President Wilson on his triumphant tour of England, during which Wilson ruffled the feathers of the British public by ignoring the hardships endured by Britain in the war. More serious diplomatic stresses developed from Wilson's conduct at the Paris Conference, and

(WEST VIRGINIA AND REGIONAL HISTORY COLLECTION, WEST VIRGINIA UNIVERSITY LIBRARIES)
Philip Laszlo was the favored portrait painter of London society in the early
twentieth century. Here, he painted a confidant, dignified Ambassador Davis
and his elegant wife, Ellen.

Davis sought continually to provide reassurance, explanation, and
context to both his government and his British hosts. As always,
England was most sensitive to its naval supremacy; and when this
seemed to have been challenged by Secretary of the Navy Josephus
Daniels in an inadvertently inflammatory speech delivered in 1919,
Davis was instrumental in reassuring the British government.

As the Irish question came once again to the forefront of
British politics, Davis was in a somewhat precarious position.
Although there was much sympathy for the Irish nationalists
in the United States, Davis was decidedly pro British. Wilson's
disastrous effort to secure American entry into the League of
Nations on a partisan basis was baffling to the British, and Davis
did much to interpret the American political scene for them. He
was a strong supporter of the League but felt that Wilson should
have sought bipartisan support and accepted at least most of
Lodge's reservations.[52]

As the ill Wilson became more withdrawn and dysfunctional, Davis and his boss, Secretary Lansing, felt increasingly isolated. As Davis recalled years later, "Then, with Wilson mute up in the White House, I had no direct communication with him. The lines of communication were all cut, and there I was, out in the trenches, without much direction from home. I just had to throw myself at them, do what I could."[53] Finally, Lansing resigned in February 1920, and Davis thought seriously about following suit but concluded it was his duty to remain through Wilson's term.

(WEST VIRGINIA AND REGIONAL HISTORY COLLECTION, WEST VIRGINIA UNIVERSITY LIBRARIES)

This photo, taken in his London office, conveyed the reserved dignity, sartorial precision, and commanding presence that so captivated Ambassador Davis's British audience.

As Davis planned to leave England in early 1921, he could look back with satisfaction over his two years. He always believed his primary duty as ambassador was to foster the unique benefits of the Anglo-American alliance; and, despite the many tensions in the relationship over those two years, he was consistently an important force in strengthening the alliance. Three unusual honors were conferred on Davis while he was in England. He was chosen president of the Birmingham and Midland Institute, a distinction previously conferred on only three predecessors—Ambassadors Lowell, Choate, and Page. He was made an honorary member of the Honorable Society of the Middle Temple, the oldest and most distinguished body of barristers in England, and was only the second American so honored. Also, he was made senior warden of Freemasons of England, a distinction never before conferred on a foreigner.[54] As he prepared to return to America, every major newspaper in London commended him for his efforts to strengthen the Anglo-American alliance.

Four days before leaving the country, Davis and his wife lunched with the King and Queen at Buckingham Palace. Over drinks the King thanked Davis for his service and friendship and then good naturedly needled Davis by predicting that Prohibition would never come to Great Britain. The King apologized for injecting one matter of business and proceeded to ask Davis to convey to President Harding the importance of British naval supremacy to world peace. On March 9, 1921, the Davises departed Victoria Station for Southampton amidst three hearty cheers from a host of friends, including the diplomatic corps and Lords Curzon, Reading, Middleton, Sandhurst, and Bryce.

Finally, as the *Olympic* put out to sea from Southampton, Davis was surprised by an honor never before given an American ambassador. A British destroyer flying the Stars and Stripes and under the command of a British admiral, suddenly appeared and passed the *Olympic*. There then followed two squadrons of destroyers, all flying the American flag, which escorted the ship to midchannel, turned around, and passed in review to the cheers of hundreds of British sailors. With "a lump in my throat as big as my fist," a beaming Ambassador Davis, ever the diplomat, signaled back a final message, "Mr. Davis is glad to have as his last sight of England the representatives of the valiant British Navy which has done so much to make the seas secure for the commerce of the world."[55] As he noted in his journal for March 9, 1921, "It is the end of a great adventure."[56]

The country lawyer from the hills of West Virginia returned to the United States a recognized and widely acclaimed leader in Congress, at the bar of the Supreme Court, and before the Court of St. James's. In his own words, Davis was on his return to America in 1921 "dead broke" after ten years of public service. The cost of the three years in London had totaled approximately $75,000 over and above his government salary, which was in line with Lansing's original estimate and which had depleted Davis's life savings.

By mid-1920, Davis had concluded he should secure his finances by practicing law at one of the major firms in New York City. Such a practice would allow him to remain involved in political life, while at the same time he could rebuild his savings, free himself from the financial stress of his London years, and return to his first love—the bar.

As he was considering his post-ambassadorial future in 1920, Davis was briefly sidetracked by the oncoming presidential election. President Wilson's health clearly precluded a third term, and William Gibbs McAdoo and A. Mitchell Palmer surfaced as the front-runners. By late 1919 there was considerable speculation that the convention could well result in deadlock, and several dark-horse candidates emerged. One of those was John W. Davis. A group of prominent West Virginia Democrats, lifelong friends of Davis, began to talk of a favorite son candidacy. The Fairmont, West Virginia, *Times* exhorted them to "launch a boom that will lead to his nomination."[57]

Former Senator Clarence Watson, a conservative West Virginia Democrat, launched the effort with a $25,000 contribution and persuaded Governor John Cornwell to write to Davis in July 1919, to encourage him to consider running. After receiving Cornwell's letter, Davis confided to his diary, "I dread the burdens of the office; have never nursed any ambition for it; would certainly not refuse a nomination if it came my way; cannot become an active candidate at this time."[58] By May 23, Davis's burgeoning candidacy achieved real momentum as evidenced by the *New York Times* editorial entitled "A Great Democrat," giving Davis a three-column endorsement and noting, "His personal qualities have won the friendship, confidence, and admiration of everyone he touched."[59] Secretary of State Lansing urged Davis to return home to campaign actively, but the Ambassador refused to leave London and remained an unofficial candidate.

As the Democratic Convention convened in San Francisco on June 21, 1920, President Wilson had indicated no preference among McAdoo, Palmer, or the other candidates; however, he had added dismissively of Davis, "He is a fine man . . . If you want to stand still, he is just the man to nominate."[60] For a conservative Democrat like Davis, this was not as backhanded a compliment as it might have first appeared. Davis was duly nominated by Governor Cornwell, and as the balloting began, his supporters wired the ambassador apprising him, "You are gaining strength," "Situation improving," "This minute it is McAdoo or Davis," etc.

As the convention lurched into its second week, much of the press thought Davis would prevail; and, ironically in light of future conflicts between the two men, young Franklin Roosevelt cast several ballots for Davis and predicted his victory. On June 28, Davis noted in his diary, "It certainly begins to look like McAdoo or myself."[61] Finally, after the fortieth ballot, Governor James Cox of Ohio was nominated as a compromise candidate who was not tied to Wilson, a wet, and a popular Democrat in the Republican stronghold of Ohio. In London Davis expressed relief when informed that Cox—and not he—had been nominated, and he returned to the United States in September to campaign in several key states for Cox.

During his visit to America in September 1920, Davis gave serious and final consideration to his future. He concluded that he would prefer to practice law in New York instead of Washington and that he did not want to establish a new firm. He weighed offers from a number of New York firms, including Sullivan & Cromwell; Chadbourner, Babbitt, & Wallace; Cravath & Leffingwell; and Stetson, Jennings, & Russell. He was also offered the general counselorship of Standard Oil of New Jersey but declined because of his resolve never to serve a single client. In the end, Davis was attracted to the people and the potential of Stetson, Jennings, & Russell. President Cleveland was senior partner of the firm during the four years between his two presidential terms. Though suffering some decline in recent years, the firm still retained an impressive group of clients, including J. P. Morgan & Co, Guaranty Bank and Trust, Associated Press, and International Paper Corporation.

Frank Polk, a longtime friend of Davis from his days in Washington, and Allen Wardwell, a more recent acquaintance, were the partners who convinced Davis of the fit and the potential. They—and the other partners at Stetson, Jennings—were the type of men with whom Davis could feel comfortable, and the firm enjoyed a fine reputation for conservatism. Davis was offered the senior partnership with 15 percent of the firm's net, which meant Davis could expect $150,000 in his first year.

The potential for the firm's future growth was evident as clients lobbied Davis to accept the offer from Stetson Jennings. Henry Davison, the leading Morgan partner, ferried Davis out to his Long Island estate on his yacht and, while golfing at Piping Rock Country Club, impressed upon him the significance which J. P. Morgan would attach to Davis's joining Stetson, Jennings. On September 27, Davis left New York by train for Hot Springs, Virginia; and, on the following day from the tranquility of his favorite spa, The Homestead, he dictated letters accepting Stetson, Jennings' offer and rejecting the others.[62]

By April 1, 1921, Davis was ensconced in the corner office—President Cleveland's old office—of Stetson, Jennings at 15 Broad Street in the heart of the Wall Street financial district. It was not long before his partners knew they had made a fortuitous decision in recruiting Davis. By mid-May, he was arguing a major case before the United States Circuit Court of Appeals in Richmond, and his ability to hold old clients and attract new ones had become apparent. He was almost immediately elected to the boards of the Rockefeller Foundation and the Carnegie Endowment, and in 1923, he was elected president of the American Bar Association.

Eighteen months after joining Stetson, Jennings, Davis made a momentous decision that determined the remainder of his career. While his name had been often circulated as a potential nominee to the Supreme Court and Chief Justice White had recommended Davis on numerous occasions, Davis was confronted squarely with this opportunity in 1922. President Harding had nominated former President Taft as chief justice in 1921, and Taft was determined to mold the court in his own conservative image. When Justice Day stepped down in 1922, Taft immediately began lobbying for Davis. Taft dispatched his former attorney general, George Wickersham, to sound out Davis. While he recognized that a lawyer could receive no higher honor than a seat on the Supreme Court, Davis had said many times that there was more "fun" on the bar's side.[63]

In addition to the "fun," he was just beginning to reap the financial rewards of a Wall Street practice, and his wife was not at all anxious to return to Washington—especially at greatly reduced compensation. As Davis explained, only half in jest, "I have taken the vows of chastity and obedience, but not of poverty."[64] Despite Taft's further efforts to bring pressure on him to accept "his patriotic duty," Davis in the end declined. Although he conceded it might have been a call to duty, there was never any sign that he regretted the decision. As he stated on a number of occasions, had the offer come earlier, when he was solicitor general, or later, when he was financially secure, he probably would have accepted.

As the nation moved toward the presidential election of 1924, Davis was recognized as a remarkable candidate. He was one of those rare men who seemed without exception to have gained the trust, respect, and love of his associates—in college, in Congress, before the bar, and in England. He brought a brilliant intellect, an easygoing graciousness, and unquestioned integrity to everything he did. And to politics he also brought a well-reasoned conservatism based on solid Jeffersonian tenets. As the Democrats nominated a candidate and perhaps turned to their last conservative nominee, they could not have found a more worthy man than John W. Davis.

Chapter Eight

ABOVE ALL THINGS, BE BRIEF

His philosophy of hard work and frugal living and piety
crowned with success might have been brought down from
some Vermont attic where McGuffey's Reader gathered
dust. But it was so old that it looked new; it was so exactly
what uncounted Americans had been taught at their mother's
knee that it touched what remained of the pioneer spirit in
their hearts; and Coolidge set it forth with refreshing brevity.
—Frederick Lewis Allen

When the Republican delegates departed Cleveland in June
1924, they had every reason to be smugly self-congratulatory.
They had successfully avoided running aground on the divisive
issues of the day—Prohibition, the Ku Klux Klan, and the
League of Nations. They had managed both to sense correctly
the conservative mood of the country and nominate a suitably
conservative candidate, while at the same time ensuring that most
progressive Republican leaders backed the party and its nominee.
Unable to disown the scandals of the Harding administration, the
GOP was able to hold itself out as the party—under its leader

Coolidge—that could arguably restore trust in the government and in ethical leadership.

It was indeed no small political accomplishment for Calvin Coolidge to emerge from the shadow of the popular Harding, consolidate his hold on the GOP—both conservatives and progressives, separate himself effectively from the Harding scandals, and secure the nomination virtually unanimously—all in less than one year. With the party united, the economy humming, and their nominee still evoking a warm response from the public, the prospects for Republican victory appeared excellent.

But exactly what kind of man had the GOP nominated? As a recent biographer of Coolidge has written, he was "a man extraordinary in his simplicity and notable in his complexity, which is to say an unusual human being who merits serious consideration."[1] As a starting point, Coolidge was without question a product of his native New England. In *Autobiography*, Coolidge quoted a New England aphorism, "The education of a child begins several generations before it is born,"[2] and this was in every sense true for him. For seven generations, the Coolidges had labored, propagated, and prospered in the inhospitable New England soil and climate as farmers, businessmen, and lawyers. They were among the early Puritans, and much of Puritanism remained in the Vermont hills in Coolidge's youth. As he once noted with considerable pride to William Allen White, "No Coolidge ever went west." Because of the harsh climate and rocky soil, many Vermonters moved west in the nineteenth century, seeking prosperity and an easier life, but the Coolidges put down roots and persevered despite all odds.[3] As biographer Gamaliel

Bradford wrote in Coolidge's time, "That temperament was the inherited, cumulative, aggravated temperament of New England, in which the sense of duty is the overriding force, and an uneasy conscience suggests that we are not in this world mainly to have a good time, or even to have a good time at all, but for some higher purpose."[4]

PLYMOUTH NOTCH, VERMONT

(BY PERMISSION OF CLARK M. GOFF)

It is impossible to imagine a more bucolic setting than Plymouth Notch, Vermont. This hamlet remained untouched by the social and economic changes of the twentieth century and provided the perfect platform for Calvin Coolidge.

In 1870, Vermont claimed slightly more than 330,000 in population and had not been touched by the successive waves of immigration into the United States from Ireland and Germany. Most Vermonters could trace their lineage back to Colonial times, and the state's agrarian way of life had been little changed by the industrial revolution. This was true for Colonel John Coolidge, who was a prosperous farmer and shopkeeper in Plymouth Notch,

Vermont, and who held a number of local and state offices during a long career. Colonel Coolidge had married a Vermont girl, Victoria Moor, and on July 4, 1872, a son, John Calvin Coolidge, was born. (The "John" was soon dropped).

Plymouth Notch was composed of a church, a school, a general store—run by John Coolidge—and three dwellings—in two of which lived Coolidges. The closest railroad link was in Ludlow, some twelve miles away, a two-hour carriage ride from Plymouth Notch. As Coolidge reminisced in later life, "Vermont is my birthright. Here one gets close to nature in the mountains, in the brooks, the lakes, the fields tilled by hand of man. My folks are happy and contented. They belong to themselves, live within their incomes, and fear no man."[5]

When Coolidge was only thirteen, his mother died, and, he later wrote that no greater grief could come to any young boy than "came to me. Life was never the same again."[6] Perhaps partially because of his wife's death, John Coolidge was to have an immeasurable impact on his son's life. Much later as president, Coolidge reflected back that his father was a man of "untiring industry and great tenacity of purpose. He always stuck to the truth." He was "decidedly a man of character."[7]

Coolidge spoke often of his father's hard work and his "strong New England trait of great repugnance at seeing anything wasted." While he was always generous and charitable—never mean-spirited—he nonetheless sternly viewed any kind of waste as a "moral wrong."[8] Another New England characteristic that young Coolidge absorbed was a total lack of pretense—and a strong aversion to anything, or anyone, pretentious. In his words, "Country life does not always have breadth, but it has depth."[9]

Colonel John Coolidge, the president's father, in front of the family home,
Plymouth Notch, Vermont.

These New England Puritan virtues—hard work, independent
thinking, lack of pretense, sense of duty, perseverance, scrupulous
truthfulness—constituted the essence of Coolidge's boyhood life
in Plymouth Notch and, not surprisingly, became the trademarks
of Calvin Coolidge the adult. When he left Plymouth Notch at
age thirteen to attend high school down in Ludlow, he was in
William Allen White's somewhat cynical term, "a museum piece,"
coming "like a waxwork figure of a Puritan boy, out of the social
museum that is rural Vermont."[10] While Coolidge never lived again
in the rural seclusion of Plymouth Notch, these "museum" virtues
to which he was exposed as a child served him well as he rose to
prominence in the modern twentieth-century political world.

John Coolidge's decision to send young Calvin to Black
River Academy in Ludlow was not an easy one but necessary. In
addition to the expense, it was a hard two-hour ride by wagon

from Plymouth Notch to Ludlow, and Coolidge was required to spend weeknights with cousins in Ludlow. For the four years of his son's secondary schooling, John faithfully drove to Ludlow by wagon every Friday to pick up Calvin and returned him on Sunday evening.

The only school in the vicinity of Plymouth Notch, Black River was a typical classical school of its day, rigorously emphasizing Latin, rhetoric, and English literature. Boys wore coats, ties, and starched shirts with stiff collars. Years later he wrote revealingly in his autobiography about spending his summer vacations riding alone on horseback for hours. He noted that a horse was "much company" and that these solitary rides were a "good occupation" for a young man. Coolidge found that the "silences of Nature have discipline all their own."[11] An appreciation of "the silences of nature" was to remain with him throughout adulthood.

As a student, Coolidge was hardworking and serious, though not particularly outstanding, and he demonstrated a consistent love of reading. In his final year at Black River, Coolidge's younger sister, Abbie, who was by then also a student at the academy, was stricken unexpectedly with appendicitis. Since the death of his mother six years before, Coolidge had been quite close to Abbie, his only sibling. He remained by her bedside day and night and was with her when she died. This second major loss in his young life left Coolidge with a seriousness that was definitely unusual for his age and that would remain with him for the rest of his life. Soon after her death, Coolidge wrote to his father, expressing his deep sorrow over the loss of Abbie; but several years later he was able to say, "We must think of Abbie as we would of a happy day, counting it as a pleasure to have had it but for a sorrow because it could not last forever."[12]

It was Coolidge's strong desire to continue his education at Amherst College, a small, regional liberal arts college in western Massachusetts with a reputation for academic rigor and social prominence, and he entered the college in September 1891. However, in the spring before entering Amherst, Coolidge experienced his first encounter with presidential politics, and the impression was lasting. The Coolidges were rock-ribbed New England Republicans, and John Coolidge was a local GOP leader and frequent local and state office holder. In 1888, Coolidge had witnessed the rejoicing among the GOP faithful of Ludlow when Benjamin Harrison reclaimed the presidency from Grover Cleveland, referring in *Autobiography* to two nights of celebration, "parading the streets with drums and trumpets."[13]

It was quite fitting for John Coolidge to take his son with him to Bennington, Vermont, in May 1891, for the dedication of a war memorial by President Harrison—in William Allen White's words, it was "a pious pilgrimage! For here were assembled to dedicate this monument all the high priests of the Republican temple."[14] Coolidge and his father attended the celebratory banquet, along with the governor of Vermont, all living ex-governors of Vermont, the secretary of war, the attorney general, and President Harrison himself.

After dinner and a round of toasts, President Harrison spoke rousingly of the American tradition of self-government and the New England town meeting. Coolidge later recorded his thoughts: As he gazed at Harrison—the embodiment of the United States—

he asked himself how it must feel to stand in those shoes and "little thought I should ever know."[15]

(COURTESY OF THE FORBES LIBRARY, NORTHAMPTON, MA)
Young Calvin Coolidge at Amherst College.

The Amherst College of Coolidge's day was some four hundred undergraduates, drawn almost exclusively from the New England and Mid-Atlantic states. Founded in 1821 by New England congregationalists, Amherst had established a reputation for fostering serious academic study and supporting several outstanding faculty members. Social life at Amherst revolved around fraternities, and not surprisingly, given his serious and generally aloof personality, Coolidge did not join a fraternity initially. As he reflected philosophically years later about the lesson he had learned in waiting until his senior year to join the fraternity, "If one will only exercise the patience to wait, his wants are likely to be filled."[16] Patience was to become a hallmark of Coolidge's political philosophy.

While the young New England socialites reveled in the Amherst fraternity life, Coolidge settled into a large boarding house on the outskirts of town for a modest $3.50 per week. A classmate recalled, "He lacked small talk, and he was never known to slap a man on the back. He rarely laughed. He was anything but a mixer."[17] He received academic recognition, winning Latin academic honors and eventually graduating cum laude. Despite his aloofness, he developed a reputation for his dry humor and oratorical ability and was chosen by his classmates to deliver the Grove Oration, a humorous address given by a senior at commencement. Coolidge developed a number of close college friendships, which would prove lifelong and significant in his later career—primarily Dwight Morrow and Harlan Fiske Stone, both of whom would be trusted advisors and appointees to key government posts.

Two distinguished Amherst professors, Charles E. Garman and Anson D. Morse, exerted a profound and lasting influence on the development of Coolidge's personal and political philosophy. Garman was a charismatic teacher who attracted an almost cultlike following among Amherst students and who "preached a homegrown brand of Christian humanism that emphasized spirituality, self-reliance, and industry."[18] Coolidge wrote years later that Garman's influence had been decisive in the development of his political philosophy. [19]

Although Morse lectured primarily on European and medieval history, Coolidge wrote, "It was when he turned to United States history that Professor Morse became most impressive."[20] Coolidge responded to Morse with keen interest and became a thoughtful student of American history, as classmates recalled Coolidge "in the library with his nose in *The Federalist*" and other serious works.[21] During his years at Amherst, Coolidge was challenged and stimulated by Morse and Garman and was able to integrate the tenets of his inherited New England Puritanism and his Republican politics with their teaching.

Having completed his undergraduate studies with some academic distinction, successfully delivered the Grove Oration at commencement, and established himself as something of a personality—an introvert with a dry sense of humor, strongly independent, someone who never seemed or tried to be something other than who he was, he decided to pursue a career in law.

Shortly before graduation, he and his close friend Dwight Morrow were discussing their futures. Morrow indicated he planned to pursue a legal career in Pittsburgh, the closest burgeoning industrial and financial center. When Morrow asked Coolidge where he planned to study law, Coolidge responded simply, "Northampton—it's the nearest courthouse."[22] Such was his attachment to his family and his region. Indeed, "no Coolidge had ever gone west." Northampton and western Massachusetts were much more like Vermont than Boston, so it was natural that Coolidge would settle there. This decision to settle in Massachusetts rather than return to Vermont was to prove critical to his future political career, leading to the state house in Boston and ultimately to Washington.

Coolidge took an apprenticeship in Northampton under two recent Amherst graduates, John Hammond and Henry Field, who had established a thriving small-town practice. Hammond was regarded as the best lawyer in the area, while Field was more of a local politician. They had heard Coolidge's Grove Oration and were impressed. Asked many years later why he had hired Coolidge, Field responded, "I liked to laugh and Calvin Coolidge was very funny."[23] After two years of apprenticeship, Coolidge passed the Massachusetts bar in 1897, and in the following year he launched his political career with election as a Republican member to the Northampton city council. This quiet, seemingly insignificant event marked the beginning of what would become a spectacularly successful thirty-year career in elective office.

In 1905, the rising young lawyer and politician married Grace Goodhue, a Phi Beta Kappa graduate of the University of Vermont and a teacher in Northampton. If ever there were a case of opposites attracting, it was this marriage. The shy, diffident, reticent, dour Coolidge somehow won the hand of a woman who was invariably viewed as charming, vivacious, and loquacious. Their marriage was by all accounts a strong one. As one biographer has written, "Like his religious faith, she gave him a reservoir of strength and security cordoned off from political affairs."[24] Coolidge paid tribute to his wife's influence when he wrote years later, "She has borne with my infirmities and I have rejoiced in her graces."[25]

With predictable Coolidge thrift, the young couple shared half of a two-family house at 21 Massasoit Street in Northampton. It was here they would live until his election as vice president, and it was back to this house they returned in 1928 when he stepped down as president. As Coolidge observed, "So long as I lived there, I could be independent and serve the public without ever thinking that I could not maintain my position if I lost my office."[26]

The following year, the Coolidges had their first son, John, and in 1908, their second son, Calvin Jr., was born. Now that he had a family to support, Coolidge took his responsibilities even more seriously and committed to live always within his income. In later life, he reflected, "I knew very well what it means to awake in the night and realize that the rent is coming due, wondering where the money is coming from with which to pay it." He saw the salutary effect of this apprehension as his commitment always to keep his expenses sufficiently low so that he could save enough to provide a cushion against any unforeseen decrease in future income.[27] As a politician, Coolidge often spoke of applying common sense to governing, and many of his political speeches contain the same principles expressed in his personal life. Refreshingly, he was a politician who lived what he preached.

From 1898 with his election to the Northampton City Council until 1906, Coolidge was subsequently elected to serve as city solicitor and clerk of the court, before winning election to the Massachusetts House of Representatives in 1906. It was here that his statewide political career began. As the wagon ride from Plymouth Notch to Ludlow and the transition from Black River Academy to Amherst had opened new vistas for him, so too the train ride across the state to Boston brought Coolidge onto a bigger stage and confirmed his calling to politics. Grace and the boys remained back in Northampton while Coolidge resided during the six-month legislative session in Boston's slightly threadbare Adams House Hotel, taking a spartan room without a private bath for $2.50 per week. Predictably, Coolidge was soon seen as a diligently hardworking representative, who never sought nor achieved the limelight. Republicans found him to be a reliable party man, while Democrats mistakenly underestimated him. A Democratic state leader speculated of Coolidge, "This fellow is either a schoolteacher or an undertaker from the country."[28]

The early twentieth-century Massachusetts political world was divided between the eastern and western areas. Eastern Massachusetts, primarily Boston and suburbs, had absorbed large numbers of Irish immigrants and was consequently a political blend of New England Protestant Republicans and urban Irish Catholic Democrats. The western region was similar in philosophy and practice to the rest of New England—heavily Republican, dominated by business and agricultural interests. Eastern Massachusetts Republicans were led by the quintessential Boston Brahmin, Henry Cabot Lodge, the imperious self-proclaimed "scholar in politics."

It was from the western area that Coolidge ascended to the statewide stage, and it was of incalculable importance and good fortune to his career that he attracted the friendship, trust, and support of Murray Crane, the acknowledged leader of Western Massachusetts Republicans. Crane was a wealthy western Massachusetts industrialist who had served ably as governor and was the state's junior senator, where he had emerged as one of the most influential national Republicans. Coolidge's critics often tried to attribute his political success to pure luck, citing Crane's sponsorship as an example, but any objective analysis would indicate otherwise.

Crane was the perfect mentor—by personality and philosophy—for Coolidge and was attracted to Coolidge for obvious reasons; for Crane was ethically above reproach, cautiously conservative but not narrowly partisan, calm in demeanor, soft spoken, always concise, and every bit as physically unimpressive as Coolidge. One of Crane's fellow senator's marveled that, although he never made a major speech or authored any landmark legislation, he was widely considered the most influential senator in Washington.[29]

A political commentator described Crane in words that could easily have been applied years later to Coolidge: "Mr. Crane was a unique figure in Massachusetts politics. He lacked much of what people generally regard as necessary in a successful man in politics. He had not a commanding presence nor was he given to the glad hand habit, so common among public men, but he possessed many attractive personal qualities which endeared him to his neighbors and friends."[30]

Indeed, Crane's political support was critical to Coolidge's steady rise from House member, 1907–09; to State Senate, 1911–13; to president of the State Senate, 1914–16; to lieutenant governor, 1916–19; and finally to Governor 1919–1920; but even more important ultimately was Crane's influence on Coolidge's philosophy of governance. In an era of political bosses, Crane stood apart. He was not personally ambitious, nor in any way corrupt. He was remarkably bipartisan, successfully advancing Republicanism by supporting sound ideas—not a rigidly partisan agenda. He was slow to act—and never before he was certain of his course. His advice was often, "Do nothing. It is more important that the law be permanently fixed than that experiments in new legislation should be tried."[31] Coolidge brought to this dynamic and successful partnership a personality, a style, and a set of personal convictions that were much like Crane's, while Crane opened political doors and served as the wise mentor and ideal role model.

As Coolidge was steadily ascending the state political ladder, the GOP was absorbing significant change with the surge in progressivism under Roosevelt, the intraparty split in 1912, and the reunification of the party by 1916 to challenge Wilson's reelection. Early in this period as progressivism reached high tide in the nation, Coolidge was, in William Allen White's words, "more than half persuaded to be a Rooseveltian,"[32] but he gradually began to discern the incompatibility of his own cautious conservatism with progressivism. As he prepared to assume the presidency of the State Senate, Coolidge observed, "It appeared to me that a spirit of radicalism prevailed which unless checked was likely to prove very destructive." He defined this spirit of radicalism as the dangerous notion that somehow the government should be "blamed because everybody was not prosperous."[33]

It was in response to these concerns that Coolidge delivered an acceptance speech in Boston in 1915, entitled "Have Faith in Massachusetts," which was immediately printed, broadly distributed, and widely hailed as a challenge to return to Republican conservatism. In this speech, "appealing to the conservative spirit of the people," Coolidge explained, "I argued that the government could not relieve us from toil, that large concerns are necessary for the progress in which capital and labor all have a common interest, and I defended representative government and the integrity of the courts." Coolidge felt the citizens responded almost immediately to this message, and he observed, "Confusion of thought began to disappear, and unsound legislative proposals to diminish."[34]

With these words, Coolidge not only solidified his standing in Massachusetts as a rising Republican star but also actually emerged onto the national stage with former President Taft congratulating him on the speech. Also of tremendous significance for his Massachusetts career was the gracious letter received from Senator Lodge. Coolidge had always been a protégé of Murray Crane, Lodge's rival for leadership of the state GOP, and had never been even acknowledged by Lodge. The scholarly senior senator had obviously read Coolidge's speech carefully—twice, in fact, as he indicated in the letter—and recognized in the speech a quality that would become a hallmark of Coolidge's political communications, "It [the speech] is not only able but you have put the propositions with epigrammatic force and often in a very original way."[35]

As Coolidge considered the logical next step in his advance, the lieutenant governorship, he established a second friendship that was to prove just as providential as that with Murray Crane. In 1915, fellow Amherst graduate and trustee Frank Stearns approached Coolidge about a legislative matter but also with the secondary motive of evaluating his qualifications for higher office. Stearns was a wealthy Boston department store owner, active financial supporter of the Republican Party, and devoted son of Amherst College. He came away from this meeting impressed with Coolidge and was soon dedicated to electing Coolidge Lieutenant Governor. Stearns proved to be a master of political public relations, and he began introducing the reticent country politician to important GOP contributors and tirelessly—and quite effectively—raising campaign funds.

Many American political leaders have had trusted confidants who were critically important in their rise to power, but it is difficult to find anyone comparable to Frank Stearns. By all accounts, he was completely dedicated to the advancement of Coolidge's career—but for reasons of "civic pride and patriotism."[36] There is no record of Stearns ever asking anything in return from Coolidge, or even offering any political advice to Coolidge. As Grace Coolidge wrote, "Mr. Stearns knew and understood the president as no other man knew and understood him. He stood by in his quiet, self-effacing ways, eager to help, but never offering advice unless it was sought."[37]

Coolidge, in *Autobiography*, paid tribute to Stearns: "While Mr. Stearns always overestimated me, he nevertheless was a great help to me. He never obtruded or sought any favor for himself or any other person." He rightly concluded that few politicians had been blessed with "so valuable and unselfish a friend."[38] Coolidge could not have written it more straight forwardly or accurately— or more understatedly. Years later Stearns wrote to Grace Coolidge, "You and I have one thing in common, at any rate. You picked out Calvin Coolidge some years ago and gave him your endorsement; more recently I picked him out and gave him the most emphatic endorsement I know how to. Of course many others can claim to have picked him out, but amongst them all I think we can shake hands over the proposition that yours was the most important endorsement and mine comes next."[39]

With the able assistance of Murray Crane and Frank Stearns and a general shift in sentiment towards the GOP, Coolidge was elected lieutenant governor, and Samuel McCall won the governorship. This McCall-Coolidge ticket bore a remarkable similarity to the future Harding-Coolidge ticket. McCall was a charismatic progressive who was an expert politician and something of a spellbinder. During the campaign the conventional wisdom was that "McCall could fill any auditorium in the state, and Coolidge could empty it,"[40] but it was Coolidge who won by a far larger margin and who ultimately became the more successful politician.

Coolidge dutifully fulfilled the obligations of lieutenant governor in the shadow of the colorful McCall, went on to win reelection to two more one-year terms, and quietly bide his time for his turn at the governorship. While it was widely assumed that he would run to succeed McCall, Coolidge held the old-fashioned notion that a candidate should not chase the office, writing, "It is much better not to press a candidacy too much, but to let it develop on its own merits without artificial stimulation."[41] Coolidge's instincts and timing were right; but, fortunately for him, Stearns was a good bit less passive.

On June 23, 1918, to no one's surprise, Coolidge entered the gubernatorial race, but the headlines focused more on the war, the initial rumblings of what would become the Red Scare, and the influenza epidemic that was terrifying the country—especially Boston, which was particularly hard hit. Coolidge was unopposed for the Republican nomination, while the Democrats selected Richard Long, a shoe manufacturer from Framingham. Coolidge ran quietly on McCall's record of moderate progressivism, combined with his own commitment to fiscal conservatism and strong support for the war.

Crane's well-oiled machine was solidly behind Coolidge, and Senator Lodge supported him with similar enthusiasm. Writing to Theodore Roosevelt, Lodge praised Coolidge as a "very able, sagacious man of pure New England type." And then speaking somewhat prophetically (in light of Coolidge's future performance as governor), Lodge went on to say that not only was he sound in his thinking, but he also has "an excellent capacity for firmness."[42]

Meanwhile, Stearns was busy organizing business leaders, power brokers, and the Amherst network into an electoral steamroller. Coolidge refused to answer the personal attacks from his opponent, saying, "I will not attack an individual."[43] Again, Coolidge correctly read the electorate and was elected governor on November 6, 1918.

(COURTESY OF THE FORBES LIBRARY, NORTHAMPTON, MA)
The Coolidges receive telephone notification of his election as governor of Massachusetts in 1918.

Up until this point, Coolidge had continued to reside in Northampton and commuted weekly to Boston during the legislative session. As governor, this arrangement was no longer possible, and he moved Grace and their two sons across the state to

Boston. Stearns offered to provide funds for renting an adequately large house in Boston from which the governor might appropriately function; but Coolidge, faithful to his views on independence, propriety, and frugality, summarily refused. When Stearns tried to give him a $5,000 gift with which to defray expected expenses, Coolidge indignantly returned the check and informed Stearns that he had sufficient savings to cover any expenses.

Instead, Coolidge rented a second room at the Adams House Hotel, raising his rent to $2.50 per day, while prudently subletting his Northampton home for $32 per month. It was widely known— and widely applauded—that the new governor traveled in Boston by streetcar, as the image of the New England Puritan was firmly established with his constituents.[44]

Coolidge had not campaigned for the governorship on any detailed platform or well-defined legislative agenda. Once elected, he announced no new major initiatives; but, at the same time, his record shows substantial activity in supporting the extension of existing government programs and services. A recent biographer offered insight into Coolidge's method of governing by noting that Coolidge has often been criticized for not promoting some sweeping government program. Such criticism fails to measure the depth of his political convictions, for "Coolidge was an atypical politician. Even more than Theodore Roosevelt did, he used the political arena as a stage to set forth a political philosophy."[45]

As Coolidge navigated through his first year as governor with customary caution, larger national and world events began to exert more influence on the Massachusetts political scene. In the wake of the Russian Revolution of 1917, continuing civil war in

Russia, and economic distress throughout western Europe, there was a pervasive, growing fear of Bolshevism. In the United States, the postwar months saw a torrent of strikes, some of which were violent and all of which were widely suspected as Communist instigated. Wilson's attorney general, A. Mitchell Palmer, aroused the public's fears by warning of communist infiltration into the labor movement, and he urged action: "We can get rid of them! And not until we have done so shall we have removed the menace of Bolshevism for good."[46]

The American labor movement had made tremendous strides towards organizing workers during the war, and one of the recently organized segments of the labor force was municipal workers in a small number of cities, including the Boston police force. A confluence of economic forces was about to ignite a serious political problem in the city of Boston. William Allen White attributed much of the crisis to economics, explaining that the relatively high wages being earned by unskilled factory laborers proved an inflammatory aggravation to the otherwise staid Boston police force. [47]

After several threats by the police to affiliate with a national labor union organization, the informal policeman's "club" applied to the American Federation of Labor (AFL) for a charter in August 1919, prompting Police Commissioner Edwin Curtis to issue an order expressly forbidding any officer from joining a labor union. These events took place against a broad backdrop of labor unrest, as various American railroads, theaters, newspapers, construction companies, and municipalities were paralyzed by striking workers. On August 11, the AFL responded promptly in granting recognition to the newly chartered Boston Police Union. The lines were drawn, and neither side showed any inclination for compromise. Boston Mayor Andrew Peters, a Democrat, attempted to reach some conciliation, while Curtis remained intractable and Coolidge watched from the State House.

When the police called the strike on September 9, Coolidge carefully consulted his attorney general before backing the authority of Commissioner Curtis to control the police and also calling in the State Guard to ensure the maintenance of order. Once order was restored, it was announced that the striking policemen would not be rehired. Samuel Gompers soon telegraphed Coolidge demanding the ouster of Curtis and the reinstatement of the union members. It was in response to Gompers that Coolidge issued his statement that reverberated throughout the nation and propelled Governor Coolidge onto the national stage: "There is no right to strike against the public safety by anybody, anytime, anywhere."[48]

This was a clear distillation of Coolidge's political style and philosophy: be cautious, move slowly, consult the law, and then act decisively and articulate it clearly. Coolidge believed that his public statements in the midst of this crisis had a "clearness of thought and revealed a power I had not before been able to express." He further saw this as confirmation that "when a duty comes to us, with it a power comes to enable us to perform it. My faith that the people would respond to the truth was justified."[49] And indeed the people did respond—over 70,000 letters and telegrams flooded the governor's office, editorials in the major dailies praised him, and Coolidge was an overnight American hero. On September 13, a perspicacious reporter for the *New York World* introduced Governor Coolidge to his readers with this revealing article:

To one who has never seen Governor Calvin
Coolidge of Massachusetts, he is a sphinx or an
enigma. He talks little. It is his silences which seem
to speak loudest, for when one ventures to put a
question to him, the answer comes in a tightening
of the governor's lean face and the closing of his lips.
He has a lean and hungry look, and the Policeman's
Union and the Central Labor Union of Boston
discovered that such men are dangerous.

Contrary to the accepted characteristics of
the usual sort of politicians, "Cal" Coolidge seldom
smiles, hardly ever does any handshaking, and has a
reputation that his word is as good as gold.

Ethnologists in search of specimens to be
preserved in bronze or marble as a reminder
of the type of true New Englanders for future
generations should come to Beacon Hill and take
the measure of this governor. He is the type of
New Englander one sees on the stage—long and
thin. He has red hair tinged with gray. A pair
of pale-blue eyes pierce the veil of silence that
usually envelopes his face. Where other men may
smile, "Cal" Coolidge is grave. Where home
folks pretend to effervesce with enthusiasm for a
visitor or the possessor of a vote, the governor is
aloof and forbidding.

Generally speaking, Governor Coolidge is a
living contradiction of that school of politicians
anxious for a career. Massachusetts politicians do not

do him homage, but few, if any, have ever discovered the secret of his success. Politicians say it would be impossible to beat Coolidge in an election with a baseball bat. He is regarded as unbeatable, and had proved himself so from the moment he entered politics. He has passed without threat or fear from member of the legislature, president of the senate and lieutenant governor to governor of the state. The governor is a Republican, but it is said that the Democrats would do anything for him, many of them as much as vote for him.[50]

In preparation for the November elections, Republicans renominated Coolidge on October 4; and, as a result of the Boston police strike, the national spotlight was focused on Massachusetts. Plagued by a severe cold, Coolidge waged an even quieter campaign than usual, while Stearns managed the campaign with all the efficiency as before. His Democratic opponent was again the hapless Richard Long, who campaigned as vigorously as in the prior year's battle. Coolidge's victory was resounding—the greatest in the state's history, with 317,774 votes to Long's 192,673.

Congratulations poured in from President Wilson, Charles Evans Hughes, Warren Harding, former President Taft, and other national leaders, as Coolidge claimed correctly that the election had been referendum on his handling of the now famous Boston police strike. Coolidge was inescapably pleased by the election's outcome, while Stearns was ecstatic about his friend's future electoral prospects. As far back as July 23, 1915, Stearns had presciently written to one of Coolidge's Amherst classmates,

"Just think what a time we will have at commencement when the president of the United States, a graduate of your Class, '95, comes back to commencement!"[51] One can easily imagine what Stearns was thinking in November 1919, as he savored the election returns.

It was astride this crest of popularity that Coolidge rode onto the national political scene in 1920 at the Republican National Convention. Coolidge acknowledged with his usual straightforwardness that it was the Boston police strike that thrust him onto the national political stage. This event "furnished the occasion and I took advantage of the opportunity. I was ready."[52]

(COURTESY OF FORBES LIBRARY, NORTHAMPTON, MA)

In 1920, newly elected Vice President Coolidge and his family greet their fellow citizens in Northampton.

With the able assistance of his longtime supporters Crane, Stearns, and Morrow, he was suddenly a creditable candidate for the presidential nomination; and, when Harding was nominated instead, a popular frenzy swept through the delegates as they demanded Coolidge for vice president. First as Harding's ticket mate and then as vice president, Coolidge settled back into a subordinate role—beginning carefully to observe the requirements of national politics and to bide his time as the loyal understudy. When the fortunes of fate struck again in 1923 with Harding's sudden death, Coolidge was ready; or, as he said to Grace, "I believe I can swing it."[53]

It had been less than one year since Harding's death when the Republicans nominated Coolidge in Cleveland, and he was still very much in the honeymoon period afforded every new president. By 1924, the American public was just beginning to understand what kind of man Coolidge was, but their first impressions were to prove accurate and enduring; Calvin Coolidge was never perceived as anything he was not. He was in almost every way the antithesis of the popular perception of the 1920s.

Instead, Coolidge manifestly embodied the straightforward simplicity, dignity, integrity, honesty, thrift, morality, and common sense upon which America had been founded. In this turbulent decade, Americans found comfort in a president who espoused and modeled these bedrock virtues. As William Allen White summed him up, "Caution, courage, and intelligent honesty were his rather simple virtues."[54]

Chapter Nine

FIGHTIN' BOB

A third party candidate had intruded into the balance of political forces—a candidate whose radical stance would serve as a foil to the conservatism of both Davis and Coolidge. The decision of Senator Robert La Follette of Wisconsin to run for president in 1924 gave the campaign a unique flavor, spicing it with a fresh and pungent radicalism that attempted to bring together the strength of factory and farm.
—David Burner

From the earliest days of the Republic, Jefferson's philosophy and vision of limited government had competed with Hamilton's advocacy of a stronger, more centralized government. As the country developed into a more capitalistic, industrialized, and urban nation after the Civil War, some Americans began to question whether the old Jeffersonian ideals of maximum individual freedom and minimal governmental interference were still applicable. In the 1880s American progressivism arose in response to what some viewed as the need for a stronger government to protect individuals from capitalism. As historian David Thelen has explained,

"Progressivism began as a series of grassroots, angry, unorganized campaigns by consumers and taxpayers to challenge the legitimacy of privileged and concentrated wealth and power."[1]

Initially, the progressive movement was nonpartisan and had at least three major strands. In the western states, farmers consistently battled with railroads, banks, and large agribusiness corporations and frequently considered themselves disenfranchised. These western farmers were generally Republicans; and as they succeeded in electing progressive Republican congressmen, a farm bloc developed within Congress, which was often at odds with the party leadership.

In the South, the populist movement also centered around small-farm owners and tenant farmers, who were economically vulnerable to the frequent boom and bust cycles of agriculture and who contended with the southern establishment. These southern progressives were all Democrats and soon formed a minority within their party. In the Northeast, urban industrial workers were attracted to various socialist movements that advanced the cause of labor. By 1880, there was a sizable minority of progressives in the northeast, primarily within the Democratic Party.

From the Civil War until 1912, the Democrats elected only one president, Grover Cleveland, and he was a conservative who believed in sound money and minimal government. The Republican presidents of this era were like-minded; and, in fact, the tariff was perhaps the most defining issue between the two parties. As progressivism took hold at the grassroots level in the 1880s and began working its way into the mainstream of both parties, it was only a matter of time before circumstances allowed for the nomination of a progressive presidential candidate.

The Democratic convention of 1896 was that time. There was a stinging backlash against President Cleveland as the convention adopted a platform condemning the gold standard and the labor injunction and attacking "Cleveland and his administration at more points and with greater vehemence than it did the Republican foe."[2]

The progressive leader who captured the Democratic Party in 1896 was Nebraska's William Jennings Bryan. In his famous "cross of gold" speech, Bryan challenged his party to throw off the yoke of the gold standard and embrace free silver; but his agenda was far wider than this. He articulated the progressive impulse for citizens to band together, strengthen the government, and confront big business. Capitalism was the problem, and government was the answer. With a righteous fury, Bryan proclaimed to the convention, "The humblest citizen in all the land, when clad in the armor of a righteous cause, is stronger than all the hosts of error. I come to speak to you in defense of a cause as holy as the cause of liberty— the cause of humanity."[3]

Philosophical battle lines were clear and quickly drawn in the election of 1896. The Republicans nominated William McKinley, an able and thoroughly orthodox Ohio conservative; and the newly emerged Populist Party pragmatically endorsed Bryan. The battle was of two competing visions of America's future. Bryan's progressivism idealized agrarianism, voicing the fears and interests of the West and the South. He fiercely opposed the industrialization of America and the interests of Wall Street and enthusiastically endorsed greater government intervention in the market. McKinley's vision was pro-growth and pro-business with a Jeffersonian view towards maximum individual freedom and limited government interference. While Bryan won the West and South, McKinley won the states with big electoral votes; and the result was a decisive electoral endorsement of America's continuing industrialization. The fight for control of the Democratic Party continued between progressives and conservatives; and in the next three elections, Bryan would be nominated again twice and a conservative, Alton Parker, once.

Within the Republican Party, progressivism was also gaining strength. The electoral base of Republican progressivism was the western states. By the mid-1880s, GOP voters in western states like Wisconsin were electing congressmen like Robert M. La Follette. Known as "Insurgents," these progressive Republicans had begun to call for "direct democracy," which meant somehow the people would "initiate policy and rule directly."[4] Their vision was to wrestle control of the government from business interests and to rely wherever possible on direct referenda to the people. Bitterly opposed by the ruling conservative leaders of the GOP, these Insurgents held sufficient votes in Congress by 1910 to control the balance of power between the traditional Republicans and the Democrats.

Also, within the GOP, there was a small number of reform-minded eastern Republicans who gravitated philosophically toward the progressives. Among this group was Theodore Roosevelt, a quintessential easterner with an affinity for things western. It was through the accidents of Roosevelt's last-minute selection as McKinley's running mate in 1900 and the president's subsequent assassination in 1901 that progressivism gained initial entry to the White House.

As president, Roosevelt was able to hold the conservative, pro-business GOP base while governing as a moderate progressive; and in the election of 1904, Roosevelt completely swept the Republican East and the progressive/Republican West, while losing only the South to the conservative Democrat, Alton Parker. In 1908, the Democrats reverted to Bryan, and this Republican coalition of business and progressives held in 1908 with Taft's election.

By 1912, progressivism had reached full flower and was a decisive factor in both parties. Roosevelt mounted a challenge to his successor, Taft, from the left, charging Taft with selling out to the conservatives; and in this process, Roosevelt moved much farther to the left than ever before in his career. When the GOP rebuffed Roosevelt and renominated Taft, Roosevelt bolted the party; and he shoved aside somewhat abruptly the Insurgent leader, La Follette, to claim the progressive mantle. As James Chace has described it, "To Roosevelt's thinking, big business required big government," and he was now ready to adopt an anti-business, progressive platform and to assert "the executive power as the steward of public welfare" as the formal leader of the Progressive [or Bull Moose] Party.[5]

Roosevelt's new radicalism reflected his deep distrust of the Jeffersonian ideals of limited government and maximum individual freedom. As Herbert Croley, editor of *The New Republic* and a Roosevelt protégé, wrote, Roosevelt was much more comfortable with the Hamiltonian legacy, which "implied government interference with the natural course of American economic and political business and its regulation and guidance in the national direction."[6] Roosevelt's 1912 campaign clearly married this Hamiltonian notion of strong government with the progressive's Direct Democracy.

On the Democratic side, progressivism was equally the central issue. Professor Woodrow Wilson had gained immediate prominence with his landslide election as governor of New Jersey in 1908. During the course of that campaign, Wilson made a prophetic admission: "A politician, a man engaged in party contests, must be an opportunist."[7] Up until that point, Wilson had been a lifelong principled proponent of Jeffersonian ideals; and his gubernatorial candidacy was initiated by the conservative Democratic bosses of New Jersey. After securing the nomination as a conservative, Wilson read the electoral winds carefully and concluded that he could only win as a progressive and that progressive reform was the future of the national Democratic Party. To the great surprise and ultimate dismay of the New Jersey bosses, Wilson thenceforth became a model progressive.

By the election of 1912, progressivism had totally transformed the American political landscape. Roosevelt's successor, Taft, who had done his best to uphold Roosevelt's progressive tradition, was suddenly the only quasi-conservative on the ballot. Wilson and the Democrats positioned themselves squarely in the progressive camp. An increasingly radical Roosevelt was attacking hard from the left. And, in the event progressivism had not moved sufficiently far to the left, Eugene Debs ran as an outright socialist. As William Allen White suggested, "Never before have we been so nearly one people, with one dominant political ideal."[8]

With a relatively small popular vote plurality of 42 percent, Wilson won a sweeping 435 to 96 vote electoral college landslide.

The conservative vote for Taft was only 23 percent, compared to a total 77 percent total for the progressives—Wilson, Roosevelt, and Debs. Progressivism was back in the White House with a decisive electoral mandate. As historian Paul Johnson has written about the progressive agenda in 1912, "The state was seen as a knight in shining armor, coming to the rescue of the poor and the weak and the victimized, and doing with objective benevolence what otherwise would be done selfishly by greedy aggregators of private wealth." It was Wilson who inaugurated the era of big government.[9]

It was the profound disillusionment following World War I, the sharp economic postwar recession, and the popular Republican reaffirmation of conservative, Jeffersonian principles that turned the country away from progressivism in 1920. Indeed, the Democrats moved back to the right themselves in nominating Ohio Governor James Cox. By 1924, progressivism was still a nonpartisan issue, with both of the major parties having sizable progressive wings. This period from the mid-1880s through the 1924 election was one of major realignment for the Republicans and the Democrats. Paul Johnson noted that, by the 1920s, progressive "do-gooders"— and the bulk of the Democratic Party—had begun to regard a strong government as a necessary defense against the excesses of corporate power.[10] After 1924, the Republicans remained on a rightward course, while the Democrats steered leftward; and there has been no major realignment since.

When Roosevelt elbowed La Follette out of the way in 1912, scars remained. The Insurgents resented Roosevelt's definition of them as "Progressives who were exceeding the speed limit," labeling them as too radical; but La Follette and the Insurgents

(COURTESY LIBRARY OF CONGRESS)

Senator Robert La Follette is here captured in a typically combative posture.

remained within the Republican Party. As his biographer David Thelen has written, "La Follette believed that the insurgent Republicans' position as the bloc holding the balance of power between regular Republicans and Democrats gave him a unique opportunity to establish a reputation as a statesman."[11]

In addition, La Follette refused to consider joining the Democrats, whose stronghold was the South where they were complicit in denying black Americans the right to vote. In the early 1920s, La Follette adroitly led his Insurgents in tilting the balance of power away from the conservative Republican leadership whenever possible, as in the repeated passage of the McNary-Haugen Bill. By late 1923, it was apparent to La Follette that the GOP was in the firm control of the very *un*-progressive

Calvin Coolidge and that the Democrats were equally unlikely to nominate a true progressive.

The Committee of Forty-Eight had been formed as a progressive political action group in 1919 by several prominent veterans of the Bull Moose Party, and political mobilization was begun in earnest in 1922 when La Follette assumed the leadership. The committee pulled together for the first time such disparate left-wing groups as labor unions, socialist leagues, and farm activist parties in an attempt to join rural and urban progressives into a cohesive entity. The result was the reestablishment of the Progressive Party in 1924.

As the Republican convention met in Cleveland in June 1924, La Follette led the Wisconsin delegation as a favorite son candidate. In several floor fights over various platform planks and in the nominating process, the Wisconsin delegation was soundly defeated and subjected to incessant heckling. The Republican convention removed all doubt from La Follette's mind as to whether he should stand as a Progressive candidate; and, in less than a month, he was back in Cleveland's Public Auditorium to accept the enthusiastic nomination of the Progressive Party.

Approximately one thousand delegates were gathered representing the National Socialist Party, the National Farmer Organization, the Women's Committee for Political Action, State Federations of Labor, the National Non Partisan League, and many other left-wing activist groups. According to *Time*, "Only Communists, cranks, and reactionaries were not wanted—and they were very much not wanted. As much as possible, these people were ruled out. No one wants less to be confounded with reds than do the pinks."[12]

The Public Auditorium dais was now decked with a great American flag flanked by huge portraits of Washington, Lincoln, Jefferson, and La Follette, removing any doubt as to whom the convention planned to nominate. Convention Chairman William H. Johnston, who was also president of the International Association of Machinists, wasted no time in his keynote address in colorfully contrasting the Progressive Party to its two rivals: "The nation has witnessed the holding of a dull and lifeless convention of political puppets in this very hall. It has also witnessed the antics of what seemed to be a disorderly mob meeting in New York City, but which responded to boss control quite obediently in its voting. In Cleveland, there was one boss. In New York, there were several. In Cleveland, there was the chill hand of approaching dissolution upon the party. In New York, the fever of class, religious, and sectional hatred burned in its veins."[13] Here was the self-proclaimed vision of the Progressives. They were to be the radical party of the people, with all the spontaneity that the Republicans lacked and without being the chaotic, boss-controlled mess that the Democrats represented. Undergirding this vision was a strong measure of self-righteousness from this coalition of—in Paul Johnson's term—"do-gooders."

Chairman Johnston went on to offer this word of guidance to the convention, "This conference is alive. It may have its moments of enthusiasm. I beg of you that it will always remain an orderly, deliberate assembly." He reminded them of their high political calling, which meant that their "enthusiasm shall not be perverted into silly demonstrations, wherein mature men behave like children and attempt to measure the strength of their convictions by their lung power or express the quality of their faith by the amount of noise they can produce. The older parties are going back to second childhood. Let us not imitate them. Let us have done with childish ways."[14] So much for fun, the Progressives were about the serious business of saving humanity.

There was certainly no suspense or spontaneity in the nominating process. The convention was of one mind that La Follette should lead them. His name was lovingly put in nomination with these stirring words: "We have a leader, that lifelong, faithful servant of the people, whose character, ability and record as a constructive statesman entitle him to take his place with the greatest men this nation has produced—with Washington, with Jefferson and with Lincoln. His name is already on your lips, his service is in your hearts, his vision is in your souls—Robert M. La Follette of Wisconsin."[15]

Unlike Roosevelt and the Bull Moose Party in 1912, La Follette and the Progressives decided not to form a party in the traditional sense but simply to put forward a presidential slate of candidates. For his running mate, La Follette wanted a Democrat, and his first choice was Justice Louis Brandeis. When Brandeis declined, he turned to Montana Senator Burton Wheeler, who had refused to support Davis because of his Wall Street ties. The Progressive platform was written by the candidate himself and called for increased government ownership of utilities and eventual nationalization of the railroads, decreased military spending, the "crushing" of all monopolies, and direct support of the farmers under McNary-Haugen.

Republicans and Democrats were quick to label the Progressive Party "radical." Bryan warned progressive Democrats against La

Follette's extremism, and Dawes commenced a withering attack on the Progressives, characterizing them as socialists and "reds." The *Washington Post* offered this assessment on its editorial page: "The fiction that the radicals can remain both within and outside of the two old parties, without forming a party of their own, will soon disappear. They call themselves 'progressives,' but their true name is radicals."[16]

At sixty-four, Robert M. La Follette was an American legend. He had been on the national stage for more than forty years where he had consistently been an uncompromising fighter for progressive causes, a renowned orator, and a masterful tactician in his Senate years. From his leadership of the progressive western farm bloc in the Senate, he waged guerilla warfare on the Republican leadership and occasionally sparked legislative victory for progressive causes.

In the surge of patriotic unity that preceded America's entry into World War I, La Follette was the courageous voice of lonely dissent. Even though he had been ill and away from the Senate for weeks in early 1924, he was a formidable candidate and revered among all progressives. He knew he was near the end of his political career and this would in all likelihood be his last run for the presidency. La Follette relished a fight; and on September 18, 1924, in New York City, he opened his campaign by declaring with anticipation, "The campaign in which we are now engaged witnesses a conflict between two principles of government as old as human history."[17]

Part Five

THE CAMPAIGN

Chapter Ten

SAY *SOMETHING!*

The President's technique was to
destroy issues by ignoring them.
—David Burner

When his friend and law partner, Frank Polk, congratulated him on the night he won the Democratic nomination, Davis responded candidly, "Thanks, but you know what it's worth."[1] It was indeed apparent to everyone that the Democratic Party had practically eliminated any chance it might have had to win the election by staging the most divisive convention in American history. A Minnesota delegate wrote to Franklin Roosevelt soon after returning home from Madison Square Garden, "We defeated ourselves in New York in June."[2] Because it was in exhaustion and desperation that the party had in the end turned to Davis, he knew that he must move quickly to heal the wounds and prepare for the general election. The urgency of the hour led him to break with precedence by appearing in person before the convention, where he appropriately addressed the delegates on the necessity of party unity.

From the very moment the gavel descended in the Garden, Davis confronted the challenges of trying to lead a hopelessly divided party. He instinctively turned for help to his law partners, offering the party national chairmanship to Frank Polk, who ultimately declined but served as a senior advisor, and handing over financial responsibility to Allen Wardwell. His old West Virginia supporter and friend, Clem Shaver, agreed to serve as national chairman when Polk declined and proved to be sadly ineffective. Several young associates at his law firm took up the remaining organizational posts for the campaign, while Davis left for Maine for two weeks of planning and daily rounds of golf. He was able to assemble an impressive group of experienced senior advisors; but it was a matter of only days before the McAdoo forces were grumbling that they were not being consulted, while the Smith supporters were soon just as disaffected. McAdoo himself announced plans to leave for an extended European trip with only a vague commitment to campaign later, and Governor Smith gave his tentative assurances that he would campaign in the East. The first order of business was clearly somehow to hold the party together.

Despite his selection as a compromise candidate, there was no doubt that Davis was a conservative; hence, his greatest challenge was to prevent the progressive wing from bolting the party. After opposing Davis's candidacy throughout the convention, William Jennings Bryan loyally swung in behind the nominee and tirelessly pled with his fellow progressives to support the ticket, which included his younger brother. However, the Democrats suffered a major setback in early August when Democratic Senator Burton K. Wheeler of Montana agreed to join La Follette as his running

(WEST VIRGINIA AND REGIONAL HISTORY COLLECTION, WEST VIRGINIA UNIVERSITY LIBRARIES)
The recently nominated Davis was here flanked by a beaming Franklin Roosevelt
and Al Smith on the steps of the Roosevelt mansion at Hyde Park in August
1924. Davis and Smith would remain lifelong friends, but their relationships with
Roosevelt were later fractured by FDR's New Deal policies.

mate on the progressive ticket. The liberal Wheeler devastatingly
justified his defection in terms that instantly resounded with every
progressive Democrat, "When the Democratic Party goes to Wall
Street for a candidate, I must refuse to go with it."[3]

Early polls showed the progressive ticket attracting disaffected
Democrats by the droves in far western, midwestern, and eastern
states. It was now clear that the desperate addition of Charlie
Bryan to the ticket as Davis's running mate had in no way stanched
the outflow of progressives. The *New York Times* quoted former
Supreme Court Justice Daniel Cohalan as saying, "The most Mr.
Davis can hope for from any progressive Democrat is silence."[4]
Similarly, a reassuring letter from Davis to Samuel Gompers on
July 17, in which Davis characterized his positions as pro-labor
and implored Gompers to meet with him, fell on deaf ears.

Gompers soon endorsed La Follette. *The New Republic* concluded that "no informed progressive can find any reason connected with his progressive convictions for supporting John W. Davis."[5] The candidate was now besieged by advice from all sides. Smith and others argued for concentrating heavily on the East, writing off the western states altogether, while Bryan and others counseled the exact opposite.

Meanwhile, as Davis labored intensely up in Maine to write his acceptance speech and to bring coherence to the campaign organization, troublesome signs of disaffection began to surface. His Maine vacation was the first tactical blunder. Democratic liberals—and soon Republicans as well—were snickering about "the luxurious retreat where the Democratic candidate was to rest from his lucrative labors in Wall Street."[6] The image of the rich Wall Street lawyer golfing at a palatial spa was brilliantly contrasted by Republican strategists to the bucolic photograph of Coolidge pitching a load of hay at his father's Vermont homestead.

Clem Shaver was proving totally deficient as a chairman both in failing to bring efficiency to the campaign and to foster a working relationship between the Smith and McAdoo camps. A revealing example of the lingering fracture surfaced at the August meeting of the Democratic National Committee. The eastern and western factions debated for two hours before approving by a majority of one Shaver's motion for three, not four, vice chairmen. As ex-Secretary of State Lansing wrote just after the election, "mismanagement and inaction" by the party had been a large factor in Davis's defeat. In October, Davis himself wrote to the 1920 nominee James Cox, "the organization does not seem to be functioning."[7]

Clem Shaver, the West Virginia Democratic operative, was Davis's ardent supporter and campaign manager in 1924. After the convention, Davis appointed Shaver national chairman of the Democratic Party.

Davis officially accepted the nomination on August 11 in Clarksburg, with a speech before an estimated 50,000 of his native West Virginians. The *New York Times* speculated that "It is not probable that a candidate for important office ever received a more cordial reception from the men, women, and children of the city in which he was born and bred."[8] Davis began by paying moving tribute to his forbears: "Among them now lie those who gave me life, and to whose high precept and example I owe all that I have ever been and all that I can hope to be."[9]

This acceptance speech contained elements that would contribute to Davis's ultimate failure as a candidate. As was his general custom, Davis wrote the speech himself, and it was carefully structured, elegantly phrased, and flawlessly delivered,

(WEST VIRGINIA AND REGIONAL HISTORY COLLECTION, WEST VIRGINIA UNIVERSITY LIBRARIES)

The favorite son, John W. Davis, arrives in Clarksburg as the Democratic nominee on August 9, 1924.

(WEST VIRGINIA AND REGIONAL HISTORY COLLECTION, WEST VIRGINIA UNIVERSITY LIBRARIES)

The 1924 presidential campaign started with Davis's acceptance speech on August 11 in Clarksburg. Thousands of enthusiastic supporters surrounded Davis's car as he attempted to reach the platform.

yet most observers felt it generally lacked the passion needed to arouse voters. Even *The Nation* wrote admiringly that President Wilson "at his best seldom surpassed Davis' beauty and occasional eloquence," but there was very little of Wilson's moral fervor.[10] This was to be a recurring criticism of Davis's campaign. Although his ability, character, and dignity were transmitted effectively, and although he spoke passionately about the corruption of the Harding administration and the need for tariff reform, it was already becoming painfully apparent that few issues divided Davis and Coolidge. In an effort to foster party unity, Davis sidestepped the most controversial issues in his Clarksburg speech, but pressure was building for him to take a more forceful stand on these issues—especially on the Klan issue.

On August 17, the *New York Times* headlined "Presidential Battle Lines Are Now Drawn" and analyzed the three candidates' acceptance speeches. It was obvious to the reporter that "the

(WEST VIRGINIA AND REGIONAL HISTORY COLLECTION, WEST VIRGINIA UNIVERSITY LIBRARIES)

At the Clarksburg campaign opening, the handsome—and unfailingly dapper—Davis struck a presidential pose by doffing his hat to his fellow citizens while grasping his cane.

record of the last four years meant one thing to Mr. Davis and something quite different to Mr. Coolidge."[11] The primary issues were identified as corruption, tariff policy, and taxation, as well as the Klan and Prohibition. While the issue of honesty in government should have afforded Davis and the Democrats their greatest opening, it was already clear that Harding's corruption had in no way stuck to Coolidge in the minds of the electorate.

The Progressive Party had ignored the Klan in its platform, and La Follette was painfully aware that his greatest potential source of votes was disaffected McAdoo Democrats, many of whom were supporters of the Klan. It was under some duress from his urban supporters, that La Follette renounced the Klan on August 5 with a noticeable lack of his usual fighting spirit and moral fervor. As a result, both factions within the Democratic Party increased pressure on Davis to take a clearer stand. Eastern, urban Democrats urged him to issue a definitive denunciation of the Klan, while southerners and some midwesterners were warning that he could lose his only solid base of electoral support if he attacked the Klan.

Davis fully realized the polarizing effects of taking a strong stand, but on August 21 at a major rally at Sea Girt, New Jersey, he spoke decisively, "If any organization, no matter what it chooses to be called, whether it be KKK or any other name, raises the standard of racial and religious prejudices, or attempts to make racial origins or religious beliefs the test of fitness of public office, it does violence to the spirit of American institutions and must be condemned by all those who believe, as I do in American ideals."[12] Davis included in his speech an appeal to Coolidge to join him in denouncing the Klan, to which there was ultimately no response.

It was revealing of both Davis's character and the gravity of this issue that, on the night before the New Jersey speech, Davis was officially approached by an officer of the KKK. He was handed a letter from the Klan, offering to deliver substantial political support in return for Davis's promise of silence. Davis read the letter, tore it in two, and handed it back to the Klansman with the terse response, "You may say there is no answer."[13]

Over the course of the campaign, Davis was the only candidate who spoke out frequently and forcefully against the Klan. While it is difficult to measure the effects of this stand on the final vote, it is clear that Davis was successful in winning over a significant number of black voters, who historically had voted Republican, and in holding many Irish Catholic and Jewish Democrats within the party. It is equally clear that many McAdoo progressives in the Midwest and western states were infuriated by Davis's stand and, in the end, forsook the Democratic Party for La Follette. By late August, it was reported that Davis and his supporters had been attacked even in eastern states such as Pennsylvania and New Jersey as "being pawns of the Roman Catholic Church."[14] The *New York Times* commented on August 24 that at least Davis's friends "found pleasure in the fact that he had expressed himself according to his personal belief, regardless of the effect on his political fortunes."[15]

As the campaign passed the traditional Labor Day starting date, the Democrats and their nominee were appropriately "terribly worried," as reported by party leader Robert Wooley to Colonel Edward House. Conversely, Republicans were growing increasingly confident. Chief Justice Taft, an admirer and friend

(WASHINGTON AND LEE UNIVERSITY)

W&L Alumni Magazine featured W&L's favorite son.

of Davis's—yet a faithful Republican, was able to write to his brother with some confidence and relief, "John Davis is too good a candidate for the Democrats to succeed with."[16] One measure of the relative strength of the two major parties and their campaigns was financial. The Republicans were well on their way to raising a record $4.3 million, while the Democrats struggled to secure $1 million.

Davis realized his only chance was in waging an aggressive, active campaign, and he dutifully committed to an exhausting 12,000-mile campaign schedule, which concentrated on the Midwest and Mid-Atlantic states. The first quarter of the twentieth century witnessed a transition from the old view that somehow the presidency was "above politics" to what is now regarded as modern presidential campaigning. With the availability of efficient rail transportation and a yawning deficit in electoral support, Davis had no alternative but to embrace the modern concept of campaigning. He engaged President Taft's throat specialist, leased a Pullman car, snatched a handful of key advisors and organizers, and launched his 12,000-mile journey.

(YALE UNIVERSITY LIBRARY)

Here John W. Davis speaks from the rear platform of his railcar on the midwestern barnstorming tour in September 1924.

Not only was the speaking schedule grueling, but Davis also insisted on writing most—and editing all—of his speeches, charging that ghostwritten speeches were "a fraud on the public."[17] By the end of the campaign, he had made over seventy formal speeches and numerous short, extemporaneous talks from the rear platform of his rail car. His staff marveled at Davis's ability day-after-day to appear prepared and organized and to speak eloquently—if not passionately—no matter how many appearances were required of him. The literary allusions, elegant structure, and crisp diction that he consistently employed in his speeches routinely sailed over the heads of most of his crowds; and the criticism was also consistent, as Robert Wooley complained, "Not once did he fire his audience."[18]

In fairness, Davis did speak with conviction—and some passion—on corruption in government, tariff reduction, and the KKK, but there was no question that he failed to rouse the electorate. He often reflected on how his training as a trial lawyer worked against him as a politician. For his whole career, he had sought to remove every trace of emotion from his oral arguments and to rely instead on the power of his reasoning and command of the facts. His legal career, before and after 1924, attests to his exceptional ability to persuade a court, but the requirements and the audience of the stump were different from those of the Supreme Court.

(WEST VIRGINIA AND REGIONAL HISTORY COLLECTION, WEST VIRGINIA UNIVERSITY LIBRARIES)

While Davis's demeanor, appearance, and delivery were impressive, he did not rouse the Democratic faithful.

In addition to his own speaking style, Davis's other major problem was with the issues. He was walking a tightrope whereon almost anything he said offended one faction or the other of his party. As a conservative, Davis could not in good conscience embrace a radical, progressive agenda. There were in fact very few philosophical differences between Davis and Coolidge. Consequently, it was difficult to bestir passion in his supporters when many of these supporters were more liberal than Davis and when his primary opponent was certainly as conservative as Davis.

September found Davis barnstorming through the Nebraska, Kansas, Indiana, and other midwestern states desperately attempting to excite the farm vote. Most often speaking from the rear platform of his rail car, he frequently castigated the GOP for "discrimination against the farmer in favor of the manufacturer" while labeling the progressive effort as "hopeless" and warning Democrats not to "waste" their votes on La Follette.[19] Meanwhile, after returning to the White House from a leisurely vacation at his father's farm in Vermont, President Coolidge appeared at a charity baseball game in Washington, celebrated his nineteenth wedding anniversary aboard the presidential yacht, and tossed out the first pitch at the World Series.

By the fall campaign season of 1924, it was apparent to all that Coolidge had neither the necessity nor the personal inclination to wage a "modern" political campaign. Perceived by virtually all commentators to hold a commanding lead, Coolidge and the Republicans had every motivation to avoid campaigning. The safe course was to run the traditional-style campaign employed most recently and effectively by McKinley and Harding. In addition to offering political prudence, this campaign style very much conformed to the personality of the nominee. Coolidge stated his intention to conduct "a dignified campaign"—a masterful contrast to the Harding image and an accurate reflection of Coolidge's personality as well.

(BY PERMISSION OF THE MARCUS FAMILY)

This drawing of Davis appeared August 31, 1924, in the *New York Times* under the headline "Campaigning With Davis in the Mid-West."

The public was not only well acquainted with Coolidge's reputation for reticence and brevity but also clearly enamored of it. Throughout his career, he had been able somehow to convert a political liability into an asset. Coolidge's predilection for a dignified, McKinleyesque campaign was further strengthened by the tragic death of his son in July 1924. While family and friends felt that Coolidge never recovered fully, there is no question that this loss drove him even further from any thought of conducting an active campaign.

Herein lay a formidable challenge for Davis. The Democrats' twofold strategy was, first, to ignore La Follette, hoping progressives would conclude he had no chance of winning and stay with the Democrats, and, second, somehow to lure "Silent Cal" into a debate over the issues. But Coolidge had no incentive to debate and refused to take the bait. On September 27 in Wilmington, Delaware, Davis's growing frustration was evident when he spoke, "Just as the historian will describe 1920 as that of 'the year of great promises,' so he will come to denominate 1924 as 'the year of the great silence.' It's a vast, pervading and mysterious silence."[20]

As Davis recalled years later, "I did my best to make Coolidge say *something*. I didn't care what it was, just so I had somebody to debate with. He never opened his mouth!"[21] Resorting to sarcasm, Davis attacked Coolidge's primary policy of silence: "If scandals break out in the government, the way to treat them is—silence. If petted industries make exorbitant profits under an extortionate tariff, the answer is—silence. If the League of Nations or foreign powers invite us into conferences on question of worldwide importance, the answer is—silence. If race and religious prejudices threaten our domestic harmony, the answer is—silence."[22] Senator Key Pittman colorfully expressed his acute frustration that his friend Davis was "flanked upon one side by a mummy and upon the other by a volcano."[23]

Davis was left no alternative but to lay out his views in a vacuum, without the aid of dialogue or debate with his adversary. Over the course of the campaign, he developed a number of themes that defined his candidacy and signaled what kind of president he would have been. The underlying theme for all Davis's positions was a Jeffersonian philosophy of government, which centered on equality of opportunity, limited government, and maximum personal freedom.

Predictably, Davis was also bitterly opposed to the Fordney-McCumber tariff, in force in 1924, which imposed the highest rates in American history. Davis had always opposed the tariff on the grounds that the government was protecting special privileges—those of the manufacturers—and he denounced the tariff as "conceived in privilege and written by those who were to benefit from it."[24] He promised repeal of the Fordney-McCumber tariff and a return to freer trade; but, on the tariff issue, Davis was caught between Coolidge and La Follette. The industrialist beneficiaries of the high tariff supported Coolidge and constantly preached to their workers that the tariff safeguarded their jobs, while the farmers, who were consistently injured by the tariff, supported La Follette's more radical remedies.

Davis opposed the tariff on the basis of refusing to protect special privileges, he similarly opposed legislation aimed at providing labor with special protection. He did not believe it was government's responsibility to aid business or labor; and, unlike La Follette, he did not take a "paternalistic" approach to labor, arguing that government "should leave adult citizens to make their own contracts."[25]

In matters of government spending and taxation, it was very difficult to distinguish Davis from Coolidge. Davis advocated reduction of the "heavy and excessive" level of government spending and the burden of taxation. He dutifully opposed the Mellon Plan, as prescribed by the Democratic platform, but his proposed across-the-board tax reductions were in no way incompatible with Mellon's. Many businessmen, such as J. P. Morgan, Jr., voiced near complete agreement with Davis's economic views but felt he should be heading the Republican ticket.

(WEST VIRGINIA AND REGIONAL HISTORY COLLECTION, WEST VIRGINIA UNIVERSITY LIBRARIES)
Here candidate Davis campaigns in Richmond, Virginia, accompanied by his close
friend Senator Carter Glass.

Because of his tenure as ambassador in London, Davis was
considerably more experienced and thoughtful in foreign affairs
than either Coolidge or La Follette. He was a supporter of the
League of Nations and a convinced internationalist, who saw no
alternative to active involvement from the United States in world
affairs. However, he was a realist concerning utopian hopes for
an end to war and resisted all efforts for unilateral disarmament.
Davis believed the United States should take its place alongside
the British Empire as a force for stability, freedom, and peace
in the world, and certainly a Davis administration would have
pursued strong Anglo-American ties. While Coolidge was not an
isolationist, as was La Follette, he did not focus much of his time
or attention on foreign affairs; and foreign policy was not an area
of paramount importance in the campaign.

The greatest social issue of the 1920s was Prohibition, and Davis and Coolidge took a similar stance: the law of the land should be enforced. Neither was a real proponent of Prohibition, nor did either advocate repeal. Davis was repeatedly labeled a wet by the progressive, pro-Prohibition McAdoo forces, which was largely a result of his warmer relationship with the Smith, anti-Prohibition wing of the party. For Davis, Prohibition was ultimately a question of personal freedom and a policy in conflict with his basic notions of limited government; but since it was the law, he supported enforcement.

By the end of the campaign, Davis had once again risen to the challenge of a new assignment with grace, humor, and distinction. He was widely praised for the moral tone of the campaign and for the thoughtful content and elegant style of his speeches. *The Nation* wrote, "Mr. Davis is an honorable and likable gentleman; he has made a skillful, persuasive campaign which is perhaps the most outstanding personal achievement of the contest."[26] Walter Lippmann, James Cox, Jesse Jones, Charles W. Eliot, and many others expressed confidence that he would have made an excellent president. Perhaps the most meaningful—certainly the most touching—tribute was from Davis's young secretary, Harold Hathaway. He marveled at Davis's grace under the strain of campaigning and concluded, "I am entirely sincere in saying that I would rather be near you in any capacity than to be myself president of the United States."[27]

And yet in the end, Davis's candidacy was not a successful one for a number of important reasons. As he and most other Democrats realized, the nomination was largely worthless as a result of the fractious convention. Lippmann was right in saying the Democrats had acted wisely under impossible circumstances by nominating a man of strong character and proven ability with little partisan baggage. But it was still an impossible task for Davis to rally the party sufficiently for a unified campaign. The issues were too divisive, the differences too great. When La Follette and Wheeler took the field for the Progressive Party, the die was cast against Davis and the Democrats.

The odds of overturning the incumbent amidst prosperous times are always long. A vote for Coolidge was generally felt to be a vote for continued prosperity, and that was an impossible

(COURTESY OF THE "DING" DARLING WILDLIFE SOCIETY)

The washing-machine salesman John W. Davis makes a sales call at the White House, only to find that Uncle Sam has already purchased a washing machine, which is being well utilized by an industrious Calvin Coolidge.

current to fight. In addition to having firmly connected Coolidge with prosperity, the Republican campaign brilliantly showcased Coolidge as the New England Puritan that he in fact was. The Democrats' hopes of tarring the Republicans with the Harding scandals faded as the image of Calvin Coolidge came into clear focus. Democratic charges of corruption seemed almost unpatriotic when hurled at the puritanical Coolidge.

The Democratic campaign machinery was weak, Davis's appointments proved ineffective, and Republicans outspent the Democrats five to one. Davis himself proved incapable of calling forth sufficient passion from his base of supporters to generate the momentum for victory. He was a great man but not a great politician; and it was his poor fortune to run against a masterful politician, who was both the incumbent and the symbol of prosperity. The *New York Times* later quoted a perceptive observation made by one of Davis's friends: "He was one of the finest racehorses that ever started on a political track, and he got the worst ride."[28]

Chapter Eleven

KEEPING COOL WITH COOLIDGE

The people know the difference between pretense and reality.
They want to be told the truth. They want to be trusted.
They want a chance to work out their own material
and spiritual salvation. The people want a government
of common sense.
—Calvin Coolidge

Calvin Coolidge's campaign for the presidency began on the day of Warren Harding's death. While all of history involves some element of coincidence, the fact that the Coolidges were in Plymouth Notch on the night of August 2, was fortuitous if not coincidental. The administration of the presidential oath early the next morning by old Colonel John Coolidge, the local notary public, in the modest living room of the Coolidge home by primitive gaslight provided the perfect launching pad for the 1924 campaign. Modern photography sped this picture to the front page of every newspaper in the country. Millions of American voters had spent their own childhoods in humble rooms much like this one with families much like the Coolidges in rural villages much like Plymouth Notch, Vermont.

The rapport between Coolidge and the public was immediate. For an America that was experiencing general anxiety about modernity—mores, social structure, and technology—in the 1920s, this scene and this man were warmly reassuring. As details of scandal involving various administration figures emerged during the following months, the public could fall back on the knowledge that the new President had not been personally involved in the wrongdoing, the belief that he was a morally incorruptible New England puritan, and the image of his solemnly taking the oath of office from his father in the most modest of circumstances. Coolidge's rise to the presidency proved to be the confluence of the right man in the right setting at the right time.

As the public mourned Harding's death, Coolidge moved quickly to bolster his support within the GOP and ensure his nomination the following year. Only two days after Harding's death, Richard Oulahan of the *New York Times* wrote that the president's death "had left the Republican party in chaos, divided into many factions, with many candidates for the Presidential nomination."[1] However, as early as August 13, *Time* was prophetically reporting, "The new President is a conservative. President Coolidge is said to have much in common with Secretary of the Treasury Mellon. He is an able politician; he has never been defeated in an election. It is not to be gratuitously assumed that he will not figure in the Republican National convention next year."[2] By October 1923, statements such as that made by Postmaster General Harry New were regularly appearing in the press: "There is no doubt whatever in my mind that Mr. Coolidge will be, as he very righteously [*sic*] should be, the nominee of the Party in 1924."[3]

Candidates Davis and Bryan arrive at the theater too late, finding Coolidge and Dawes already seated in the row reserved "Honesty—1924".

Coolidge was something of a transformational figure in the party in that he was neither part of the old conservative, Stalwart wing nor part of the Roosevelt progressive faction. Philosophically far more attuned to the Stalwarts, he was perhaps best seen as part of the next generation of conservative Republicans as apart from the conservative club that had ruled Congress and the party since Mark Hanna's time. In the first six months of his presidency, Coolidge was masterfully able to deflect the taint of scandal with his own reputation for integrity; to unify, lead, and invigorate his cabinet and administration; to reach out subtly, but decisively, to Republican progressives like Senator Borah to hold them in the party; to circumvent old Stalwarts, such as Coolidge's longtime Massachusetts adversary, Henry Cabot Lodge; and to use, with expert skill, both radio and photography to establish himself as an icon of American values and economic prosperity. William Allen White declared it "a major miracle in American politics . . . Calvin Coolidge had remade the Republican Party."[4] It was, indeed, a political accomplishment of breathtaking proportions.

By the time Republican delegates convened in Cleveland the following June, Coolidge's nomination was a foregone conclusion, and the convention was universally proclaimed the dullest in American history. The platform adopted at Cleveland had been spoon-fed to the convention by Coolidge, and it suited his reelection campaign perfectly. "Economy" and "common sense" were to be the themes of his campaign, and the platform called for "rigid economy in government" and "reduction of taxes of all the people."

Earlier that year, Coolidge's 1924 State of the Union address had focused heavily on tax reduction; the Mellon Plan, and his Lincoln Day address further laid out his economic program. Always a master at distilling his thought into a succinct but memorable quotation that the public could both understand and remember, Coolidge simply proposed, "I want taxes to be less, that the people may have more."[5]

Two of Coolidge's deeply ingrained personal traits shaped his 1924 campaign. His demeanor, manner of speech, manner of dress, and personality all bespoke a reserved dignity. Throughout his political career, Coolidge always expressed a deep respect for public office and a sense of duty to uphold the dignity of the office. On the day the Coolidges moved into the White House, Coolidge pulled aside the head usher, Ike Hoover, and instructed him, "I want things as they used to be—before!"[6] He had been offended by the informality and raucousness of the Harding White House.

Coolidge once explained to his advisor Bruce Barton that no president should conduct the business of the government on the telephone. He felt it was decidedly undignified.[7] In Massachusetts, he had always refrained from attacking his opponents and had never campaigned actively. Predictably, Coolidge held the soon-to-be old-fashioned view that the presidency should be above campaigning. Early in 1924 he expressed his intention to run a "dignified" campaign without resort to whistle-stopping tours and frenetic speaking schedules.

In addition, Coolidge was himself famously taciturn. Brevity had become his trademark, and he had successfully nurtured the image of the reticent New Englander. The American public was well aware that hanging on the Coolidges' living room wall in Northampton was a needlepoint sampler that read:

> A wise old owl lived in an oak
> The more he saw, the less he spoke,
> The less he spoke, the more he heard,
> Why can't we be like that old bird?[8]

He had no hesitation in applying the wisdom of this sampler to the 1924 political campaign. As he commented during the campaign, "I don't recall any candidate for president that ever injured himself very much by not talking."[9] To the contrary, the public seemed to relish the well-known stories of this stone-faced politician's refusals to talk. To the hostess who reported to Coolidge that her husband bet she could not get more than two words out of the president, he responded, "You lose." Another favorite: During the campaign, a newsman cornered him inquiring, "Mr. President, what do you think about Prohibition?" "No comment," he replied. "What about unemployment?" "No comment," was his reply. "Please comment on the world situation." "No comment," again was his reply. As the disappointed reporter started to leave, Coolidge cautioned, "Now remember, don't quote me."[10] As William Allen White concluded, "Coolidge had the sour manners of a stern and rockbound New England spinster," yet the public embraced him with real affection—and some curiosity. He was a highly successful politician, but his success broke all the conventional political rules.[11]

Whatever question there might have been about whether Coolidge would conduct a low-key campaign was answered on July 7 when tragedy unexpectedly struck the Coolidge family. Sixteen-year-old Calvin Coolidge, Jr., died at Walter Reed Hospital in Washington. A week earlier he had sustained a minor toe injury while playing tennis at the White House. The resulting blister became infected; and, without the aid of antibiotics, blood poisoning developed.

Coolidge's running mate, Charles Dawes, dined with the President on July 2 and reported, "While I did not realize that there was anything serious about Calvin's illness I think the president must have sensed it from the first. He seemed to lose all

(COURTESY OF THE FORBES LIBRARY, NORTHAMPTON, MA)

The Coolidges with sons John and Calvin, Jr. This photo was taken on the steps at
the White House in mid-1924, only weeks before young Calvin's death.

interest in the conversation and the dinner soon ended. As I passed
the door of Calvin's room I chanced to look in. The president was
bending over the bed. I think I have never witnessed such a look
of agony and despair that was on the president's face. From that
moment on I felt a closeness to Coolidge I never felt before, and
have never lost. I had gone through the same great sorrow that he
faced." Dawes too had lost a son several years before.[12] His son's
death plunged Coolidge into deep despair. His wife remembered
that he would sit for hours, alone in the White House, wondering
somehow, "If I had not been president . . ." Coolidge himself wrote
later that with Calvin's death, "the power and the glory of the
presidency went with him."[13]

(COURTESY OF THE FORBES LIBRARY, NORTHAMPTON, MA.)
This poignant photo captures the grieving President and Mrs. Coolidge
at the July 1924 funeral of Calvin, Jr.

The Republican campaign strategy was simple but brilliant: ignore the opponents, claim complete credit for the nation's prosperity, dispatch Dawes to rouse the GOP faithful, and let Coolidge be Coolidge by showcasing his virtues and character. The political setting in 1924 allowed for Coolidge, as the incumbent running during economic prosperity, to ignore his opponents. Indeed, there was no incentive for Coolidge to respond to Davis or La Follette.

In American politics, it has always been virtually impossible to unseat an incumbent in the midst of prosperous times—especially if the incumbent is well liked; and it was here that Coolidge had proven a masterful politician. In less than one year, he had captured the imagination of the public, established himself as a symbol of traditional American values, and become synonymous with the prosperity of the day. While his detractors at *The Nation*

(COURTESY OF THE "DING" DARLING WILDLIFE SOCIETY)

Calvin Coolidge, the hardworking woodcutter, ignores the political clamor of the 1924 campaign and continues to work quietly on "the people's business."

complained, "The Coolidge myth has been created by amazingly skillful propaganda," the public was fascinated. Coolidge's campaign advisor and advertising whiz, Bruce Barton, explained that the three "essentials of effective advertising are (1) brevity, (2) simple words, (3) sincerity," and his client had mastered them all.[14]

At the outset of the campaign, with Coolidge grieving the loss of his son and not planning to campaign actively even later in the campaign, Charles Dawes was commissioned to take the Republican message out to the country. He proved to be an excellent complement to Coolidge. A fiery orator, Dawes loved his assignment and especially relished attacking La Follette. After describing the Progressives as socialists who "fly the Red Flag," Dawes would demand of the crowd, "Where do you stand, with the president on the Constitution with the flag, or on the sinking sands of socialism?"

As Dawes was preparing to leave on a western speaking tour, Coolidge wrote a revealing letter of instruction to him. The president counseled, "The more simple you can keep it, the better you will like it. If you keep as much as you can to an expression of general principles, rather than attempting to go into particular details of legislation, you will save yourself from a great deal of annoying criticism." As a P. S., Coolidge added "Whenever you go anywhere, take Mrs. Dawes along."[15]

On August 3, the one year anniversary of his elevation to the presidency, reporters asked Coolidge what he considered his primary accomplishments of his first year, and he replied tersely that "the general public perhaps was a better judge" than himself.[16] This was quintessential Coolidge, the nonpolitician, pointedly turning away the kind of question that most politicians yearned for and could speak to for hours.

In his acceptance speech on August 14, Coolidge characteristically held to the central themes of his campaign and ignored Davis and La Follette. He defended the existing tariff and strongly endorsed Mellon's tax reduction plan. To no one's surprise, he said, "I favor the American system of individual enterprise, and I am opposed to any general extension of government ownership and control. I believe not only in advocating economy in public expenditure, but in its practical application and actual accomplishment."[17]

In foreign affairs, he sounded an internationalist note by offering cooperation with the struggling countries of postwar Europe and by indicating he would lead the United States to join the World Court. Perhaps the most prescient statement in the speech was when he sounded the note for what he called "common sense," saying, "The people know the difference between pretense and reality. They want to be told the truth. They want to be trusted. They want a chance to work out their own material and spiritual salvation. The people want a government of common sense."[18]

With the requisite acceptance speech behind him, Coolidge retreated to his father's Vermont farm to rest and recover from the loss of his son. But there Coolidge was not unmindful of his image and used photography to contrast sharply his vacation to that of Davis, his hapless Democratic opponent, who was golfing at a fashionable spa in Maine. While en route to his father's farm

(COURTESY OF FORBES LIBRARY, NORTHAMPTON, MA)
The Republicans brilliantly portrayed Coolidge as himself—a New Englander with agrarian roots.

in an entourage of expensive automobiles, Secret Service men, photographers, and reporters, Coolidge had the chauffeur stop, whereupon the president donned a set of overalls over his suit and began pitching hay. The photographers readily obliged, and soon every newspaper in the country treated their readers to this bucolic scene from the presidential vacation.

During this same vacation, the photographers recorded another classic incident that received wide distribution. President and Mrs. Coolidge were joined in Vermont by a trio of eminent American capitalists—Henry Ford, Thomas Edison, and Harvey Firestone—to discuss economic issues and, no doubt, to praise administration policies that had fostered the current prosperity. The picture of the president and his wife, seated with their distinguished guests in front of the modest, clapboard Coolidge homestead, spoke volumes to the American public. These three capitalists symbolized the American prosperity that the nation was enjoying, while the setting was as familiar and reassuring as the average American's childhood recollections of a Sunday afternoon at their grandparents' farm. Millions of Americans were thought to have been chuckling approvingly over their morning coffee at the sight of 'Ol Silent Cal up on the farm in Vermont with those big-shot millionaires.

In addition to the expert deployment of campaign photographs, Coolidge had developed a surprisingly good rapport with the press. Despite his well-honed image of the stone-faced, taciturn New Englander, he could often be almost garrulous in off-the-record conversations with reporters. They seemed genuinely to like him; and, throughout his presidency, Coolidge received generally favorable press coverage. In the new medium of

The great economic boom of the 1920s meets small-town America. Here, left to right, Harvey Firestone, President Coolidge, Henry Ford, Thomas A. Edison, Mrs. Coolidge, and Colonel Coolidge (standing, Russell Firestone) confer in Plymouth Notch in 1924.

radio, Coolidge found another strategic ally. Contrary to popular belief, it was Coolidge, not Franklin Roosevelt, who was the first president to utilize the radio effectively.

Unlike most politicians of his day, Coolidge did not have a booming speaking voice, but rather a somewhat high-pitched voice with a precise New England accent. While singularly ineffective in large auditoriums, Coolidge's voice was made for radio. A *New York Times* reporter wrote of his use of the radio, noting that Coolidge had quickly adapted himself to this new technology. Coolidge himself recognized that he was not a rousing orator and once confided to a friend, "I am very fortunate that I came in with the radio."[19] In his five years as president, Coolidge delivered sixteen radio addresses, which effectively gave him direct access to the American public.

Coolidge and his Republican strategists were determined to ignore John W. Davis and the Democrats, and the campaign's primary slogan, "Keep Cool with Coolidge" was designed to draw the synonymity between the president and the present prosperity. On a less positive note, the Republicans launched another slogan, "Coolidge or Chaos." The premise behind this slogan was that neither Davis nor La Follette, but only Coolidge, could hope to win an outright electoral college majority, therefore a vote for anyone other than Coolidge would result in throwing the election into the House of Representatives. The Republicans sought to conjure up fears that, in the House, progressive Democrats would dump Davis and, along with La Follette Progressives, support the Democratic vice-presidential nominee Bryan. This somewhat convoluted argument was expressed as a warning to voters, particularly in the East who had never supported William Jennings Bryan, that "A vote for Davis is a vote for Bryan, a vote for La Follette is a vote for Bryan, a vote for Coolidge is a vote for Coolidge."[20] As developed on the editorial page of the pro-Republican *New York Herald Tribune*, "The explanation of how the election might go to Bryan was originally an interesting plaything of an idea, but now it is being developed into a campaign bogey. The question of whom the House would elect is a matter of conjecture. Probably it would not be Coolidge. Both Democrats and Progressives are united against him."[21]

As the campaign passed its traditional Labor Day starting date, Coolidge seldom ventured away from the White House; and in the few instances in which he did speak, he assiduously avoided all controversy. In late September, he appeared in Philadelphia to

This 1924 cartoon shows a young Calvin Coolidge whistling
past the political graveyard.

deliver a placid civics lecture on "The Causes of the American
Revolution." On September 21, he addressed the Holy Name
Society in Washington on the importance of religious faith in
American life; and, similarly, he appeared in early October before
a convention of Methodists where he again identified religious
faith as "the foundation of our independence."[22]

Finally, on October 24, Coolidge delivered a major address
on economic issues to the United States Chamber of Commerce,
meeting in Washington. It was here that the president laid out
clearly his conservative economic philosophy. He warned against
the "thousands upon thousands of organizations ceaselessly

("THE WHIRLWIND CAMPAIGN" BY ROLLIN KIRBY
REPRODUCED WITH PERMISSION FROM LAUREN POST.
PRINT COURTESY OF INDIANA UNIVERSITY LIBRARY, BLOOMINGTON, IN)

This cartoon captures both the strategy of the Coolidge campaign and the
frustration of Davis's campaign. It was clear there was no incentive for the
incumbent Coolidge to campaign—and he did not.

clamoring and agitating for Government action that would
increase the burden upon the taxpayer by increasing the cost of
Government"; and he solemnly pledged himself to "the practice
of public economy and insistence upon its rigid and drastic
enforcement." He decried the growth in the American tax burden
over the twenty years preceding Harding's election, stating, "It is
no wonder that under these almost despotic exactions the morale
of the country began to break down. Its vitals were eaten out.
Business began to languish, and agriculture proved unprofitable."
He continued by extolling the benefit of the Coolidge/Mellon
policies, "The present policy of the Government has been to pay
off the national debt and reduce the national expenditures, and the

burden of taxes has been cut in two. A policy of economy has as its sole object the benefit of all the people." After a comprehensive defense of the Mellon tax plan, Coolidge concluded by describing his philosophy of government with eloquence and clarity:

> The Government can help to maintain peace, to promote economy, to provide a protective tariff, to assist the farmers, to leave the people in the possession of their own property, and to maintain the integrity of the courts.
>
> But after all, success must depend on individual effort. It is our theory that the people make the Government, not that the Government makes the people. Unless there abides in them the spirit of industry and thrift, of sacrifice and self-denial, of courage and enterprise, and a belief in the reality of truth and justice, all the efforts of the Government will be in vain.
>
> I believe in the existence of these virtues. I do not think the fathers of the land are going to barter away their property or their liberty. I do not think the mothers of the land are going to abandon the rich heritage that belongs to their children.[23]

This speech was not only classic Coolidge, it was classic conservatism. The Republicans wisely broadcast the speech nationally; it defined Coolidge's campaign and, indeed, his presidency. Except for the brief reference to tariffs, this speech could have been delivered just as enthusiastically by John W. Davis.

But, even though the country embraced the conservative message, it was clearly looking to the incumbent rather than to his challenger for presidential leadership.

(U.S. SENATE COLLECTION/CENTER FOR LEGISLATIVE ARCHIVES)

Clifford Berryman captured the partisan rush to curry favor with the tax-paying voter.

By mid-August, the press was full of talk about the use of radio in the upcoming campaign. The *New York Times* devoted a full page to providing instructions on how to use the "home radio" and speculating on the political impact on the new technology.[24] As Election Day approached, the Republicans turned repeatedly to their new ally, the radio. Republican campaign manager, John Tilson, boasted, "We literally filled the air with Republican addresses from the various studios during the entire month of October."[25]

Coolidge's election eve speech was heard coast-to-coast by the largest audience ever recorded. Journalist Bruce Bliven estimated, "Calvin Coolidge's speeches have been heard by at least ten times as many people as have heard any other man who ever lived." Blevins perceptively concluded that these radio addresses established a link between the voters and Coolidge and provided "a powerful reason to vote in his favor."[26]

(COURTESY OF FORBES LIBRARY, NORTHAMPTON, MA)

President Coolidge was photographed more than any of his predecessors. Here he greets Hall of Fame pitcher Walter Johnson in Washington Stadium.

In one final photo opportunity, Republican campaign managers hauled chairs and a table out onto the rear lawn of the White House and assembled a host of photographers to record President and Mrs. Coolidge's casting their absentee ballots. With the White House looming in the background and Grace Coolidge, wearing a necklace of ivory elephants, smiling admiringly, the president held aloft a large envelope holding their marked ballots. All the while, the accommodating press photographers snapped pictures for the Election Day newspapers.[27]

On November 4, in his last press conference before the election, Coolidge, with classic understatement, said, "I have conducted a campaign that I think will not leave me anything to be sorry for, whether I am elected or not."[28] In summary of the campaign, it could well be said that Coolidge had been dealt a winning hand; and, to his credit, he played it flawlessly.

Chapter Twelve

A PROGRESSIVE WHIMPER

When Progressives divide among themselves reaction wins.
—Samuel Gompers

The framers of the Constitution held political parties in generally low esteem, but fortunately they devised a system that fostered a strong two party system. There are inexorable forces within the American constitutional system that have discouraged the fracturing of parties and rewarded the party that can sustain the support of a majority of the electorate—at least a majority of the electoral college. Over the course of presidential election history, third parties have appeared with some regularity; however, their appearance has generally signaled some major realignment between the two dominant parties, rather than the emergence of a new permanent political party.

This was the case of the Progressive Party in 1924. Historian David Burner has written, "Third parties prepare the way for major periods of political realignment—the road to the Roosevelt coalition of 1936, in other words, began in 1924. The Progressive

Party seems to have functioned for many voters as a way station between the Republican and Democratic parties."[1] As the country swung to the right in the 1920s under Republican leadership and the Democrats followed suit by nominating Davis in 1924, the progressives in both parties felt disenfranchised.

With the nomination of Republican La Follette and Democrat Wheeler, progressives from both parties were urged to leave their historical moorings on principle and support the Progressive Party ticket. This was no idle threat to the two established parties; for, as recently as 1912, the electorate had delivered a whopping 69 percent of the popular vote to the two progressive presidential candidates. In the months leading up to the Republican convention, Coolidge had assiduously courted the progressive Republican

O-O-OH! THERE'S SOMETHING STIRRING IN THE WOODS!

(COURTESY OF INDIANA UNIVERSITY LIBRARY, BLOOMINGTON, IN)

The cartoonist captures the concern of the two major parties over the 1924 resurrection of the Progressive Party.

senators in an attempt to subvert any third party effort, and Davis's most immediate challenge as the Democratic nominee was to hold the progressives within the party.

La Follette uncharacteristically bowed to tradition and did not attend the Progressive convention, but he did dispatch his son, Robert La Follette, Jr., to deliver his acceptance speech. Introduced as "a chip off the old block," young La Follette laid out the challenge for the faithful. There was no doubt in the nominee's mind that "the time has come for a militant political movement, independent of the two old party organizations and responsive to the needs and sentiments of the common people." The paramount issue of 1924 was "to break the combined power of the private monopoly system over the political and economic life of the American people." Free market capitalism was the problem, and expanded government was the Progressives' answer. After calling for "sacrifice, courage, and unsparing activity," La Follette assured his partisans of his "full confidence of success," in response to which the convention erupted in sustained applause. While the convention did express great heartfelt enthusiasm for La Follette, there is no record that it descended "back to second childhood" with the unseemly floor demonstrations which the Progressive chairman had attributed to the philistine Republicans and Democrats and against which he had cautioned these serious, high-minded delegates.[2]

Immediately following the Cleveland Progressive convention, La Follette received a boost from Eugene Debs and his Socialist Party. Although Debs was ill and could not attend the Socialist Party convention, he urged his party to endorse La Follette, which it did by a decisive vote. Debs had been a creditable third party candidate in 1912, garnering almost one million votes. Debs's endorsement simultaneously offset the Progressives' disappointment in Samuel Gompers's warning against the futility of third party candidacies.

From the Republican side, it was soon apparent that Coolidge had succeeded in subverting any sizable defection of progressives, as Senator William Borah and other progressive Republican leaders reluctantly signaled their intention to support the GOP nominee. On the Democratic front, McAdoo was visibly cool towards Davis and offered only the most tepid support, but William Jennings Bryan resolutely enlisted to do his utmost for Davis and the party. Columnist David Lawrence reported later in the campaign that Bryan was drawing "enormous" crowds reminiscent of his previous campaigns and concluded, "He has kept many wavering, progressive Democrats from going to La Follette."[3]

The earliest polls indicated strong and growing strength for La Follette—especially in the West and in the major American cities. In California, the *Literary Digest* reported Coolidge and La Follette running neck and neck with Davis far behind. The Scripps chain of newspapers endorsed La Follette, and the Hearst papers reported a poll of major cities that had La Follette running ahead of Coolidge. Early reports of La Follette's strength in the West even resulted in rumors that Coolidge was considering the possibility of a swing through the western states. At the outset, betting odds ran 16 to 1 against La Follette, but by mid-September the odds were only 6 to 1. Newspaper polls in September were predicting Progressive victory in Wisconsin, Minnesota, the Dakotas, Nebraska, Nevada, and Montana. Many pundits were convinced the election might well result in an electoral college stalemate and ultimately be settled by the House of Representatives. Intellectuals wrote impassioned endorsements in the *Nation* and *New Republic*. Every variety of left-wing activist flocked to the La Follette banner, including civil rights leader W. E. B. DuBois, birth-control activist Margaret Sanger, socialist Norman Thomas, social worker Jane Addams, and political organizer Harold Ickes.

In a September 18, 1924, speech in New York City opening his campaign, La Follette laid out clearly the need for a new Progressive Party, "Opposed to these two old parties is the great Progressive movement. While the Progressive organization has been built up in a very brief period, the great body of public sentiment and opinion which supports it has been of slow growth and is deeply rooted. It has taken years of betrayal and a long line of shameful abuses on the part of the Democratic and Republican parties to convince the people that they must organize for political action outside both old parties in order to find relief."

This speech was a manifesto of progressivism, vowing to make government the active, corrective tool through which to implement "the people's will" on myriad issues. From agricultural prices to telephone rates to control of the judiciary, La Follete set out an expansive role for governmental action under "direct democracy" of the people. He concluded with his sweeping vision of the United States taking its place at the head of "the tidal wave of democracy that is sweeping the world" in order to "outlaw war, to abolish conscription, and to place in the hands of the people of every country the decision upon the declaration of war. It will mean the end of war and dawn of peace for all the world."[4]

After the Republicans indecisively sidestepped the Ku Klux Klan issue at their convention and the Democrats were torn asunder by the same issue, La Follette confronted a difficult political choice. The Progressive platform, which was written by La Follette himself, made no mention of the Klan. Many progressive Democrats, who had supported McAdoo and were attracted to La Follette, were also sympathetic to the KKK, while many of the old Bull Moose Republicans were stoutly opposed to the Klan. Under strong pressure from the latter group, La Follette somewhat reluctantly spoke out against the KKK in early August.[5]

La Follette's tepid condemnation was followed by a much more forceful attack by Davis on August 21, which was followed by Coolidge's studied silence. The Klan did not in the end seem to be a decisive factor in the vote. McAdoo supporters were

(AP/WIDE WORLD PHOTOS)

Scenes like this Ku Klux Klan rally in Oklahoma were widespread in all regions of the country—not just the South—throughout the 1920s.

not generally deterred from backing La Follette, many eastern Democrats were reassured by Davis's strong anti-Klan stance, and Coolidge seemed to attract conservatives on both sides of the Klan issue.

For all the political heat generated by the Prohibition issue among the voting public, this issue did not seem to be a defining one for any of the three candidates—certainly not La Follette. For years La Follette had tried desperately to avoid this issue. He realized how important Prohibition was to many evangelical Christian Progressives, but he in no way viewed it as central to the Progressive agenda. Privately, he shared fellow Progressive Hiram Johnson's exasperated outburst, "Damn the liquor question, anyway," but publicly La Follette was far more cautious.[6] While announcing his personal opposition to Prohibition, he ultimately supported the constitutional amendment under the somewhat convoluted argument of letting the people decide the issue at the state level. Basically, all three candidates supported enforcing the law; and, since none of the three was a strong advocate of Prohibition, the voters were left to make their ultimate choice based on other issues.

La Follette's positions on the League of Nations and foreign policy in general were somewhat complex, and it was not entirely clear what role they played in the 1924 election. La Follette had long advocated some form of international organization dedicated to securing world peace, and he had no conservative inhibitions about surrendering American sovereignty in foreign affairs. However, he came to view the Versailles Treaty as totally flawed and considered it an instrument to thwart the growth of democracy around the world. La Follette was adamantly opposed both to European colonialism and to any form of American internationalist foreign policy. He condemned the Allied effort to suppress revolutionary Russia and advocated recognition of the Soviet Union.

La Follette found himself in the unique position of having opposed American entry into World War I and then subsequently opposing the League of Nations; and, consequently, he was quite convincingly skewered on the Senate floor by Democratic leader Gilbert Hitchcock because "he voted against the war, and now he votes against peace."[7] In essence, La Follette was an American isolationist who abhorred war. His opposition to American involvement in World War I had been widely unpopular at the time; but postwar disillusionment had begun to set in by 1924, and his opposition to Wilsonian internationalism was by then very palatable to progressives.

As for Davis, Coolidge—and especially his tax policies—was the defining issue for La Follette's candidacy. La Follette and Davis hardly ever referred to each other, but focused their attacks almost exclusively on Coolidge. La Follette believed that World War I had "openly enthroned Big Business in mastery of Government" and that the Republican ascendancy of the 1920s had fulfilled what Wilson had started.[8] Coolidge's commitment to minimal government intervention in the market place and Mellon's tax policies were anathema to La Follette, who advocated government initiatives into the control of farm prices, utility rates, trade regulation, and a multitude of labor matters. Whereas Coolidge and Davis believed taxation was only constitutionally sanctioned for supporting basic government functions, La Follette was a steadfast advocate of taxation as a tool of wealth redistribution.

Presaging FDR's frustration with the judiciary in the next decade, La Follette condemned the Supreme Court's consistent reluctance to sanction governmental interference in the market place. When the Court struck down the second child-labor law in 1922, La Follette fulminated, "We cannot live under a system of government where we are forced to amend the Constitution every time we want to pass a progressive law;"[9] and his solution was to promote a constitutional amendment to allow a congressional override of the Supreme Court. This was not a particularly widely discussed issue in 1924, but it was on this issue that Davis strongly attacked La Follette.

As with most third party efforts, the Progressives experienced chronic financial and organizational problems. La Follette turned to a trusted group of Wisconsin supporters, who had never had the challenge of mounting a national effort, to organize the campaign. National Treasurer William Rawleigh soon despaired of "the apparent lack of business ability and capacity" within the organization.[10] Perhaps it should not have been altogether too surprising that so anti-business a campaign as La Follette's had not attracted the best business ability. Throughout the campaign money remained tight with contributions totaling less than $250,000 nationally. Of these contributions, labor unions accounted for more than 20 percent. The campaign committee had to abandon plans to organize the southern states because it would have cost $15,000.

The ultimate challenge for La Follette was to sell his Progressive agenda in a year of economic prosperity. The message that government can solve myriad problems has always been more appealing in the midst of an economic crisis where the electorate has begun to doubt the ability of the market to function or to seek some mitigation of the economic pain of market self-correction. While the situation looked dire to devout Progressives, it did not to most American voters. As the economy continued to improve throughout 1924, and, especially as farm prices strengthened in the western states, the betting odds lengthened by October to 35 to 1 against a La Follette victory.

By mid-October, the last major polls by the *Literary Digest* and the Hearst papers showed La Follette and Davis running neck and neck for second place; but Coolidge was expanding his lead, and Davis was gaining ground. The Republicans' subtle exploitation of the Coolidge Prosperity and their not-so-subtle slogan "Coolidge or Chaos" were overpowering. The conservative policies of Coolidge and Mellon were producing remarkable economic results, and the voters were not interested in jettisoning them to embrace governmental activism.

When the votes were in, La Follette had won only 16 percent of the popular vote and carried only his home state, Wisconsin; however, he had run second in eleven states and run quite strong in the major cities. The Republicans had been successful in casting La Follette as "a menace to prosperity."[11]

La Follette's wife, Belle, had pled with him not to run in 1924. She knew his health was poor and feared the race would cost him his life. Only after realizing how desperately he wanted to achieve the presidency did she relent, but she was right. His health declined steadily after the November election, he sought recovery in Florida, and never resumed his active Senate career. Robert La Follette died on June 18, 1925, four days after his seventieth birthday. In summary of his career, *Time* wrote, "He was a fighter. He was uncompromising. He was a lonely leader. He inspired some. He angered others. He was loyal to ideals rather than to party. He was true to his causes, and too sure of his convictions. He was too fierce a warrior to be a great general."[12]

While his 1924 run for the presidency fell short, it was a transformational event in American political party history. The major party realignment marked by the 1924 election was significantly influenced by the La Follette candidacy. Progressive Republicans were shaken loose from their historical party moorings of more than a generation and ultimately found a home in the Democratic Party, which turned away from its Jeffersonian roots in the years following 1924. As the victorious Republicans held steady on a conservative course, the Bryan Democrats determined to guide their party leftward to claim the progressive banner. As William Jennings Bryan vowed the morning after Davis's defeat, "It was a severe defeat and we must begin at once on the campaign of 1928."[13] Bryan and his progressive Democrats were soon joined by many La Follette Progressives in realigning the Democratic Party as the left-of-center party in America.

Chapter Thirteen

LANDSLIDE!

I knew I hadn't any more chance than a snowball in Hell.
—John W. Davis

Both Coolidge and Davis concluded their campaigns on the same note. Coolidge spoke to the press on November 4 and expressed his confidence that he had conducted a campaign that required no apologies.[1] Similarly, Davis wrote to his friend Lord Charnwood one week after the election that he had said nothing he did not believe. Although he humorously corrected this contention in subsequent years by admitting that he had uttered one slight falsehood in the campaign, "I went around the country telling people I was going to be elected, and I knew I hadn't any more chance than a snowball in Hell."[2]

By Election Day, little suspense remained. While polls taken early in the campaign had shown La Follette winning enough votes possibly to throw the election into the House of Representatives, later polls correctly foresaw Coolidge receiving an outright majority. Even as early as mid-August, the *New York*

"THEY'RE OFF!"

(BY PERMISSION OF THE MARCUS FAMILY)

This drawing by Edwin Marcus appeared in the *New York Times* and depicted "the high tide of conservatism" as the conservatives—Davis on his donkey and Coolidge astride his elephant—lead La Follette out of the starting gate.

Times reported the bookies had declared Coolidge a three-to-one favorite.[3] The final *Literary Digest* poll, conducted in late October, predicted Coolidge would win 56.6 percent of the popular vote. Newspaper editorials were running heavily in Coolidge's favor.

On October 26, the *New York Times* gave Davis a ringing endorsement entitled "The Question of Fitness":

> The personal fitness of John W. Davis to be president of the United States is not challenged by anybody worth serious consideration. In character, in training, in aptitudes, in experience, in grasp of the largest problems confronting the nation, Mr. Davis has demonstrated to all impartial minds that he is well qualified for the presidency. His bitterest political opponents do not deny that he is attractive,

able, eloquent, well-stored with knowledge, fitted forth with principles which he can both avow and defend.[4]

As Davis doggedly barnstormed the country, he could clearly sense state and local Democrats distancing themselves from the national ticket. The St. Louis *Post-Dispatch* wrote, "On the Democratic side there was only John W. Davis, making an able, eloquent but lonely campaign, with little money, a poor organization and not much support from the leaders of the party."[5] To the delight and good fortune of the Republicans, the central issue of the campaign became Coolidge himself.

With the economy continuing to strengthen and prosperity becoming both more ubiquitous and seemingly more secure, there was clearly no compelling reason for the electorate to dislodge the president. La Follette and Davis both had to define themselves and their candidacies in relation to Coolidge; and this was far easier for La Follette than Davis. As the only bona fide progressive in the race, La Follette was able not only to differentiate his candidacy on the issues but also to arouse genuine passion among his liberal following. As a fellow conservative, it was much more difficult for Davis to present any compelling contrast of his candidacy to Coolidge. H. L. Mencken correctly perceived Davis's dilemma when he wrote, "Dr. Coolidge is for the Haves, and Dr. La Follette is for the Have Nots, but whom is Dr. Davis for?"[6]

On election night, Coolidge and his wife awaited the returns in the White House, while the Davises gathered at Frank Polk's townhouse in New York with the Lansings, the Wardwells, and the Polks. By early evening, it was apparent the Republicans had won decisively. Voter turnout was low, 51 percent; and in the popular vote, Coolidge received 15.7 million votes (54 percent); Davis 8.4 million votes (29 percent); and La Follette 4.9 million votes (17 percent). Davis's percent of the popular vote was the lowest of any Democrat ever. In the electoral college, Coolidge totaled 382 votes; Davis 136; and La Follette 13.

As compared to the election of 1920, Harding had won 60 percent of the popular vote and 400,000 more votes than Coolidge, but Harding's had been a two-way race. The breadth and depth of the 1924 victory contrasted the national strength of the Republican Party with the relative weakness of the Democrats. Coolidge achieved a clean sweep of the eastern states; carried all of the west except for La Follette's home state, Wisconsin; and even won the border states of Kentucky, Maryland, Missouri, and Davis's own, West Virginia. (West Virginia was traditionally a Republican state. In the eight presidential elections from 1896 until 1932, it voted Republican in every election except in 1912, when Theodore Roosevelt split the GOP vote.) Davis was left with only the eleven states of the old Confederacy plus Oklahoma, leading Walter Lippmann to comment, "the Democratic party is more or less indestructible because of its stable base in the Solid South."[7]

As *Time* magazine observed on November 17, 1924, "Two landslides for the same party two election years in succession are unusual. It implies that twice in succession the country has been thoroughly roused." The *New Republic* concluded, "The election of 1920 was a great Democratic defeat. This election is a great Republican victory."[8] The Republican landslide of 1924 validated the Harding victory of 1920 and decisively demonstrated the

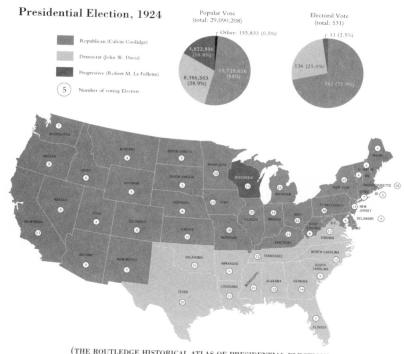

Presidential Election, 1924

Popular Vote
(total: 29,090,208)

- Other: 155,833 (0.5%)
- 4,822,856 (16.6%)
- 15,725,016 (54%)
- 8,386,503 (28.9%)

Electoral Vote
(total: 531)

- 13 (2.5%)
- 136 (25.6%)
- 382 (71.9%)

Republican (Calvin Coolidge)

Democrat (John W. Davis)

Progressive (Robert M. La Follette)

(5) Number of voting Electors

(THE ROUTLEDGE HISTORICAL ATLAS OF PRESIDENTIAL ELECTIONS,
YANEK MIECZKOWSKI, ROUTLEDGE, 2001)

Map of the Electoral College Vote

country's satisfaction with minimalist government, Mellon tax policy, and Coolidge's puritan values. Unlike the three-man race of 1912, which was won by Wilson with a slim plurality, the 1924 election produced a significant Coolidge majority. In addition, the 1912 election—the high point of progressivism—resulted in a combined Democratic/Bull Moose endorsement of progressivism with 69 percent of the popular vote, while the 1924 conservative Republican/Democratic total was 83 percent of the popular vote. The country had been roused, and Progressivism decisively repudiated.

(COURTESY OF THE "DING" DARLING WILDLIFE SOCIETY)

The victorious Coolidge charges over the election goal line leaving Davis and
La Follette badly battered far down the field.

At the outset of the campaign there was much debate over which party would suffer more because of the Progressive challenge. As Davis declared years later, "When La Follette first came out, I thought there was some dividend in that for me. Not a month had gone by, however, before I discovered clearly that for every vote he was taking away from Coolidge he was taking anywhere from two to three from me. Instead of being an advantage, it was a distinct loss."[9]

An analysis of the final vote indicates that the Democrats were hurt far more than the Republicans. Approximately 60 percent of the counties carried by La Follette were carried by Wilson in 1916. Even more conclusively, the following table of the congressional and presidential vote shows that, while Coolidge's vote was only 4 percent below the Republican House vote, Davis's vote fell a whopping 13 percent below the Democratic House vote:

A Comparison of the 1924 Presidential and Congressional Vote

	Republican %	Democrat %	Progressive %
President	15.7 million (54%)	8.4 Million (29%)	4.9 million (17%)
Congressional	14.8 million (58%)	10.7 million (42%)	--------------(--%)

SOURCE: ARTHUR M. SCHLESINGER JR., EDITOR, HISTORY OF AMERICAN PRESIDENTIAL ELECTIONS, VOL III 1900–1936, (NEW YORK: CHELSEA HOUSE, 2001), "ELECTION OF 1924," 2491.

A further analysis by region is helpful in analyzing where La Follette's candidacy hit each party the hardest. In New England, virtually all of La Follette's strength seemed to come from the Democrats, as the Republicans achieved an identical 61 percent of both the presidential and the House votes. In the southern and border states, what few votes La Follette received came almost equally from the two parties; and in the western Midwest, the damage was also about even. In both the Midwest and the mountain states, the Democrats suffered heavier losses; and in the Pacific states, both parties suffered substantial losses.

Percentages of 1924 Presidential and
Congressional Vote by Sections

Section	Congressional Vote		Presidential Vote		
	Dem.	Rep.	Dem.	Rep.	Prog.
New England	39%	61%	26%	61%	12%
Southern/border	60%	40%	57%	37%	6%
Midwest	34%	64%	23%	58%	19%
Western Midwest	35%	65%	25%	52%	23%
Mountain	46%	54%	25%	50%	25%
Pacific	23%	77%	12%	55%	33%

SOURCE: ARTHUR M. SCHLESINGER JR., EDITOR, *HISTORY OF AMERICAN PRESIDENTIAL ELECTIONS*,
VOL III 1900–1936, (NEW YORK: CHELSEA HOUSE, 2001), "ELECTION OF 1924," 2489.

Fortunately for the Democrats, the Progressive Party did not outlive Robert La Follette; the 1924 election proved a watershed event in the ultimate emergence of the Democratic Party as the liberal—or progressive—party in twentieth century American politics. The success of Coolidge in 1924 secured the conservatives' hold on the Republican Party and persuaded the La Follette Republican progressives to seek a permanent home outside the GOP. Similarly, the Democrats became convinced after Davis's defeat that they could not successfully challenge the GOP from the right, and no conservative Democrat has been seriously considered as the party nominee since Davis. When Senator La Follette died in 1925, the Progressive Party died; and the Democrats were the primary beneficiaries.

As for the impact of the major issues on the election outcome, none was as important as Coolidge himself. As the *Boston Transcript* accurately assessed the campaign, "Calvin Coolidge was *the* issue, and to the President belongs the victory."[10] The Ku Klux Klan issue seemed to cut both ways for Davis. The presence of Bryan on the ticket convinced many eastern Democrats to stay at home, even though Davis had denounced the Klan; and conversely, Davis's condemnation of the Klan apparently pushed McAdoo supporters towards La Follette. While his position on the Klan was not popular in many areas of the South, it did not seriously erode Davis's vote there. Coolidge's rather oblique criticism of the Klan and his refusal to join Davis's explicit renunciation of the Klan did not diminish his Republican support. The Prohibition issue seemed to work against Davis to La Follette's advantage, as eastern Democrats often referred to Davis as a wet and interpreted his references to "personal liberty" as anti-Prohibition. The League of Nations did not figure decisively in the election. La Follette's isolationism no doubt kept some Wilson Democrats in the party, and there was no strong differentiation between Davis's and Coolidge's foreign policy positions. The Republican's strongest issue was prosperity—or the "belly issue" as Davis called it—and neither La Follette's radicalism nor Davis's me-too conservatism could shake the voters' faith in the link between prosperity and Coolidge conservatism.

The impact of technology on presidential campaigns was first felt to a significant degree in 1924. Radio was in its infancy in 1920 and was not a factor in the election. Only one station broadcast the 1920 election results to a small number of listeners. By 1924, however, a network of over five hundred stations carried Coolidge's campaign speeches throughout the country. The Republicans wisely allocated the considerable sum of $120,000 in the campaign budget to radio, and the payoff was huge. Strapped for cash, the Democrats and Progressives were unable to match the Republicans, and Coolidge had the airwaves to himself.

The Republican National Committee understood the power of this new technology, although Committeeman George Baker resorted to hyperbole when he predicted, "It [radio] will knock the nonsense out of politics." But Bruce Barton, Coolidge's advertising guru, was correct in predicting the radio "enables the president to sit by every fireside and talk in terms of that home's interest and prosperity."[11] Similarly, the Coolidge campaign grasped the potential of modern photography. Coolidge himself loved staging the carefully scripted "impromptu" moments, and his managers perfected the art of making the photographs "more real than reality." As with radio, the Republicans dominated the country's front pages with creative, captivating photography. In many ways, Coolidge's 1924 campaign was the first of the modern media era.

One interesting manifestation of the claim that the 1924 election ranked as a high point of American conservatism was the electoral influence of J. P. Morgan & Co. The House of Morgan was unquestionably the foremost symbol of capitalism in postwar America. Its partners seemed always to be involved throughout foreign and domestic policymaking, and the firm's ties to both parties and both candidates in 1924 were extremely strong. J. P. "Jack" Morgan, Jr., was an outspoken admirer of Coolidge, commenting, "In a somewhat long life, I have never seen any President who gives me just the feeling of confidence in the Country and its institutions, and the working out of its problems, that Mr. Coolidge does." Morgan senior partner Dwight Morrow was Coolidge's classmate, lifelong friend, and presidential advisor.

On the other hand, Davis was Morgan's lawyer; and, in the words of the firm's chronicler, "He had exactly the right credentials for a Morgan man: debonair and dignified, he favored a larger U. S. role in Europe, supported the League of Nations, and opposed the welfare state and a progressive income tax. He was also a devout Anglophile and one of the Duke of Windsor's lawyers." In addition, Davis was "Jack" Morgan's neighbor on the north shore of Long Island and his regular backgammon partner. "By 1924, the House of Morgan was so influential in American politics that conspiracy buffs couldn't tell which presidential candidate was more beholden to the bank."[12]

(COLLECTION OF ALBERT FELDSTEIN, WESTERN MARYLAND REGIONAL LIBRARY)
Campaign buttons, 1924.

Despite the magnitude of Coolidge's presidential victory, his coattails were surprisingly short. The Republicans gained a relatively modest 22 seats to give them a total of 247 House seats, while the Democrats lost 24 seats and were reduced to 183 seats. The various left-wing parties gained 2 seats to hold a total of 4. The Republicans scored their congressional gains in all areas of the country except the South. In the Senate, the Republicans added 4 seats to hold a modest majority with 50 seats, the Democrats 40 seats, and the La Follette Republicans 6 seats. Several Democratic gubernatorial candidates mounted strong campaigns and successfully bucked the Coolidge landslide, such as New York's Al Smith, who defeated Theodore Roosevelt, Jr.

In the wake of his loss, Davis's spirits were buoyed by scores of letters congratulating him on the high moral tone and philosophical integrity of his campaign. Friends such as Newton D. Baker, Jesse Jones, and Robert Lansing wrote admiringly; and even the daughter-in-law of William Gibbs McAdoo, whom Davis had labeled as "distinctly unfriendly," wrote, commending Davis for having "kept his idealism intact," unlike many of his Wall Street friends.[13]

Davis never displayed any bitterness over the election and was soon entertaining his friends with humorous stories of the campaign. He loved to read the letter of the earnest Prohibitionist who was concerned about Davis's past affiliation with "a bar association." Another favorite was about "Marty," a young Irish woman in Brooklyn who exclaimed to her ward boss after meeting Davis, "you kin tell you mon he kin park his shoes under my bed anytime he wants."[14] As the titular head of the Democratic

Party, Davis continued after the election to speak out on various national issues and to offer advice to the Democratic National Committee from time to time, but he was soon back in his Wall Street office where he resumed his position at the pinnacle of the nation's legal profession.

After La Follette's death, Davis spoke perceptively of his Progressive opponent in his 1929 Princeton lectures, "The Progressive movement of 1924 under La Follette was of an even more [than previous third party efforts] opportunistic character. It sought to capitalize all the discontent with either the Democrats or the Republicans, the war, the weather, the crops or the taxes, hoping, no doubt, that factors of a permanent cohesion might develop and that a true third party might arise. It, too, exhausted all its force with a single effort, and after the death of its leader, it disappeared, leaving not a sign to mark its passing."[15] La Follette did not live to see the ultimate realignment of the two parties in which the Democrats were to become America's progressive party and the ascendancy of liberalism under FDR.

Calvin Coolidge was left with a bittersweet victory. His election triumph was at once both personal and monumental, and it had been achieved with virtually no strings attached. He had made no promises to gain the nomination or to win the election. He had remade the Republican Party in his conservative image and molded the campaign completely around both his personality and his philosophy. And yet the death of his son robbed him of the great joy that should have accompanied such a victory. Friends and family concluded that Coolidge was a different man after young Calvin's death. William Allen White revealed the poignant story that Grace Coolidge, in November, 1924, began to crochet a bedspread comprised of eight squares—each square representing a remaining month in their White House tenure. He wrote, "She and the President alone in their sorrow—talked it over many times, month by month, as she finished each square, and they counted the months until they should be home in Northampton and away from the grinding pressure of the Presidential job."[16]

Part Six

AFTER 1924

Chapter Fourteen

THE TWENTIES ROAR ON

We live in an age of science and of abounding accumulation
of material things. These did not create our Declaration [of
Independence]. Our Declaration created them. The things of
the spirit come first. Unless we cling to that, all our material
prosperity, overwhelming though it may appear, will turn
to a barren scepter in our grasp.
—Calvin Coolidge

Following the election of 1924, as a victorious Calvin Coolidge
prepared to assume the presidency in his own right, he delivered
three major addresses that were to define his administration. On
December 3, he sent his annual State of the Union message to
Congress, and in it he sounded his renewed call for lower taxation.
In early 1924, Coolidge and Mellon had proposed a 25 percent tax
cut for all taxpayers; but the president had reluctantly compromised
with Congress and signed the Simmons-Longworth bill, which
reduced the surtax to a maximum rate of 40 percent. Coolidge
made it clear to Congress that he viewed his election victory as a
mandate for lower taxes and contended that "the larger incomes of

the country would actually yield more revenue to the government if the basis of taxation were scientifically revised downward." The *Washington Post* offered a summary that could have been applied to Coolidge's entire political career, "The concise, straightforward presentation of facts with regard to the state of the Union, the short simple sentences which can be understood without effort, and the common sense of the whole message combined to make a strong appeal." The message was received with bipartisan acclaim as the "best message Mr. Coolidge has sent to the Capital."[1]

(COURTESY OF THE "DING" DARLING WILDLIFE SOCIETY)

The hardworking, puritanical President Coolidge ignores the adulation of the public and remains focused on his "regular job."

On January 17, 1925, he delivered the second of his major addresses before the American Society of Newspaper Editors; and it was here that he uttered those famous, and much misunderstood, words, "The chief business of the American people is business." Coolidge had simply observed that Americans "are profoundly concerned with producing, buying, selling, investing, and prospering in the world," while he proceeded to praise idealism and condemn materialism: "It is only those who do not understand our people, who believe our national life is entirely absorbed by material motives. We make no concealment of the fact that we want wealth, but there are many other things we want much more. We want peace and honor, and that charity which is so strong an element of all civilization. The chief ideal of the American people is idealism." His message was clear: Prosperity is the result of the character of the American people not the government. Historians, however, have too often lifted "The chief business of the American people is business" quotation out of context and portrayed Coolidge as a tool of big business.

In his third major speech, the Inaugural Address on March 4, 1925, Coolidge was widely praised for his comprehensiveness and brevity, "rarely equaled by the utterances of presidents" according to the *Washington Post*. Here again Coolidge drove home his basic theme:

> I want the people of America to be able to work less for the government and more for themselves. I want them to have the rewards of their own industry. That is the chief meaning of freedom. Until we can re-establish a condition under

which the earnings of the people can be kept by
the people, we are bound to suffer a very distinct
curtailment of our liberty.

Coolidge preached economy in government as a cardinal
virtue. To him it was immoral for the government to take one penny
more from the taxpayer beyond what was absolutely necessary
in order to maintain law and order and provide the most basic
services of government. Mellon believed, "The Government is
just a business and can and should be run on business principles,"[2]
which included balancing the budget and reducing the public
debt. Coolidge and Mellon were of like mind and were equally
determined to practice economy in government by lowering
taxes and reducing government spending. Modern historians have
generally failed to understand the moral dimension of Coolidge's
philosophy and have instead simply viewed him as a mouthpiece
for big business. The *Washington Post* perceptively captured the
essence of Coolidge and his philosophy in this editorial comment
on his address:

> Few persons, probably, have considered economy
> and taxation as moral issues. But Mr. Coolidge so
> considers them, and his observations give a fresh
> impression of the intensity of his feeling on this
> subject. He holds that economy, in connection with
> tax reduction and tax reform, involves the principle
> of conservation of national resources. A nation
> that dissipates its resources falls into moral decay.
> Extravagance lengthens the hours and diminishes

the rewards of labor. "*I favor the policy of economy,*" says Mr. Coolidge, "*not because I wish to save money, but because I wish to save people*" [emphasis added]. He would protect those who toil by preventing the waste of the fruits of their toil. The burden of taxation is excessive. It makes life more meager, and falls hardest upon the poor. The United States is fortunate above other nations in the opportunity to economize. It is at peace and business activity has been restored. "The collection of any taxes which are not absolutely required, which do not beyond reasonable doubt contribute to the public welfare is only a species of legalized larceny," is Mr. Coolidge's vigorously expressed conclusion on the subject of economy.[3]

The federal income tax was introduced in 1913 with the highest bracket set at 7 percent; but by the end of World War I, Congress had enacted huge increases on all levels of income. On incomes exceeding $1 million, the rate stood at a whopping 77 percent. The economy was in a steep recession when Harding's administration began, and Secretary Mellon believed substantial tax reductions were needed to boost growth. The Revenue Acts of 1921 and 1924 achieved modest reductions. Finally, in February 1926, Coolidge and Mellon achieved the comprehensive congressional victory they had long sought: The Revenue Act of 1926 was passed by overwhelming majorities in both houses of Congress. This sweeping legislation removed fully one-third of the 1925 taxpayers completely from the tax rolls, halved the estate tax, and repealed the gift tax. Progressives mounted fierce resistance in the Senate, characterizing the bill as tax relief for the rich; however, the bill returned over 70 percent of the tax reductions to taxpayers with incomes below $10,000 per year. Nebraska's Senator George Norris charged that Andrew Mellon's personal tax reduction was larger than the aggregate reduction of all the citizens of Nebraska.[4] Secretary Mellon did not bother to rebut this charge, but historian Thomas Silver has retorted that "in 1924 Andrew Mellon paid *more* federal taxes than all the people of Nebraska put together."[5]

These tax cuts fostered unprecedented economic growth through the 1920s: GNP grew at an astounding annual average rate of 4.7 percent, while the unemployment rate declined from 6.7 percent to 3.2 percent and consumer prices remained stable. As Mellon and Coolidge accurately forecast, by the end of the decade the rich were paying more taxes; and, with the tax exemption on the first $4,000 of annual income, most Americans now owed no income tax at all. Between 1922 and 1928, the number of taxpayers earning over $100,000 quadrupled, while the average income reported by this bracket increased 15 percent. Similarly, those taxpayers in the $10,000 to $100,000 bracket increased 84 percent. For the lowest bracket, those earning below $10,000, the number actually declined, leading Silver to conclude, "It is only a tiny exaggeration to say that Coolidge and Mellon completely removed the burden of federal income taxation from the backs of poor and working people between the time Coolidge entered the residency and the time he left."[6] Equally pleasing to Mellon and Coolidge was that gross tax receipts grew substantially, creating annual surpluses and allowing for federal debt reduction. As a modern economist has written, "The tax cuts of the 1920s were the first federal experiment with supply side income tax rate cuts. The Mellon tax cuts restored incentives to work, save, and invest, and discouraged the use of tax shelters."[7]

Against this backdrop of reduced taxes and limited government interference, the American economy surged forward to achieve record prosperity. As Paul Johnson has written, "Prosperity was more widely distributed in the America of the 1920s than had been possible in any community of this size before.[8] Millions of Americans entered the middle class and attained a measure of economic security they had not known before. The greatest driver of the 1920s economy was the automobile. In 1915 Americans owned two and a half million cars; and, by 1929, there were fully 23 million automobiles registered. This mammoth industry was the largest customer for steel, rubber, and gasoline and provided work for millions of American workers. It was Henry Ford who converted the automobile from a rich man's toy to an everyday necessity by relentlessly driving down costs and reducing the price of his cars.

A second major driving innovation of the 1920s was the radio. Modern radio transmission began in 1920 when station KDKA in Pittsburgh broadcast the election returns to a few dedicated hobbyists with crystal sets. By 1930, there were over 600 stations nationwide, while annual consumer expenditures for radio equipment exploded from $60 million in 1922 to $400 million in 1925.[9] The radio tied together the country as nothing ever had. Politicians, marketers, educators, entertainers, and preachers could now reach into the remotest corners of the nation, and the effects

(COURTESY OF FORBES LIBRARY, NORTHAMPTON, MA)
Coolidge was the first American president to utilize the radio, and he expertly used it to his great advantage.

were profound. Gradually, rural areas connected to urban centers, traditional family ties were weakened, the general level of speech improved, and, in general, a more common culture emerged.

Consumer installment credit greatly assisted the growth of the automobile and the radio. Before the twenties, America was still a puritanical society that valued savings over consumption and "pay as you go" over "easy credit." Between 1920 and 1928, installment sales quintupled to over six billion dollars. Auto makers were enticing drivers to "Pay as you ride," while advertisers exhorted consumers to buy a radio and "Enjoy while you pay."[9]

Suddenly middle America had access to time-saving appliances, furniture, automobiles, and radios through installment credit; and manufacturers were bombarding consumers with advertisements. Modern advertising was born in the early 1900s; and, by 1925, advertising revenue accounted for over 70 percent of media revenue. National ad campaigns were launched in newspapers, magazines, and radio for every conceivable product, creating universally recognized slogans such as "I'd walk a mile for a Camel," "The Pause that refreshes," "Good to the last drop," and on and on and on.

Very quickly this 1920s prosperity became generally known as "Coolidge Prosperity." Coolidge's fiscal and tax policies were credited for igniting the country's economic growth, and the president's New England Puritanical character provided a reassuring link to America's past in the midst of a rapidly changing social order. Walter Lippmann mused in 1926, "The politicians in Washington do not like Mr. Coolidge very much, for they thrive on issues, and he destroys their business. But the people like him, not only because they like the present prosperity, but because they trust and like the plainness and nearness of Calvin Coolidge himself. This is one of the most interesting conjectures of the age."[11]

In the off-year elections of 1926, Republicans suffered losses that were relatively small by historical off-year standards. The GOP House majority decreased by ten seats, and the Senate loss was seven seats; but the Republicans retained control of both Houses. This nominal control was somewhat deceptive in that the reduced GOP majorities gave the progressive, western farm bloc decisive leverage in the Senate and caused Coolidge problems in the new session. Neither in 1924 nor in 1926 did Coolidge even attempt to provide coattails to influence the election of larger Republican majorities, yet the strength of the party and the president's popularity were sufficient to provide working control of the Congress.

(COURTESY OF FORBES LIBRARY, NORTHAMPTON, MA)

These two photos of President Coolidge vacationing out West delighted the public.

Coolidge's greatest congressional challenge was over passage of the McNary-Haugen Bill. The roots of this legislation were in the boom/bust cycle in the farm belt from 1914 to 20. Before and during the war, farm acreage and production exploded to meet international demand, and the price of farmland rose commensurately. This boom was followed by a sharp collapse in farm prices, thousands of bankruptcies, and deep economic anguish, resulting in political unrest across America's midwestern farm belt.

The McNary-Haugen Bill first emerged in 1924 as a plan whereby the government would purchase domestic agricultural surpluses and sell them overseas, raising domestic farm prices. Eastern and southern opposition defeated the bill in June, 1924; but the progressive farm bloc resurrected the bill in the following session. Proponents of McNary-Haugen picked up strength in the 1926 congressional elections and also won over certain key Republican converts, including Vice President Dawes and Agriculture Secretary Wallace. Coolidge, supported strongly by Mellon, voiced opposition during the congressional debate, but the bill easily passed both Houses, only to be promptly vetoed by Coolidge.

In his veto, the president forcefully characterized this legislation as a radical intrusion of the federal government into the free market. He gravely warned against granting "almost unlimited control of the agricultural industry" to a twelve-man board that could "not only fix the price which the producers shall receive for their goods, but can also fix the price which the consumers of the country shall pay for these commodities." In a Jeffersonian argument that was repeatedly articulated by John W. Davis in opposing New Deal legislation in the 1930s, Coolidge further decried the idea of "equalization": "This so-called equalization fee is not a tax for purposes of revenue in the accepted sense. It is a tax for the special benefit of particular groups."[12] McNary-Haugen was again passed by Congress in 1928, and again Coolidge wielded his veto. The two defining congressional battles of his administration were those over taxes and McNary-Haugen.

Reflecting the underlying strength and growth of the American economy, the stock market began a steady, spectacular climb in mid-1921 that culminated in late 1929. The Dow Jones Industrial Average sextupled from 63.90 to 381.17 over these eight years as the stock market became a highly visible symbol of the Coolidge Prosperity. Just as many consumer products such as appliances and automobiles had previously been affordable only by the rich, so too equity investments enjoyed a far broader following than ever before. The emergence of investment trusts and the availability of low interest rate margin loans helped to fuel the market. Inevitably, as in every bull market, greed became the primary motivation; by 1928, rank speculation was driving the market to new heights.

(COURTESY OF FORBES LIBRARY, NORTHAMPTON, MA)
This is one of few photos capturing a smiling President and Mrs. Coolidge.

From early 1928 until the market crash in the fall of the following year, the Dow Jones Industrial Average more than doubled. As John Kenneth Galbraith has written, "Until the beginning of 1928, even a man of conservative mind could believe that the prices of common stock were catching up with the increase in corporation earnings, the prospect for further increases, the peace and tranquility of the times, and the certainty that the Administration then firmly in power in Washington would take no more than necessary of any earnings in taxes. Early in 1928, the nature of the boom changed. The mass escape into make-believe started in earnest."[13]

While Coolidge warned of the moral danger of "gross materialism" and Hoover fretted about the "growing tide of speculation," the public remained confident; and Hoover was elected in a landslide over Al Smith in 1928. The inevitable day of reckoning came in October 1929, with the Great Crash. Primarily because of the length and severity of the Great Depression, which followed the crash, Galbraith observed that "A whole generation of historians has assailed Coolidge for the superficial optimism which kept him from seeing that a great storm was brewing at home and more distantly abroad. This is grossly unfair."[14]

Always, in the final stages of a bull market, greed becomes the primary motivator; investors are loath to consider caution, and the result is a precipitous correction. As Paul Johnson has written, "Business downturns serve essential purposes. They have to be sharp. But they need not be long because they are self-adjusting." Such downturns require patience from the public and the government; but, because any downturn is by definition painful, it is difficult for the public and its government to exercise patience.[15]

In the severe recession of 1920–21, the Harding administration had reduced taxes, cut government spending, and exercised patience, while allowing the market and the economy to self-adjust. In 1929, Herbert Hoover chose not to follow suit. Contrary to popular mythology, Hoover greatly increased government spending, incurring an unprecedented peacetime government deficit of $2.2 billion in 1931. In marked contrast to Coolidge, Hoover not only practiced interventionism with the implementation of his Reconstruction Finance Corporation, the Emergency Relief and Construction Act, and the Agricultural Marketing Act, but also his interventionism was accompanied by what Johnson termed "an incessant activist rhetoric."[16] At the same time, he increased tax rates on higher income taxpayers; and these Hoover policies were vastly expanded by the succeeding Roosevelt administrations.

It remains a matter of fierce debate among historians and economists as to whether the crash of 1929 would have become the eleven-year-long Great Depression had the government followed the Harding-Coolidge-Mellon policies instead of those of Hoover and FDR. In any event, historians have tended to look back over the painful reality of the Great Depression and conclude, with no creditable substantiation, that the Coolidge Prosperity was unsound and somehow responsible for all that followed.

As Coolidge's term ended in 1928, he rode a crest of unparalleled popularity. The Coolidge Prosperity had indeed been a five-year period that in many ways represented the "Last Arcadia." America was at peace abroad, and economic activity was robust by every measure. Technological advances were transforming how people lived, worked, and played, and these new innovations brought an improved standard of living to every class of society.

(COURTESY OF FORBES LIBRARY, NORTHAMPTON, MA)
One of Coolidge's last major speeches at the dedication of the
Washington War Memorial in 1928.

Taxes were low, and government was minimal. Political pundits
and historians have found it difficult to reconcile somehow the
results of the Coolidge Prosperity with the man himself.

How could such a seemingly simple man as Calvin Coolidge,
who adhered so closely to old-fashioned virtues and conservative,
Jeffersonian government, have captured the respect, admiration, and
even affection of the American public as they entered the modern
era? After pondering the Coolidge phenomenon for eight years,
Walter Lippmann finally concluded at the end of Coolidge's tenure
that "Americans feel, I think, that they are stern, ascetic and devoted
to plain living because they vote for a man who is. Thus we have
attained a Puritanism *de luxe* in which it is possible to praise the classic
virtues, while continuing to enjoy all the modern conveniences."[17]

Chapter Fifteen

LAWYER'S LAWYER

*I do not like to have John W. Davis come into my
courtroom. I am so fascinated by his charm and eloquence
that I always fear that I am going to decide in his
favor irrespective of the merits of the case.*
—Judge Learned Hand

It did not take Davis long to shake off the effects of the election
and get back to his first love—the bar. After the election, he
complained of feeling like a "sucked orange"; but, on returning
from a Mediterranean cruise with Nell, he was soon back in his
Wall Street office. In his absence and in eager anticipation of his
return, Davis's admiring partners had renamed the firm Davis Polk
Wardwell Gardiner & Reed. (From 1925 to the present, the firm
has retained the first three names, though "Gardiner and Reed"
were later dropped and others added. For many years the name
has been simply Davis Polk & Wardwell, commonly referred to as
"Davis Polk." It remains one of the nation's premier law firms.)

Davis always led the firm by example. During his thirty-
four-year tenure, Davis Polk grew from thirty to one hundred

partners. Through this period, Davis chaired the partners' meetings where he set the firm's overall tone and direction; delegated the administrative duties successively to Lansing Reed, Frank Polk, and then George Brownell; and consistently led the partners in the attraction of major clients. He personally resisted the profession's trend toward specialization. While he used the resources of a large firm, he always prepared his own briefs and did his own drafting, adamantly contending that, "no six lawyers can draft anything."[1]

In 1954, as he looked back on his long career, Davis explained clearly how his Wall Street practice was a reflection of what he had learned as a small town lawyer: "I still think of the lawyer as an advocate and an adviser. That has helped to keep me from going into something like tax-work. I'd have been a flat failure . . . There is one thing you've got to learn as a country lawyer, and that is to take care of yourself, to be confident in your own decisions and efforts."[2] Herein lies the secret of Davis's success as a lawyer. He was valued by clients both as an adviser and as an advocate. Clients engaged him because they trusted him completely and because of the soundness and quality of his advice, but also they knew that he was an exceptional advocate before the bench. Many lawyers excel at one or the other of these two primary roles, but few have matched Davis in the mastery of both.

There are many examples of Davis's functioning as adviser and advocate with a host of clients over the years. One of the most visible and famous of such relationships was Davis's role as lead counsel for J. P. Morgan & Co. during the Pecora Senate hearings of 1933. As was often the case, the base of Davis's client relationship was personal. As a neighbor and regular backgammon partner of

"Jack" Morgan, Davis knew him to be a man of personal integrity and knew that Morgan's—and Morgan's father's—personal integrity was reflected throughout the bank. Since his return from England in 1920, Davis had served as lead counsel to J. P. Morgan & Co. and, on a wide range of issues, had provided sound counsel upon which was built a solid relationship as adviser.

When the national spotlight turned to Wall Street in 1933 following the market crash and the election of FDR, congressional hearings commenced under the leadership of the crusading former district attorney of New York, Ferdinand Pecora. A fervent progressive with many anticapitalist convictions, Pecora predictably turned to investigate what was then the premier private bank in the world, J. P. Morgan & Co. Equally predictably, Morgan then turned to his trusted adviser, John W. Davis. From his own days in Congress, Davis had developed a deep cynicism regarding congressional hearings. He believed Congress was full of politicians who prayed regularly, "Lord, let the limelight shine on me, just for the day;" and he viewed Pecora's committee from this deeply skeptical perspective.[3]

Personally, Morgan was a thoroughly shy man who had always avoided publicity and was now thrust onto the front pages to his total discomfort. Two widely viewed photographs provide eloquent summary of Davis's role as adviser. In one, Davis is discreetly—almost tenderly—whispering advice into the ear of his besieged client. He was at Morgan's side throughout the exhausting testimony; and, because of both his personal friendship with Morgan and his sound counsel, Davis was able to navigate through the hostile hearings to a successful conclusion.

(BETTMANN/CORBIS)

This photo captured Davis's role as counsel and advisor to J. P. Morgan, Jr., in the famous Pecora congressional hearings of 1933.

In the second photograph, Davis and Pecora were seen conferring, each with cigar in hand—the appearance of two friends having an amicable chat. There is no question that Davis was unsympathetic with Pecora's political views and contemptuous of the political motivations behind the hearings; however, throughout his career, Davis was always able to establish warm rapport with his adversaries through his gracious personality. Davis's remarkable ability to engage adversaries on a personal level, while hammering hard on the issues at hand, was of tremendous value in securing a favorable outcome for his clients, whether arguing a case before the court or appearing before a hostile committee.

After commanding an exhausting, three-month rearguard action for his client involving sharp exchanges with Pecora over a host of issues and retreating strategically when necessary, Davis was able to secure for Morgan what was probably the best

Here Davis, as advisor and counsel to J. P. Morgan, confers with antagonist Ferdinand Pecora during the sensational 1933 congressional hearings.

outcome possible in light of the committee's—and the public's—hostility. Pecora concluded in the end that J. P. Morgan & Co. was not involved in speculative activities that had characterized the operations of many of the banks.[4] While Davis was frustrated that he had not been able to deliver a more complete vindication, which was probably not even a reasonable objective, he could take great solace in the letter of thanks and appreciation from Morgan and his thirteen partners to Davis: "Words are entirely insufficient to express our deep sense of gratitude to you and your associates through these past three months of work and strain. Without your wisdom and sympathetic interests we should have been at a loss how to prepare for the examination before the Senate Committee; without your great legal ability we should not have known how, or to what extent it was wise, to defend our rights against the attacks of the Counsel for the Committee. For this and for the tireless work of yourself and all your associates, we wish to express our heartfelt thanks and our true gratitude."[5] Davis's consistent ability to elicit such trust and gratitude from major clients was the foundation upon which Davis Polk's practice was built over the years.

It was always easy to caricature Davis as the prototypical Wall Street lawyer who represented America's largest companies and presided as senior partner over one of the nation's most prestigious corporate law firms; however, as his obituary pointed out, he had represented a long list of unpopular underdogs. In his early years as a lawyer, Davis represented "Mother" Jones, a famous union organizer in West Virginia and Eugene V. Debs, a father of the national socialist movement; and from his Wall Street platform at Davis Polk, he later represented conscientious objector Rosika Schwimmer, immigrant Isador Kresel, and atomic energy scientist J. Robert Oppenheimer. Davis saw no inconsistency between his conservative views and the arguing of these civil rights cases. On the contrary, he viewed his role in these cases with pride, as an extension of his belief in Jefferson's individual liberty.

Although Davis had returned to full engagement as senior partner of his firm, he was also the titular head of the Democratic Party following the 1924 election. He never harbored any illusions about the decisiveness of his defeat and accurately perceived the party would naturally look elsewhere for active leadership. Since he had never seen himself as a politician and fully understood that "the man who is out of politics more effectively than any other is a defeated presidential candidate," Davis did not seek to exert any leadership of the Party.[6]

Instead, he did from time to time provide counsel as an elder statesman. Davis testified frequently before congressional committees on the constitutionality of various domestic issues and the advisability of various foreign policy issues. In 1929, he gave the Stafford Little Lectures at Princeton, which were published under the title *Party Government in the United States*, and in which he explained the Jeffersonian concepts that underlay both the historic Democratic Party and his own political philosophy. He here identified the "profound and lasting" struggle between paternalism and individualism—or "between the conservative and the liberal view of government and society." In words that clearly foreshadowed his future denunciation of Roosevelt and the New Deal, he warned against paternalistic government that offered "a transcendental faith in the power and wisdom of the State and the human agencies it must employ. In laws and still more laws lies the cure for every human ill, and fallible men when inducted into office are presumed to receive a mystic baptism of unselfish wisdom that fits them to administer the most intimate of their neighbors' affairs."[7]

In the years approaching the 1928 election, Davis grew increasingly sympathetic to Al Smith. He appreciated the support Smith had given him in 1924, and he believed the urban Catholic Democrats would tear the Party apart if their man were denied the nomination in 1928. More importantly, Davis had come to believe Smith was truly of presidential stature, as he explained to his friend Lord Shaw, "High society is pained at the thought of his entering the White House," but Davis saw through these superficial distractions and found Smith to be a leader of uncommon courage and ability—as well as refreshingly witty and candid.[8]

While not endorsing Smith, Davis provided valuable assistance to his campaign by attacking religious discrimination, especially widespread anti-Catholic sentiment. On January 18, 1928, Davis wrote that "as a non-Catholic—who dissents on pretty much every point of Catholic doctrine—I am willing to go to the mat at any time on the right of a Catholic to hold any office for which he is qualified."[9] Smith's Tammany backers did not seek Davis's counsel, nor did he seek to provide a major role in the campaign. During the campaign, Davis made a sizable $10,000 pledge, chaired a national committee of lawyers for Smith, and made a nationally broadcast radio address entitled "Religion and Politics."

In this radio speech, he appealed to both Jefferson and Lincoln, who belonged to no church, and concluded, "If a member of one faith is to be excluded today from a civil right or opportunity or privilege, is to be declared by reason of his creed unfit or unsafe for public place or honor, what faith may not be trodden down tomorrow. 'He only is free,' says the maxim, 'who lives among free men.'" On the following morning, October 12, 1928, a *New York Times* front-page headline heralded "Davis Denounces Bigotry in Campaign." The article reported that "Mr. Davis saw in the issue of religious liberty and civic equality the gravest problem this country had faced since the settlement of slavery," and reprinted Davis's speech in its entirety.[10]

Following Smith's defeat in 1928, the subsequent market crash, and the ensuing depression, Davis became somewhat more active in seeking to guide the party's direction as it approached the 1932 election. The Democrats' prospects for victory brightened as the country slumped deeper into recession. Davis went to the 1932 convention in Chicago as a delegate-at-large, hoping to influence the nomination of a conservative candidate. He received a rousing ovation when he spoke to the convention and was able to influence the adoption of a relatively conservative platform, but Davis was not successful in securing the nomination for either Newton D. Baker or Harry F. Byrd, his two favorite conservative candidates. For some time Davis had believed Franklin D. Roosevelt was too unpredictable to make a good President, even warning, "if that man is elected, he will ruin the United States."[11] Nonetheless, Davis announced his support for the ticket and began attempting to hold the party to the conservative platform adopted at the convention.

Unlike many subsequent historians, Davis recognized the philosophical difference between President Hoover and his two predecessors. Harding and Coolidge were essentially Jeffersonians who consistently advocated minimal government intervention, whereas Herbert Hoover was far more of an interventionist. Presaging his later attacks on the New Deal, Davis condemned Hoover's administration as following "the road to socialism at a rate never equaled in time of peace by any of its predecessors." Walter Lippmann posited that Hoover was the forerunner of the New Deal, Davis wrote to Lippmann to express his complete agreement:

> I think that Hoover did make an unprecedented departure when he assumed that the national government is charged with the responsibility of the successful operation of the country's economics and the maintenance of a satisfactory standard of life for all classes in the nation. I do

not believe that doctrine myself, first in point of right and second in point of power and capacity. Nothing but mischief, to my way of thinking, can come from any government attempting tasks which lie beyond its power to accomplish. This is one of them.[12]

In the *New York Times* on October 30, 1932, in an article entitled "Why I Am a Democrat," Davis made the case for Roosevelt by harkening back to the party's Jeffersonian principles: "Any nation that continues to spend more than it receives is headed for inevitable disaster; neither a nation nor a man can find solvency by borrowing; neither he nor it can spend its way into prosperity nor beg itself into comfort . . . If the Democratic Party is successful, it will balance the budget . . . Instead of striving to give every man a share of governmental help, borrowing from impoverished Peter to pay poverty-stricken Paul, it will aim to make it possible for every man to help himself."[13] Davis's eloquent campaign appeal was soon to be replaced by his profound disillusionment with the New Deal.

After Roosevelt's landslide election, Davis continued to challenge the incoming administration to adhere to the party's Jeffersonian ideals. On March 5, 1933, as FDR assumed the reins of government, Davis authored a major article in the Sunday *New York Times*, entitled "The Torch Democracy Keeps Alight— Jefferson's Inspiration, Says John W. Davis, Is Still the Beacon of the Past." As clearly as any conservative Democrat has ever written, Davis laid out the Jeffersonian precepts of government:

The chief aim of all government is to preserve the freedom of the citizen. His control over his person, his property, his movements, his business, his desires should be restrained only so far as the public welfare imperatively demands. The world is in more danger of being governed too much than too little.

It is the teaching of all history that liberty can only be preserved in small areas. Local self-government is, therefore, indispensable to liberty. A centralized and distant bureaucracy is the worst of all tyranny.

Taxation can justly be levied for no purpose other than to provide revenue for the support of the government. To tax one person, class or section to provide revenue for the benefit of another is none the less robbery because done under the form of law and called taxation.[14]

As FDR and the Democrats began to construct their policies, Davis's worst fears were soon realized. Over the first twelve months of the new administration, the internal philosophical struggle was decisively resolved, and a leftward course was set after considerable seesawing back and forth from right to left. By the summer of 1934, Davis complained that "the administration has moved away from me rather than I from the administration"[15]; and it was in August 1934, that he took the most active political position of his post–1924 career.

Along with other prominent conservatives of both parties, Davis founded the American Liberty League as a defender of Jeffersonian liberalism. He served for a time as executive director and headed the Lawyers' Committee. Under Davis's active direction, the committee studied the constitutionality of the myriad New Deal laws and challenged those laws it believed were unconstitutional. In several instances, Davis himself appeared as amicus curiae before the Supreme Court in attempting to thwart the administration. In one of these cases, *United States v. Butler,* Davis offered a stirring defense of federalism and persuaded the Court to invalidate the first Agricultural Adjustment Administration.

Davis viewed the Liberty League as a nonpartisan, educational institution that would expose the dangers of the New Deal and convince the public of the merit of Jeffersonian principles. He viewed with alarm the speed with which FDR and Congress were centralizing government and intervening in the economic affairs of the nation, warning "those who stand for the old order must make themselves heard or the day will come when it will be too late for protest to be heard, much less followed."[16]

During the formation of the Liberty League, Davis delivered a major address at the University of Virginia—appropriately "Mr. Jefferson's University"—in July 1934. Warmly introduced by his old friend Senator Carter Glass, Davis condemned governmental attempts to undermine capitalism, decried economic planning, underscored the sanctity of property rights, pled for the return to greater individual freedom, and concluded with an eloquent, heartfelt plea for constitutional restraint:

Every government of whatever kind professes always to be acting only for the public good. The bloodiest tyrants in history claimed no less. The limitations which our Constitutions seek to impose, however, are not intended to prevent Government and its agents from doing those things which no one could wish to do on any pretext, but rather to fix the bounds which can not be exceeded even by conscious rectitude and righteous people. If these bounds can be over passed at will by the mere magic of the grand, omnific word "emergency," surely they are made of gossamer.[17]

Davis did not fail to appreciate the urgency of the Great Depression, but he saw as far more important the danger to the foundation of the American republic. His concern was that the New Deal "cure" was far worse than the disease. In retrospect, the wisdom of his words resonates in the history of growing government intervention—most often justified as a response to an "emergency."

The Liberty League was unsuccessful in convincing the public to abandon the New Deal; and at least a part of the reason was its lack of partisanship. The major political party realignment that began after 1924 had not been fully completed. There was still a significant conservative minority in the Democratic Party that sided with Davis, while the Republicans were wary, in the face of New Deal popularity, of declaring themselves unequivocally the party of conservatism.

The Liberty League sought to articulate and advance a conservative philosophy without providing the political party vehicle through which to govern. The League did, however, provide a rallying point for conservatives during their dark days under the New Deal and arguably was an important midway point in the ultimate realignment of the parties. While the Democrats remained on a consistently leftward tack after 1932, the Republicans did not conclusively embrace conservatism until 1964 nor bring it back into the White House until 1980.

In addition to his leadership of the Liberty League, Davis's corporate practice brought him regularly into court to challenge the New Deal. He argued against the Frazier-Lemke Act, the Public Utility Holding Act of 1935, the original Agricultural Adjustment Administration, and the Wagner Act. Six times he represented corporate or individuals in tax cases. He argued against the unconstitutionality of certain government regulations on electric utilities, oil companies, and railroads. In three cases, he defended corporations against antitrust charges. While not always successful in court, Davis was able to prevail more often than not; and, in so doing, he emerged as a national spokesman for conservatism and earned himself the sobriquet "Public Enemy No.1" inside FDR's White House.[18]

In reminiscing years later on these New Deal court battles, Davis singled out the *United States v. Butler* case as a particular "abomination" in which the court ruled, to Davis's profound dismay, that "the spending power was a part of the general welfare clause, and that Congress could spend for any purpose it thought was for the general welfare"—contrary to a hundred years of court precedence. With remarkable prescience, he predicted the results: "This case makes the government a grab-bag, and the real political urge is 'Who shall get the largest share?' Now, I don't believe that popular government can survive once that doctrine is accepted. That is what every popular government has gone down under. That idea of government as a juicy melon is poison. If you continue to administer it, with every administration what is a privilege or grant today becomes a right tomorrow."[19]

In the 1936 election, it came as no surprise that Davis broke with the Democratic Party and endorsed Alf Landon for president. In his 1929 lectures on party government at Princeton, Davis had counseled to "stay with your party as long as you can without losing your self-respect."[20] Nonetheless, it was front-page news on October 21, 1936, when Davis broke officially with the New Deal and urged his fellow Democrats to back Landon. After introducing himself as "an active and I can truly say a belligerent Democrat for forty years" who had been honored by the party "beyond my highest hopes," he ruefully concluded that "I must speak the truth as I see it without fear and without evasion." The *New York Times* published the entire text of the speech in which Davis launched a blistering broadside attack on the New Deal:

> It [the traditional Democratic Party] has opposed centralization in government as the sure road to tyranny and has demanded the preservation of the local self-governing power of the states. It has denounced wasteful government expenditure which takes from the mouth of labor the bread that it has earned. It has asserted that taxes could be justly laid only to provide the revenue necessary to

support the legitimate functions of the government and that taxation for any other purpose was no different from confiscation.

Whether business is better today than it was yesterday, or will be better or worse tomorrow than it is today, is a poor guide for people who are called upon to decide what sort of government they want to live under both today and tomorrow and for the long days after. If they found their government on the shifting sands of unsound principles, it will make no lasting difference whether business is good or bad.

It is a painful dilemma that confronts a Democrat who still holds to the creed of Democratic liberalism. What can he do, therefore, as a Democrat and an American, but stand up, speak up, and on Election Day take his judgment and his conscience with him into the polling place and make his protest there.[21]

His was much more a conviction that Roosevelt must be defeated than an endorsement of Landon. If not defeated, FDR would, in Davis's words, "press on from one crazy experiment to another;" however, he was not "greatly inspired by Brother Landon"—especially his tariff, foreign policy, and farm policies. When a fellow West Virginian wrote to ask if he thought Jefferson would have voted for Landon, Davis replied that he was "damn glad Old Tom is dead" and would not have to wrestle with that decision.

In 1940, Davis enthusiastically backed Wendell Willkie as a man of "great capacity and lofty purpose." He contributed to Democrats for Willkie and was much drawn to Willkie's internationalism. When asked, "Are you still a Democrat," Davis shot back, "Yes, *damn* still!"[22] While Davis wholeheartedly supported FDR's foreign policy leading up to and throughout World War II, he backed Dewey somewhat reluctantly in 1948. In 1952, Davis was an enthusiastic supporter of Eisenhower, drawn by his internationalism and moderate conservatism.

Davis always viewed himself as a "liberal" in the original sense as defined by Locke and Jefferson. By the 1930s, the term "liberal" had been appropriated by the progressives; and an old-fashioned Jeffersonian liberal like Davis was more likely to be called a "conservative." As Amity Shlaes, a modern historian, explained, "The president [FDR] made groups where only individual citizens or isolated cranks had stood before, ministered to those groups, and was rewarded with votes. Roosevelt's move was so profound that it changed the English language. Before the 1930s, the word 'liberal' stood for the individual; afterward, the phrase increasingly stood for groups."[23]

In 1937 Davis wrote to his friend Dr. Francis Pendleton Gaines, president of Washington and Lee, "I have never thought of myself as an indurated Tory. On the contrary, I have gloried in the name of liberal, which I interpret to mean a love for the greatest liberty consistent with public order. The great trouble with our modern 'liberals' is that they think liberalism means exceeding liberality with other people's money."[24] Davis never officially left the Democratic Party, but by his death in 1955 it was clear that his "self-respect" was leading him out of the Party. There is no reason to doubt that, had he lived another twenty years, he would have joined the vast majority of his fellow conservative Democrats in defecting to the GOP.

Davis's life and career post-1924 showed every indication of personal contentment. The liberal Louis Brandeis inquired of Davis to a mutual friend, who replied that Davis seemed to him quite happy. Brandeis then mused that he was not at all surprised because Davis loved his work as a lawyer—and he loved "good living."[25] Davis himself said many times that his first love was the law, and his partners and associates testified often to his joie de vivre in the practice of law. As Davis once said, "There's no exhilaration in the world that exceeds being clearly seized of your case, convinced that you've got the answer for all your adversary's propositions, and then to stand up and let him have it!"[26]

This photo of the Davises was taken on their daughter Julia's wedding day at Mattapan, the Davis home in Locust Valley, Long Island.

In addition, his Wall Street practice afforded him an enviable lifestyle. His ten-acre estate at Locust Valley was comfortable, if not palatial, and surrounded by neighbors who were socially compatible with the Davises. Also, Davis maintained a large Fifth Avenue apartment that overlooked Central Park, a small cottage at Yeamans Hall near Charleston, South Carolina, and a fishing camp on the Sebatis River in New Brunswick, Canada. A staff of six or seven servants included Charles Hanson, Davis's valet and devoted friend, who returned with him from England in 1923 and served him until Davis's death. Davis maintained memberships in several country clubs and six of New York City's most prestigious eating clubs. He and Nell typically spent a month every year in England visiting friends from his days as ambassador, and often they accompanied "Jack" Morgan on his yacht for Mediterranean cruises. In later years his doctor sent Davis to Yeamans Hall for at least a month every winter to avoid some of the New York cold. Indeed, Brandeis's assessment was probably right.

Mattapan, the Davises' commodious house in Locust Valley, Long Island, New York, was their summer retreat for over thirty years. Davis's third-floor study looked out over St. John's Church, Lattingtown, to Long Island Sound.

The last two of Davis's 140 cases before the Supreme Court provided a fitting conclusion to his appellate career. The first of these cases was known as the steel seizure case in which Davis argued that President Truman had violated the constitution when he seized control of the steel industry to avert a strike in wartime. At age seventy-nine, Davis stood at the pinnacle of his appellate career and argued with his utmost conviction that Truman's action was not only a "usurpation of power without parallel in American history" but also a "reassertion of kingly prerogative, the struggle against which illumines all the pages of Anglo-Saxon history."[27]

If ever there were the perfect confluence of events and the man, it was this case and John W. Davis. Convinced for the past twenty years that the government was dangerously overreaching its constitutional bounds, Davis had become the appellate champion of constitutional restraint. When President Truman received his attorney general's opinion that he could, in case of emergency, seize the steel mills, Republic Steel sought Davis's counsel. In a detailed, eleven-page opinion, Davis responded that the president did not have such authority. The crisis intensified as Truman's demagogic radio address failed to bring the steel company executives into submission. The president refused to invoke the Taft Hartley Act, a showdown of massive consequences resulted, and the Supreme Court agreed to hear the case.

Davis had not been involved in the case since delivering his opinion to Republic Steel some months before, but it was at this point that the industry's battery of lawyers came to him with the request that he make the sole argument before the Court. What greater testament could there have been to the reverential respect in which Davis was held by his peers than to have received this assignment in his seventy-ninth year?

On May 12, clad in his traditional formal morning suit, Davis rose to make his 138th argument before the Supreme Court. A reporter for the *Herald Tribune* wrote that Davis seemed "to personify the spirit of constitutionalism, his voice that of history itself."[28] Over the next eighty-seven minutes a packed courtroom was treated to a flawless performance by the greatest legal advocate in modern American history. He drew repeatedly on the conservative Jeffersonian principles learned first from his father and later from Tucker and Graves at Washington and Lee, here applied expertly to the facts at hand; and, finally in conclusion before the crowd's rapt attention, he concluded dramatically with Jefferson's own words, "In questions of power, let no more be said of confidence in man, but bind him down from mischief by the chains of the Constitution."[29]

Many of the following morning's papers prominently displayed a photograph of Davis striding confidently across the plaza of the Supreme Court. As Justice Learned Hand reported, he and his wife were finishing breakfast when she held up a copy of the *Herald Tribune* picture of Davis and said, "There, now that's the picture of a *really* distinguished man." Hundreds of congratulatory messages flooded Davis's office, but the greatest tribute was the Court's 6–3 ruling that the steel seizure had been unconstitutional.[30]

Davis's final argument before the Court was in *Briggs v. Elliott*, the South Carolina companion case to *Brown v. Topeka Board of Education*. This case involved the appeal of a ruling that upheld the constitutionality of segregation in South Carolina. Governor James

(WEST VIRGINIA AND REGIONAL HISTORY COLLECTION, WEST VIRGINIA UNIVERSITY LIBRARIES)

This photo captured a confident John W. Davis striding across the Supreme Court
Plaza after arguing the steel seizure case. It was after seeing this photo in the
morning newspaper that Justice Learned Hand's wife turned to her husband and said
of Davis, "Now there's a *really* distinguished man."

Byrnes of South Carolina, a longtime friend of Davis's, appealed to
Davis to take the case, which he did with relish.

Davis viewed this case as a clear-cut matter of stare decisis
and states' rights. He was confident that the Supreme Court would
uphold the highly esteemed Judge Parker's lower court opinion,
which rested squarely on precedent. Davis wrote to Byrnes that he

did not believe the Fourteenth Amendment removed control of education from the states and concluded, that the Court had already decided this very question in at least three previous cases.[31]

Davis and South Carolina had the weight of precedent on their side, while the opposition relied on social science, morality, and appeals to conscience. When opposing counsel, Thurgood Marshall submitted a brief predictably filled with comments by sociologists, Davis expressed profound exasperation. "I can only say that if that sort of 'fluff' can move any court, God save the state!"[32] For Davis and many conservatives, segregation—at least in the courts—was not a moral or sociological issue but a constitutional issue. Marshall and the civil rights advocates viewed segregation through an entirely different prism.

The pairing of Davis against Marshall was historic in itself. The seventy-nine-year-old WASP, a pillar of the establishment, was pitted against the forty-five-year-old, black civil rights advocate. Marshall, who later became a Supreme Court justice himself, retained throughout his long career what was often perceived as a tough edge, perhaps the result of years of racial discrimination. However, Marshall always spoke admiringly of Davis as "the greatest solicitor general we ever had. You and I will never see a better one. He was a great advocate, the greatest." As a law student at Howard, Marshall often slipped over to the Supreme Court to hear Davis argue cases. "Every time John Davis argued, I'd ask myself, 'Will I ever, ever . . . ? And every time I had to answer, 'No, never.'"[33]

Over three hundred people packed the Supreme Court chamber on December 9, 1952, as Chief Justice Vinson convened the hearing. The hopes of millions of black Americans and the

(BETTMANN/CORBIS)

Here Davis discusses his last case before the Supreme Court with
opposing attorney Thurgood Marshall.

fears of millions of white southerners were focused on the Court,
as Davis and Marshall made their arguments. Several days after
the trial, Davis wrote, "Unless the Supreme Court wants to make
the law over, they must rule for me."[34] That was a pretty good
summary, and indeed Marshall was asking the Court to do just
that. Immediately after the arguments, when the justices first met
briefly to discuss the case, there appeared to have been a 5–4
majority in favor of upholding segregation; however, by spring,
the Court had turned 6–3 against upholding it. It was at this point
that the Court decided to ask for a reargument on five questions.

By December 7, 1953, when the reargument was held, a new
chief justice, Earl Warren, had been installed; and he was eager
both to put his stamp on the court and to atone for his role as
governor of California in the internment of Japanese-Americans
during the war. Again, the duel between Davis and Marshall was
intense but argued from two very different viewpoints. *Time*

reported that Davis, now past his eightieth birthday, was "a white-maned, majestic figure in immaculate morning attire who looks type-cast for the part. Some of his friends were sorry to hear him, at twilight, singing segregation's old unsweet song. But the popularity of a case rarely cuts any ice with John W. Davis. In the 29 years since his defeat for the presidency, Davis has all but faded from popular memory; in his own profession, he is a living legend. Most Davis Polk business never reaches a courtroom at all. But the courtroom is still the showcase of the legal profession, and John W. Davis the acknowledged star of the show."[35]

Davis solemnly warned the Court against sitting "as a glorified board of education" and appealed to the law's reverence for precedence. As law professor and constitutional scholar Alexander Bickel has noted, "No one hearing Davis emphasize how pervasive and how solidly founded the present order was could fail to be sensitive to the difficulties encountered in uprooting it."[36]

Again, Davis was certain the Court could not fail to uphold his argument, which was so firmly undergirded by the most basic principles of Anglo-Saxon law. Yet, on May 17, 1954, Chief Justice Warren produced a unanimous opinion that ruled segregation unconstitutional under the Fourteenth Amendment and uprooted "the present order." Warren had done a masterful job of crafting a short, decisive opinion, overcoming the objections of several justices who were inclined to dissent until the very final discussions. Davis was truly devastated by the opinion, not because of his devotion to segregation, but because he clearly foresaw the danger of the Court's arbitrary loosening of those "chains of the Constitution," which Jefferson saw as the necessary restraint on government. In the *Briggs* ruling Davis correctly discerned the danger of what was later to be decried by conservatives as the Warren Court's "judicial activism." He sadly observed to one of his partners that the opinion was "simply unworthy of the Supreme Court of the United States."[37]

On April 13, 1953, shortly before the conclusion of the segregation case, Davis observed his eightieth birthday amidst honors from all sides. A *New York Times* editorial saluted him by observing that, whenever he spoke the word "Constitution," "there is a resonance in his voice that gives life and power to plain, old-fashioned American words. His is still a voice that commands respect."[38] Governor Byrnes presented him a resolution of appreciation from the legislature of South Carolina for his work on the segregation case. The British Consul General, on behalf of Queen Elizabeth II, presented Davis with the Honorary Knight

(WEST VIRGINIA AND REGIONAL HISTORY COLLECTION, WEST VIRGINIA UNIVERSITY LIBRARIES)

This photo of Davis as senior partner of Davis, Polk, and Wardwell was taken in his Wall Street office shortly after he argued his final case before the Supreme Court in 1954.

Grand Cross of the Order of the British Empire, the highest civilian distinction for a foreigner. His partners presented him with a resolution of their affection, addressed to "Our Beloved John W. Davis." He concluded the day by granting an interview to the *New York Times* in which he said, "The greatest changes I've seen in law stem from the relationship between the citizen and his government, with an ever-widening field of government interference." He correctly prophesied that the agencies of governmental intervention "which once set up cling like barnacles to a ship."[39]

Davis's last two years were very difficult for him. Nell had died in 1943; and by 1953, most of his lifelong friends were also gone. While he continued to go to his office until shortly before his death, his doctor restricted his travel; and, because of his unsteadiness on his feet, he did not appear in Court after the segregation case. He relied more and more heavily on Hanson, who reflected that although Davis always maintained a reserved distance, "He treated me always as a friend, always as a friend."[40] In these last years, he grew closer than ever before to his daughter Julia. She visited him daily, usually having breakfast with him in his apartment.

While on his traditional winter sojourn at Yeamans Hall in 1955, Davis contracted pneumonia and was taken to hospital in Charleston. During the next three weeks he was well enough to receive regular visits from Julia and her husband, Governor Byrnes, Edwin Sunderland, and others. Finally, on March 24, 1955, he died quietly after suffering cardiac arrest. Over one thousand mourners filled the Brick Presbyterian Church in New York for his funeral. Davis was buried beside Nell in Lattingtown Cemetery, Locust

Valley, in the beautiful forty-acre park landscaped by Frederick Law Olmstead. A plain granite headstone bears his name and the following appropriate verse lovingly selected by Julia: "Mark the perfect man, and behold the upright; for the end of that man is peace." Psalm 37:37.

Fitting tributes were posted in newspapers around the country. The *New York Times* concluded, "He was a solid citizen of absolute integrity and of great ability."[41] The *Washington Post* perceptively described his as "a gentleman in the sense that Confucius used that much abused word—a superior man, with a courtliness that came from a fine intellect and a warm heart and a gently manner. In whatever circle he moved, there was none other who seemed so fitted to be at the head of the table. To that place his fellows instinctively beckoned him. Nobody can say what kind of President he would have made, but one can say with confidence that John W. Davis had a sense of statesmanship."[42]

The simple granite tombstones of John and Nell Davis in Lattingtown Cemetery, Locust Valley, Long Island, New York.

Chapter Sixteen

AMERICAN SPHINX

I have found in the course of a long public
life that the things I did not say never hurt me.
—Calvin Coolidge

In late July 1927, President Coolidge informed his surprised
secretary that he did not plan to run for reelection the following
year. He explained that if he were to run and win in 1928, he would
serve as president for almost ten years, which was too long in his
opinion for any man to hold the office. Coolidge planned to make
the announcement at a regularly scheduled press conference at 9
a.m. on the morning of August 2. The Coolidges were vacationing
in Rapid City, South Dakota, and the president's secretary, Everett
Sanders, suggested delaying the announcement until noon, because
of the time difference, so that the stock market would be closed
back East. Shortly before noon, Coolidge summoned Sanders and
handed him a slip of paper on which he had written this terse
announcement: "I do not choose to run for president in nineteen
twenty-eight."[1]

The president then instructed Sanders quite specifically to copy the sentence economically onto just enough small slips of paper so that each member of the press could receive one. When the press assembled at noon, Coolidge asked Sanders to shut the door while the clearly amused president preceded to hand each reporter a slip of paper. Once the distribution was complete, Coolidge opened the door without saying a word and let the befuddled reporters race to file their stories. Immediately there was debate about the wording of the statement. Was it a categorical refusal to run, or did it hint at availability to a draft? Many journalists and politicians believed—or wanted to believe—that Coolidge was open to a draft, but he never gave any indication that his statement was not definitive. The statement was pure Coolidge—simple, terse, delphic.

Why did Coolidge refuse to run in 1928? In *Autobiography* he explained that he had in fact never intended to run for reelection in 1928 and had decided to announce his intention sufficiently early in order that the GOP could select his successor with due deliberation. In addition to expressing his belief that no man should serve as president for more than eight years, he went on to note, that it is impossible for politicians—especially presidents—to avoid the "malady of self-delusion. They are always surrounded by worshipers."[2] The loss of his son, Calvin, Jr., in 1924 remained a fresh wound, and Coolidge acknowledged that he never felt the same about the presidency after his son's death. Years later, Mrs. Coolidge recalled his commenting in typical homespun language, "It is a pretty good idea to get out when they still want you."[3]

Coolidge's withdrawal—or apparent withdrawal—cleared the way for his ambitious commerce secretary, Herbert Hoover, to secure the nomination. Coolidge had inherited Hoover in the Harding cabinet and retained him throughout his administration. Neither Coolidge nor Mellon liked Hoover—either personally or politically. They correctly saw Hoover as much more of an interventionist than themselves and worried that he would significantly expand the role of government. In addition, they viewed him personally as somewhat abrasive and pushy. Because it was apparent that Hoover had quite willingly taken on assignments that normally would have fallen to other cabinet members, it was a Washington joke that "Hoover was Secretary of Commerce and Undersecretary of all other departments." Coolidge often referred to Hoover, the world-famous engineer, as "Wonder Boy."[4] Under Hoover, the Commerce Department was the only cabinet-level department whose budget grew substantially during Coolidge's years in office, a fact which endeared Hoover to neither Coolidge nor Mellon.[5]

President Coolidge flanked by his Secretary of Commerce and successor Herbert Hoover.

The Republicans nominated Hoover on the first ballot at their Kansas City convention, where he was hailed as a combination of "the old-fashioned virtues of Coolidge with the new technology of the 1920s."[6] The Democrats, in a remarkably placid convention, nominated New York Governor Al Smith. As in 1924, the big issue was "Coolidge Prosperity," while an unfortunate secondary issue was Smith's Roman Catholicism.

Hoover campaigned squarely on Coolidge's record, and Coolidge delivered several speeches on behalf of Hoover. The result was a resounding endorsement of "Coolidge Prosperity," as Hoover trounced Smith 58 percent to 41 percent in the popular vote and 444 to 87 in the electoral college. Had Coolidge run, his margin would probably have surpassed Hoover's.

On December 4, Coolidge sent his final State of the Union message to Congress, and the themes were familiar. The message understandably began with optimism: "No Congress of the United States ever assembled, on surveying the state of the Union, has met with a more pleasing prospect than that which appears at the present time." He extolled the importance of both tax and debt reduction and reviewed the usual issues relating to agriculture and the tariff.

In closing, he sounded his final, oft-repeated call for conservative government: "The end of government is to keep open the opportunity for a more abundant life. Peace and prosperity are not finalities; they are only methods. It is too easy under their influence for a nation to become selfish and degenerate. This test has come to the United States. Our country has been provided with resources with which it can enlarge its intellectual, moral, and spiritual life. The issue is in the hands of its people. Our faith in man and God is the justification for the belief in our continuing success."[7] This was Coolidge's last official reminder to the public that the strength of the Republic lay in the people—not in the government. The government's primary role was to provide stability and opportunity for free individuals to excel.

In the four-month transition period, President-elect Hoover planned to take a month-and-a-half tour of South America to focus attention on foreign relations and economic affairs within the western hemisphere. In addition to his wife, he planned to take along a considerable number of his staff and requested that President Coolidge make available a U. S. battleship. With predictable parsimony, the president suggested a cruiser as "it would not cost so much." While Coolidge did eventually relent and provide a battleship, there was no indication of any close cooperation between the old and new administrations—hardly a surprise in light of Coolidge's oft-spoken reservations about "Wonder Boy."[8]

In his final months in office, Coolidge was besieged with financial offers for his post-presidential years; and he signed a contract with *Cosmopolitan Magazine* for his memoirs at the astounding rate of five dollars per word. Beyond this, banks, brokerage houses, and other financial firms proposed lucrative offers, but Coolidge reacted with appropriate caution. In declining one such offer, he wrote, "Whatever influence I might have, came to me because of the position I have held, and to use that influence in any competitive field would be unfair." He went on to observe that many of the offers he received would never have been made had he not been president, and that his acceptance of any such offer would have been a misuse of the office.[9] True to his lifelong respect for public office, he refused to do anything that would diminish the dignity of the office or the trust with which it was held by the public.

Cabinet officers hosted the Coolidges in a series of farewell dinners, among which the most elaborate was that hosted by the president's friend and economics advisor, Secretary Mellon. As inauguration day approached, Coolidge obligingly observed, "The best thing I can do for the Hoover administration is to keep my mouth shut."[10] While he personally catalogued his letters and packed his White House files in meticulous fashion, the stock market sustained a December sell-off, quickly followed by a recovery. In less than five years the Dow had more than tripled. The Giant Bull Market, as it was commonly known, was truly unprecedented, and it was universally hailed as an integral part of the Coolidge legacy. Secretary Mellon had recently counseled that, "There is no cause for worry. The high tide of prosperity will continue."[11] And the country remained confidant.

True to his Yankee industriousness, Coolidge was up at 6:30 a.m. on his last morning as president and seated in his office where he signed a final stack of bills and executive orders. The morning papers saluted his "rugged integrity" and recalled how the country had turned "with relief and confidence to the unchallenged simplicity and purity" of his character.[12] The president left a parting salute to economy, his favorite theme of government, in pocket vetoing the Dale-Lehibach civil service retirement act. This bill had been passed unanimously by Congress and offered a modestly liberalized retirement annuity to civil servants with thirty or more years of service. It was widely believed that Coolidge

(COURTESY OF FORBES LIBRARY, NORTHAMPTON, MA)

Howard Chandler Christy was America's foremost portrait painter in the 1920s. Here are his handsome presidential portraits of the Coolidges.

would sign the measure, but he declined without offering a word of explanation.[13]

The photographs of the day captured a beaming President-elect Hoover riding alongside a typically dour President Coolidge, as they left the White House for the Capitol. Hoover later reported that Coolidge had offered a few words of parting advice to him as they motored down Pennsylvania Avenue, noting that, as president, "You have to stand every day three or four hours for visitors. Nine-tenths of them want something they ought not to have. If you keep dead-still they will run down in three or four minutes. If you even cough or smile they will start up all over again."[14]

One of the most memorable events came at the conclusion of the swearing in ceremony, when the hitherto solemn Coolidge suddenly smiled broadly while shaking hands with the new president. As the *Washington Post* reported, "There had been nothing seen like it since the man from Northampton had come to Washington. It was like watching a man unsling his haversack at the top of a hard climb. It caught the crowds as thousands ejaculated their surprise, 'Look at that grin!' The several hundred reporters who had covered Coolidge for eight years were as dumbfounded as if they had seen a chunk of New England granite burst into flame."[15]

After Hoover's inaugural address the Coolidges quickly departed the Capitol for Union Station and the ride to Northampton and retirement. Before boarding the train, Coolidge commented tersely, "Good-bye. I have had a very enjoyable time in Washington."

Coolidge was soon to write in *Autobiography* that because the American republic draws its presidents from the people, "It is a wholesome thing for them to return to the people. I came from them. I wish to be one of them again."[16] In keeping with these thoughts, he and his wife returned to the modest, rented duplex at 21 Massasoit Street and resumed the life they had left some fifteen years before. In *Autobiography* and a number of magazine articles, Coolidge predictably focused far more on his philosophy and personal values than on his political achievements.

Thanks to his lifetime of consistent frugality, Coolidge was a wealthy man. As governor and later as president, he had saved much of his salary and was reported to have a net worth of more than $400,000 when he returned to Northampton. He was determined to stay out of the public spotlight, but he found himself constantly fending off business proposals, reporters, and

(FORBES LIBRARY, NORTHAMPTON, MA)
The modest house on Massasoit Street in Northampton to which the Coolidges
returned after his presidency.

tourists. By 1930, the need for greater privacy led Coolidge to purchase a handsome residence called "The Beeches" located on the edge of town on nine secluded acres. After refusing countless business offers, he accepted a directorship of New Life Insurance Company and agreed to lead a number of prominent charitable boards.

Coolidge determinedly avoided all political involvement. He was careful not to offer advice to his successor, nor did Hoover seek his advice. He traveled monthly down to New York City for board meetings, and he and Grace visited Florida occasionally during the winter months. He worked daily from the same second story office where he had practiced law and which was still spartanly furnished with two straight back chairs, a bookcase, and a small wooden desk on a bare wooden floor. Grace Coolidge renewed her commitment to the Northampton Congregational church, and her husband joined her regularly at Sunday services.

(COURTESY FORBES LIBRARY, NORTHAMPTON, MA)

Coolidge thought it important that leaders "return to the people" after their term in office. Here in 1929, again as a citizen of Northampton, he sits on the porch of the house where he lived for years before his presidency.

In the months following Coolidge's retirement, the stock market began to show unsettling signs, and in October the Great Crash occurred. With his savings invested in a diversified portfolio of blue chip securities and with his usual tightfisted control of personal spending, Coolidge did not suffer personally to any substantial extent in the downturn. He supported Hoover and the Republicans as they sought to mitigate the severity of the depression despite his concern about government's expanding role.

In the early years of the depression, Coolidge remained popular and there was even nostalgic speculation in 1932 that the Republicans might renominate him. He supported Hoover's unsuccessful campaign for reelection in 1932 by delivering a nationally broadcast radio address from Madison Square Garden on October 11 and another radio address on Election Eve.

With the Democratic landslide of 1932, Coolidge felt the nation had entered "a new era to which I do not belong, and it would not be possible for me to adjust to it." He referred to the "socialistic notions of government" embraced by his successor and fellow Republican Herbert Hoover as well as those of the newly elected Franklin Roosevelt. In the weeks following the election, Coolidge confided to a close friend, "The election went against us more heavily than I anticipated. I suppose that, since it had to be, it is just as well that the Democrats have it lock, stock, and barrel." He went on clearly to foresee greater experimentation with government legislation, and he warned that the times called for renewed commitment to reduce government spending and taxes.[17]

Aside from his concern over the direction of the country, Coolidge's health was now declining rapidly. In late December, he complained to his former secretary, "The fact is I feel worn out. I know my work is done."[18] On New Years Day, 1933, his old Amherst classmate, Charles Andrews, visited Coolidge and reported his friend's saying, "I am too old for my years. I am afraid I am all burned out."[19] It was shortly thereafter, on January 5, that Coolidge rose earlier than usual, went downtown to his office, and read the morning papers, which were filled with unwelcome news of the incoming administration. He returned to The Beeches in midmorning, spoke to the gardener on his way into the house, and went up to his second floor bedroom, where he collapsed and died alone at age sixty-one.

The reservoir of popular goodwill for Coolidge was soon evident. The *New York Times* headlined, "City Shocked by News of Death." The New York Stock Exchange immediately lowered its massive flag to half-mast, as flags were likewise lowered around the nation. In New York City, Cardinal Hayes voiced "profound regret," Evangeline Booth of the Salvation Army lamented that "a pillar has fallen in our midst," and Al Smith averred his "great admiration." Former Treasury Secretary Mellon wired a tribute from aboard the *S. S. Majestic* en route from Europe, commending the president's "sincerity and soundness of judgment." President Hoover proclaimed thirty days of mourning in tribute to Coolidge's "lifetime of devotion to our country," while Congress adjourned both houses to attend a service of prayer and thanksgiving.[20]

The following day's newspapers were filled with tributes to Coolidge. His role in the Boston police strike of 1919 was widely recounted. The *New York Times* retold how his friends had warned him not to issue that famous declaration because they felt it would end his political career: "'Very likely,' he said; and signed it." The article went on to chronicle how the nation turned gratefully to him as "a man of the highest integrity and honesty" amidst revelations of the Harding scandals.

Numerous mentions were made of his humor. "What is your hobby?" a woman asked him at a Washington dinner party. "Holding office," he said seriously. His taciturnity, thrift, honesty, lack of pretense, and humility were roundly lauded; and his career-long commitment to individual freedom, limited government, and reduced taxation was duly noted. The *Times* eloquently summarized his service, "All during his life he never changed his character or methods. He listened, he assimilated, and he waited until there appeared what seemed to be the soundest course. He did not try to make circumstances; but, when they appeared in the right configuration, he acted. Otherwise, he waited. His distinguishing characteristic was his ability to wait in silence. At first it made him a subject of ridicule. Eventually his silence was regarded as a heroic manifestation and became a legend."[21]

Coolidge was appropriately buried on Saturday, January 7, avoiding any undue disruption to the weekday business and personal life of Northampton citizens. After a simple, dignified service at the Congregational Church, a funeral motorcade proceeded to Plymouth Notch, Vermont, for the president's burial. In a cold winter rain, the thirtieth president of the United States was returned to the rocky New England soil from whence he came. A plain headstone bears simply the name, Calvin Coolidge, the dates, and the presidential seal.

This simple granite tombstone marks the grave of the thirtieth president on a hillside outside Plymouth Notch, Vermont.

Perhaps the most surprising source of praise for Coolidge came from H. L. Mencken, a cynic not known for praising anyone or anything, who wrote perceptively of Coolidge, "If the day ever comes when Jefferson's warnings are heeded at last, and we reduce government to its simplest terms, it may very well happen that Cal's bones now resting inconspicuously in the Vermont granite will come to be revered as those of a man who really did the nation service."[22]

EPILOGUE

We cannot say "the past is the past"
without surrendering the future.
—Winston Churchill

"Fightin' Bob" La Follette was guilty of only slight exaggeration when he commenced his 1924 campaign with the reference to "a conflict between two principles of government as old as human history." Twentieth-century American political history was certainly dominated by the conflict between the left and the right over the proper role of government; and, much to the surprise of many mid-twentieth-century historians and economists, the clash was not resolved with the coming of FDR and the New Deal. The late twentieth-century ascendancy of conservatism in the United States under Reagan—and abroad under Thatcher and others—has assured the continuation of this conflict. Vigorous debate continues to rage over the political and economic aspects of the Coolidge Prosperity, the New Deal, the Great Society, and the Reagan Revolution.

The pertinence of this debate is obvious today as the United States again has changed course with the election of Barack Obama in 2008. American voters continue to be offered a fundamental choice between two very different forms of governance. The philosophy of La Follette and the Progressives was essentially that of Franklin Roosevelt, Lyndon Johnson, and now Obama, and the twenty-first-century Democratic Party, while the philosophy of Davis and Coolidge was essentially that of Reagan and the twenty-first-century Republican Party.

Often a national change of political course is justified because of economic emergency. The most severe economic emergencies of the past century were suffered before the elections of 1920, 1932, and 1980. The conservative policies that were adopted after 1920 and 1980 were quite different from the liberal policies followed after 1932; and the economic results were equally dissimilar. In the years immediately following both 1920 and 1980, Harding, Coolidge, and Reagan sharply cut taxes and simultaneously reduced federal domestic spending, while Roosevelt raised taxes and vastly increased government spending in the years after 1932. The 1920s and 1980s were periods of growth and economic prosperity, while the 1930s was a period of prolonged deflation and economic stagnation. Coolidge's presidential record and his well-reasoned speeches in support of his 1920s policies and Davis's brilliantly argued rebuttals to New Deal liberalism were significant chapters in the history of American conservatism. As America now adopts policies in reaction to the first economic emergency of the new century, it would do well to examine the 1920s and to consider the lives, the words, and the warnings of two of America's greatest conservatives, John W. Davis and Calvin Coolidge.

APPENDIX

The Votes in the 1924 Election

States	Popular Vote			Electoral Vote	
	Coolidge and Dawes, Republican	Davis and Bryan, Democrat	LaFollette and Wheeler, Progressive Socialist, and others	Coolidge and Dawes	Davis and Bryan
Alabama	45,005	112,966	8,084	—	12
Arizona	30,516	26,235	17,210	3	—
Arkansas	40,564	84,795	13,173	—	9
California	733,250	105,514	424,649	13	—
Colorado	195,171	75,238	69,945	6	—
Connecticut	246,322	110,184	42,416	7	—
Delaware	52,441	33,445	4,979	3	—
Florida	30,633	62,083	8,625	—	6
Georgia	30,300	123,200	12,691	—	14
Idaho	69,879	24,256	54,160	4	—
Illinois	1,453,321	576,975	432,027	29	—
Indiana	703,042	492,245	71,700	15	—
Iowa	537,635	162,600	272,243	13	—
Kansas	407,671	156,319	98,461	10	—
Kentucky	398,966	374,855	38,465	13	—
Louisiana	24,670	93,218	—	—	10
Maine	138,440	41,964	11,382	6	—
Maryland	162,414	148,072	47,157	8	—
Massachussetts	703,476	280,831	141,284	18	—
Michigan	874,631	152,359	122,014	15	—
Minnesota	420,759	55,913	339,192	12	—
Mississippi	8,546	100,476	3,494	—	10
Missouri	648,486	572,753	84,160	18	—
Montana	74,138	33,805	65,876	4	—
Nebraska	218,585	137,289	106,701	8	—

APPENDIX

	Popular Vote			Electoral Vote	
States	Coolidge and Dawes, Republican	Davis and Bryan, Democrat	LaFollette and Wheeler, Progressive Socialist, and others	Coolidge and Dawes	Davis and Bryan
Nevada	11,243	5,909	9,769	3	—
New Hampshire	98,575	57,201	8,993	4	—
New Jersey	676,277	298,043	109,028	14	—
New Mexico	54,745	48,542	9,543	3	—
New York	1,820,058	950,796	474,925	45	—
North Carolina	191,753	284,270	6,697	—	12
North Dakota	94,931	13,858	89,922	5	—
Ohio	1,176,130	477,888	357,948	24	—
Oklahoma	226,242	255,798	41,141	—	10
Oregon	142,579	67,589	68,403	5	—
Pennsylvania	1,401,481	409,192	307,567	38	—
Rhode Island	125,286	76,606	7,628	5	—
South Carolina	1,123	49,008	620	—	9
South Dakota	101,299	27,214	75,355	5	—
Tennessee	130,882	158.537	10,656	—	12
Texas	130,023	483,586	42,881	—	20
Utah	77,327	47,001	32,662	4	—
Vermont	80,498	16,124	5,964	4	—
Virginia	73,359	139,797	10,379	—	12
Washington	220,224	42,842	150,727	7	—
West Virginia	288,635	257,232	36,723	8	—
Wisconsin	311,614	68,096	453,678	—	—
Wyoming	41,858	12,868	25,174	3	—
	15,725,003	8,385,586	4,826,471	382	136

WISCONSIN GAVE 13 ELECTORAL VOTES TO LA FOLLETTE AND WHEELER.

ACKNOWLEDGMENTS

The research staffs of the Calvin Coolidge Collection at The Forbes Library, the West Virginia Regional and Historical Collection at the West Virginia University Libraries, the University Collections at Washington and Lee University, and the Sterling Library at Yale University have provided invaluable research assistance. Photography editor Sharon Donahue professionally managed the securing of permissions for the illustrations. Editors Jay Hodges and Lari Bishop, designer Brian Phillips, Justin Branch, and Matthew Donnelley of Greenleaf Book Group LLC were consistently diligent, constructive, and patient in preparing the manuscript for publication. University of North Carolina graduate student Robert Ferguson was a very able research assistant, who offered keen insights on numerous aspects of this book. Finally, a special word of thanks is reserved for Dr. Taylor Sanders, professor of history at Washington and Lee University, for his suggestions, corrections, guidance, and perspective.

NOTES

Preface

1. Paul Johnson, *Modern Times* (HarperCollins, 1991), 219.
2. Walter Lippmann, *Men of Destiny* (McMillan, 1927), 26.
3. Ibid., 212.
4. Robert Sobel, *Coolidge: An American Enigma* (Regnery Publishing Co., 1998), 194.
5. Allen Nevins and Henry Steele Commager, *A Pocket History of the United States* (Washington Square Press, 1967), 410.
6. *Wall Street Journal*, October 28, 2008, "Get Ready for the New New Deal," Paul Rubin.
7. Paul Johnson, *A History of the American People* (HarperCollins, 1997), 718.
8. William H. Harbaugh, *Lawyer's Lawyer: The Life of John W. Davis* (Oxford University Press, 1973), 248.

Chapter One: The Country Turns Right

1. James Chace, *1912: The Election that Changed the Country* (Simon & Schuster, 2004), 3.
2. Ibid., 7.
3. *History of American Presidential Elections, Volume III, 1900-1936*, "Election of 1924" by David Burner, (McGraw Hill, 1971), 2372.
4. Irving Stone, *They Also Ran: The History of the Men Who Were Defeated for the Presidency*, (Doubleday, 1944), 30.
5. Ibid., 31.
6. Frederick Lewis Allen, *Only Yesterday, An Intimate History of the 1920's*, (Harper & Row, 1931), 5.
7. Johnson, *A History of the American People*, 655.
8. Allen, *Only Yesterday*, 108.
9. *The New Republic*, March, 1921.

10. David Greenberg, *Calvin Coolidge* (Henry Holt, 2006), 31.

11. Ibid., 32–33.

12. Calvin Coolidge, *The Autobiography of Calvin Coolidge* (Cosmopolitan Book Co., 1929), 158.

Chapter Two: Coolidge's America: Arcadia or Babylon?

1. Yanek Mieczkowski, *The Routledge Historical Atlas of Presidential Elections* (Routledge, 2001), 90.

2. Allen, *Only Yesterday*, 39.

3. Ibid., 34.

4. Sobel, *Coolidge: An American Enigma*, 222.

5. *Messages and Papers of the Presidents*, "Acceptance Speech, 1920," Volume XVIII, 9647.

6. Johnson, *A History of the American People*, 709.

7. Ibid., 709.

8. Ibid., 708.

9. David Cannadine, *Mellon: An American Life*, (Random House, 2006), 287.

10. Allen Nevins and Henry Steele Commager, *A Pocket History of the United States* (Washington Square Press, 1967), 408.

11. Arthur M. Schlesinger, Jr., *The Cycle of American History* (Houghton Mifflin, 1986), 365.

12. Cannadine, *Mellon: An American Life*, 320.

13. Johnson, *A History of the American People*, 710.

14. Sobel, *Coolidge: An American Enigma*, 234.

15. This quote was reported by several sources, including Senator George Pepper of Pennsylvania and presidential portrait artist Charles Hopkinson.

16. William Allen White, *A Puritan in Babylon: The Story of Calvin Coolidge* (Simon Publications, 2001), v.

17. Johnson, *A History of the American People*, 712.

18. Ibid.

19. Lippmann, *Men of Destiny*, 13.

20. Greenberg, *Calvin Coolidge*, 60.

21. "The New President Coolidge," *Outlook*, August 15, 1923, 580.

22. Amity Shales, *The Forgotten Man* (HarperCollins, 2007), 38.

23. Sobel, *Coolidge: An American Enigma*, 242.

24. Ibid., 245.

25. Cannadine, *Mellon: An American Life*, 316.

26. *The Quotable Calvin Coolidge*, Peter Hannaford, editor (Images from the Past, Inc., 2001), 151.

27. Nevins and Commager, *A Pocket History of the United States*, 410.

28. Johnson, *Modern Times*, 27.

29. Johnson, *A History of the American People*, 718.

Chapter Three: The Democrats

1. Johnson, *A History of the American People*, 637.

2. Ibid., 639.

3. Ibid., 640.

4. Harbaugh, *Lawyer's Lawyer: The Life of John W. Davis*, 205.

5. Ibid., 206.

6. *New York Times*, "A Great Democrat," May 23, 1920.

7. Huntley, *The Life of John W. Davis*, 133

8. Theodore A. Huntley, *The Life of John W. Davis* (Duffield & Company, 1924), 127.

9. Harbaugh, *Lawyer's Lawyer: The Life of John W. Davis*, 196.

10. Johnson, *A History of the American People*, 682.

11. Sobel, *Coolidge: An American Enigma*, 280.

Chapter Four: The Republicans

1. Samuel Eliot Morison and Henry Steele Commager, *The Growth of the American Republic* (Oxford University Press, 1962), Vol. I, 439.

2. Ibid., 650.

3. Edmund Morris, *Theodore Rex*, (Random House, 2001), 30.

4. Ibid., 484.

5. *The Quotable Calvin Coolidge*, 131.

6. Cannadine, *Mellon: An American Life*, 310.

7. Allen, *Only Yesterday*, 116.

8. Ibid., 117.

Chapter Five: The Public Auditorium: Cleveland

1. Johnson, *Modern Times*, 223.

2. Sobel, *Coolidge: An American Enigma*, 227.

3. Greenberg, *Calvin Coolidge*, 46.

4. Ibid., 46.

5. *The New Republic*, March, 1924.

6. Greenberg, *Calvin Coolidge*, 64.

7. Thomas B. Silver, *Coolidge and the Historians* (Carolina Academic Press, 1982), 108.

8. *History of American Presidential Elections, Volume III, 1900-1936*, "Election of 1924" by David Burner, 2378.

9. *News & Observer*, June 10, 1924.

10. *New York Times*, June 10, 1924.

11. Ibid.

12. *Herald Tribune*, June 10, 1924.

13. Paul F. Boller, *Presidential Campaigns* (Oxford University Press, 2004), 219.

14. *New York Times*, June 11, 1924.

15. Boller, *Presidential Campaigns*, 218.

16. *News & Observer*, June 14, 1924.

17. *New York Times*, June 13, 1924.

18. Sobel, *Coolidge: An American Enigma*, 242.

19. *New York Times*, June 14, 1924.

Chapter Six: Madison Square Garden

1. *Washington Post*, June 25, 1924.

2. *New York Times*, May 23, 1920.

3. John W. Davis, "Reminiscences by John W. Davis" (Columbia University Oral History Project, 1954), 149.

4. Huntley, *The Life of John W. Davis*, 133.

5. Ibid., 134.

6. Ibid., 135.

7. Ollinger Crenshaw, *General Lee's College* (Random House, 1969), 312.

8. *W&L Alumni Magazine*, January, 1980.

9. *News & Observer*, June 25, 1924.

10. Stone, *They Also Ran: The History of the Men Who Were Defeated for the Presidency*, 331.

11. *Washington Post*, June 26, 1924.

12. Ibid.

13. *News & Observer*, June 28, 1924.

14. Ibid.

15. *Washington Post*, June 26, 1924.

16. *News & Observer*, June 26, 1924.

17. Ibid., June 30, 1924.

18. *Washington Post,* June 30, 1924.

19. Boller, *Presidential Campaigns*, 218.

20. *News & Observer*, July 2, 1924.

21. *Washington Post*, July 2, 1924.

22. Ibid., July 5, 1924.

23. *History of American Presidential Elections, Volume III, 1900-1936,* "Election of 1924" by David Burner, 2469.

24. Robert K. Murray, *The 103rd Ballot* (Harper & Row, 1976), 228.

25. *Washington Post*, July 5, 1924.

26. *News & Observer*, July 5, 1924.

27. Ibid., July 6, 1924.

28. Robert K. Murray, *The 103rd Ballot* (Harper & Row, 1976), 228.

29. Ibid., 219.

30. *News & Observer*, July 9, 1924.

31. Harbaugh, *Lawyer's Lawyer: The Life of John W. Davis*, 219.

32. Walter Lippmann, "The Setting for John W. Davis," *Atlantic Monthly*, October, 1924.

Chapter Seven: The Most Perfect Gentleman

1. *News & Observer*, July 9, 1924.

2. Walter Lippmann, "The Setting for John W. Davis," *Atlantic Monthly*, October, 1924.

3. John W. Davis, "Reminiscences by John W. Davis," 18.

4. Ibid., 26.

5. Huntley, *The Life of John W. Davis*, (Duffield & Co., 1924), 26.

6. John W. Davis, "Reminiscences by John W. Davis," 31.

7. Ibid., 28–30.

8. Ibid., 26.

9. Huntley, *The Life of John W. Davis*, 26.

10. Harbaugh, *Lawyer's Lawyer: The Life of John W. Davis*, 15.

11. Crenshaw, *General Lee's College*, Chapter 19.

12. Harbaugh, *Lawyer's Lawyer: The Life of John W. Davis*, 15.

13. Huntley, *The Life of John W. Davis*, 50.

14. John W. Davis, "Reminiscences by John W. Davis," 29.

15. Harbaugh, *Lawyer's Lawyer: The Life of John W. Davis*, 17–19.

16. Ibid., 20.

17. John W. Davis, "Reminiscences by John W. Davis," 24–26.

18. Ibid., 32.

19. Ibid., 34.

20. Frederick A. O. Schwartz, III, "The Political Career of John W. Davis" (Harvard University unpublished dissertation, 1957), 4.

21. John W. Davis, "Reminiscences by John W. Davis," 41.

22. Ibid., 57.

23. Harbaugh, *Lawyer's Lawyer: The Life of John W. Davis*, 33.

24. Ibid., 32.

25. John W. Davis, "Reminiscences by John W. Davis," 62.

26. Huntley, *The Life of John W. Davis*, 64.

27. Ibid., 68.

28. Harbaugh, *Lawyer's Lawyer: The Life of John W. Davis*, 65.

29. Ibid., 69.

30. John W. Davis, "Reminiscences by John W. Davis," 63.

31. Huntley, *The Life of John W. Davis*, 77.

32. Harbaugh, *Lawyer's Lawyer: The Life of John W. Davis*, 81.

33. Ibid., 83.

34. Huntley, *The Life of John W. Davis*, 88.

35. Harbaugh, *Lawyer's Lawyer: The Life of John W. Davis*, 87.

36. John W. Davis, "Reminiscences by John W. Davis," 85–86.

37. Schwartz, "The Political Career of John W. Davis," 23.

38. Harbaugh, *Lawyer's Lawyer: The Life of John W. Davis*, 101.

39. Ibid., 106.

40. Ibid., 101–102.

41. Davis, "Reminiscences by John W. Davis," 88.

42. *The Ambassadorial Diary of John W. Davis*, edited by Julia Davis and Dolores A. Fleming (West Virginia University Press, 1993), 216.

43. Harbaugh, *Lawyer's Lawyer: The Life of John W. Davis*, 102–3.

44. Letter from John W. Davis to John J. Davis, January 14, 1915.

45. *The Ambassadorial Diary of John W. Davis*, 2.

46. Huntley, *The Life of John W. Davis*, 110–111.

47. *Washington Post*, September 17, 1918.

48. Ibid., 112.

49. Letter from John W. Davis to Ellen B. Davis, September 23, 1918.

50. Harbaugh, *Lawyer's Lawyer: The Life of John W. Davis*, 147.

51. Ibid., 146.

52. Schwartz, "The Political Career of John W. Davis," 34.

53. John W. Davis, "Reminiscences by John W. Davis," 133.

54. Huntley, *The Life of John W. Davis,* 119.

55. John W. Davis, "Reminiscences by John W. Davis," 148.

56. *The Ambassadorial Diary of John W. Davis*, 415.

57. Huntley, *The Life of John W. Davis*, 128.

58. *The Ambassadorial Diary of John W. Davis,* edited by Julia Davis and Dolores A. Fleming (West Virginia University Press, 1993), August 2, 1919, 125.

59. *New York Times,* May 23, 1920.

60. Harbaugh, *Lawyer's Lawyer: The Life of John W. Davis*, 173.

61. *The Ambassadorial Diary of John W. Davis*, 305.

62. Harbaugh, *Lawyer's Lawyer: The Life of John W. Davis*, 184.

63. Ibid., 191.

64. Ibid., 192.

Chapter Eight: Above All Things, Be Brief

1. Sobel, *Coolidge: An American Enigma*, 15.

2. Coolidge, *The Autobiography of Calvin Coolidge*, 37.

3. White, *A Puritan in Babylon: The Story of Calvin Coolidge*, 10.

4. Gamaliel Bradford, *The Quick and the Dead* (Houghton Mifflin, 1931), 106.

5. Allen, *Only Yesterday, An Intimate History of the the 1920's,* 22.

6. Coolidge, *The Autobiography of Calvin Coolidge*, 13.

7. Ibid., 10.

8. Ibid., 11.

9. Ibid., 13.

10. White, *A Puritan in Babylon: The Story of Calvin Coolidge*, 22.

11. Calvin Coolidge, *The Autobiography of Calvin Coolidge*, 43.

12. Sobel, *Coolidge: An American Enigma*, 30.

13. Coolidge, *The Autobiography of Calvin Coolidge*, 45.

14. White, *A Puritan in Babylon: The Story of Calvin Coolidge*, 30.

15. Coolidge, *The Autobiography of Calvin Coolidge*, 49.

16. Ibid., 50.

17. Greenberg, *Calvin Coolidge*, 20.

18. Ibid., 20.

19. Coolidge, *The Autobiography of Calvin Coolidge*, 65.

20. White, *A Puritan in Babylon: The Story of Calvin Coolidge*, 37.

21. Sobel, *Coolidge: An American Enigma*, 33.

22. David Greenberg, *Calvin Coolidge*, 20.

23. Sobel, *Coolidge: An American Enigma*, 43.

24. Greenberg, *Calvin Coolidge*, 22.

25. White, *A Puritan in Babylon: The Story of Calvin Coolidge*, 62.

26. Coolidge, *The Autobiography of Calvin Coolidge*, 95.

27. Ibid., 97.

28. Sobel, *Coolidge: An American Enigma*, 62.

29. Ibid., 64.

30. Michael E. Hennessey, *Four Decades of Massachusetts Politics* (G.P. Putnam, 1924), 162.

31. Ibid., 158.

32. White, *A Puritan in Babylon: The Story of Calvin Coolidge*, 71.

33. Coolidge, *The Autobiography of Calvin Coolidge*, 107.

34. Ibid., 107–8.

35. Sobel, *Coolidge: An American Enigma*, 87.

36. Ibid., 93.

37. Grace Coolidge, *The Real Calvin Coolidge* (Boston, 1935), 247.

38. Coolidge, *The Autobiography of Calvin Coolidge*, 113.

39. Grace Coolidge, *The Real Calvin Coolidge*, 249.

40. White, *A Puritan in Babylon: The Story of Calvin Coolidge*, 123.

41. Coolidge, *The Autobiography of Calvin Coolidge*, 121–2.

42. Sobel, *Coolidge: An American Enigma*, 111.

43. Ibid., 114.

44. Greenberg, *Calvin Coolidge*, 27.

45. Sobel, *Coolidge: An American Enigma*, 119.

46. Ibid., 122.

47. White, *A Puritan in Babylon: The Story of Calvin Coolidge*, 145.

48. Calvin Coolidge, *The Autobiography of Calvin Coolidge*, 134.

49. Ibid., 135.

50. *The New York World*, September 13, 1919.

51. Ibid., 95.

52. Coolidge, *The Autobiography of Calvin Coolidge*, 141.

53. Greenberg, *Calvin Coolidge*, 44.

54. White, *A Puritan in Babylon: The Story of Calvin Coolidge*, 150.

Chapter Nine: Fightin' Bob

1. David M. Thelen, *Robert M. La Follette and the Insurgent Spirit*, (Little, Brown & Co., 1976), vii.

2. Louis W. Koenig, *Bryan: A Political Biography of William Jennings Bryan*, (G. P. Putnam's Sons, 1971), 189.

3. Ibid., 195.

4. Chace, *1912*, 102.

5. Ibid., 104.

6. Ibid., 59.

7. Ibid., 61.

8. Thelen, 79.

9. Johnson, *A History of the American People*, 637.

10. Ibid., 636.

11. Thelen, *Robert M. La Follette and the Insurgent Spirit*, 83.

12. *Time*, July 14, 1924.

13. *Time*, July 24, 1924.

14. *Time*, July 14, 1924.

15. Ibid.

16. *Washington Post*, July 6, 1924.

17. *History of American Presidential Elections, Volume III, 1900-1936*, "Election of 1924" by David Burner, 2540.

Chapter Ten: Say *Something!*

1. Harbaugh, *Lawyer's Lawyer: The Life of John W. Davis*, 221.

2. *History of American Presidential Elections, Volume III, 1900-1936*, "Election of 1924" by David Burner, 2476.

3. Ibid, 2479.

4. *New York Times*, August 3, 1924.

5. Schwartz, "The Political Career of John W. Davis," 66.

6. Gil Troy, *See How They Ran* (Harvard University Press, 1996), 150.

7. Schwartz, "The Political Career of John W. Davis," 65.

8. *New York Times*, August 12, 1924.

9. Ibid.

10. *The Nation*, August 20, 1924.

11. *New York Times*, August 17, 1924.

12. Text of the speech is in Davis Papers, Sterling Library, Yale University.

13. Harbaugh, *Lawyer's Lawyer: The Life of John W. Davis*, 229.

14. *New York Times*, August 31, 1924.

15. *New York Times*, August 24, 1924.

16. Harbaugh, *Lawyer's Lawyer: The Life of John W. Davis*, 226.

17. Ibid., 235.

18. Troy, *See How They Ran*, 150.

19. *Washington Post*, September 14 and 21, 1924.

20. *Washington Post*, September 21 and 28 and October 5, 1924.

21. Schwartz, "The Political Career of John W. Davis," 70.

22. *New York Times*, October 26, 1924.

23. Troy, *See How They Ran*, 150.

24. Schwartz, "The Political Career of John W. Davis," 72.

25. Ibid., 74.

26. *The Nation*, November 15, 1924.

27. *New York Times*, March 25, 1955.

Chapter Eleven: Keeping Cool with Coolidge

1. White, *A Puritan in Babylon: The Story of Calvin Coolidge*, 295.

2. *Time*, August 13, 1923.

3. *Time*, October 1, 1923.

4. White, *A Puritan in Babylon: The Story of Calvin Coolidge*, 296.

5. *The Quotable Calvin Coolidge*, 151.

6. White, *A Puritan in Babylon: The Story of Calvin Coolidge*, 247.

7. Sobel, *Coolidge: An American Enigma*, 35.

8. "The New President Coolidge," *Outlook*, August 15, 1923.

9. *The Quotable Calvin Coolidge*, 134.

10. Boller, *Presidential Campaigns*, 218.

11. White, *A Puritan in Babylon: The Story of Calvin Coolidge*, 260.

12. Robert Gilbert, *The Mortal Presidency* (Basic Books, 1992), 36.

13. Troy, *See How They Ran*, 147.

14. Ibid., 148.

15. *History of American Presidential Elections, Volume III, 1900-1936*, "Election of 1924" by David Burner, 2485.

16. *New York Times*, August 3, 1924.

17. *Messages and Papers of the Presidents*, "Coolidge's Acceptance Speech," Volume XVIII, 9642.

18. *The Quotable Calvin Coolidge*, 48.

19. Sobel, *Coolidge: An American Enigma*, 302–3.

20. *Time*, September 29, 1924.

21. Ibid.

22. *The Quotable Calvin Coolidge*, 139.

23. *A Compilation of the Messages and Papers of the Presidents*, Volume XVIII (Bureau of National Literature, 1930), 9428.

24. *New York Times,* August 17, 1924.

25. Greenberg, *Calvin Coolidge*, 104.

26. Ibid.

27. *Time*, November 10, 1924.

28. Sobel, *Coolidge: An American Enigma*, 305.

Chapter Twelve: A Progressive Whimper

1. *History of American Presidential Elections, Volume III, 1900-1936*, "Election of 1924" by David Burner, 2487.

2. *Time*, July 14, 1924.

3. *Raleigh News & Observer*, October 14, 1924.

4. *History of American Presidential Elections, Volume III, 1900-1936*, "Election of 1924" by David Burner, 2541.

5. Harbaugh, *Lawyer's Lawyer: The Life of John W. Davis*, 229.

6. Thelen, *Robert M. La Follette and the Insurgent Spirit*, 139.

7. Ibid., 152.

8. Ibid., 156.

9. Ibid., 173.

10. Ibid., 185.

11. Ibid., 189.

12. *Time*, June 29, 1925.

13. Koenig, *Bryan: A Political Biography of William Jennings Bryan*, 626.

Chapter Thirteen: Landslide!

1. Sobel, *Coolidge: An American Enigma*, 305.

2. Davis, "Reminiscences by John W. Davis," 149–150.

3. *New York Times*, August 10, 1924.

4. *New York Times*, October 26, 1924.

5. *Saint Louis Dispatch*, November 6, 1924.

6. Troy, *See How They Ran*, 150.

7. *History of American Presidential Elections, Volume III, 1900-1936,* "Election of 1924" by David Burner, 2487.

8. *New Republic,* November, 1924.

9. Davis, "Reminiscences by John W. Davis," 151.

10. Boller, *Presidential Campaigns,* 220.

11. Troy, *See How They Ran,* 148.

12. Ron Chernow, *The House of Morgan* (Simon & Schuster, 1990), 254.

13. Harbaugh, *Lawyer's Lawyer: The Life of John W. Davis,* 246.

14. Davis, "Reminiscences by John W. Davis," 152–3.

15. John W. Davis, *Party Government in the United States* (Princeton University Press, 1929), 17.

16. White, *A Puritan in Babylon: The Story of Calvin Coolidge,* 309.

Chapter Fourteen: The Twenties Roar On

1. *Washington Post,* December 4, 1924.

2. David Cannadine, *Mellon,* 316.

3. *Washington Post,* March 5, 1925.

4. Sobel, *Coolidge: An American Enigma,* 326.

5. Silver, *Coolidge and the Historians,* 111.

6. Ibid., 130.

7. Veronique de Rugy, "1920's Income Tax Cuts" (Cato Institute, March 4, 2003).

8. Johnson, *A History of the American People,* 718.

9. *American Heritage History of the 20's and 30's,* Ralph Andrist, editor, (American Heritage Publishing Co, 1970), 28.

10. *This Fabulous Century* (Time Life Books, New York, 1969), 99.

11. Walter Lippmann *Men of Destiny,* (McMillan, 1927), 15.

12. *Messages and Papers of the Presidents* "Coolidge's Veto of McNairy Haugen Bill," Volume XVIII, 9658.

13. John Kenneth Galbraith, *The Great Crash, 1929* (Time, inc. 1961), 17.

14. Ibid.

15. Johnson, *A History of the American People,* 735.

16. Johnson, *Modern Times: The World from the Twenties to the Nineties,* 244.

17. *This Fabulous Century,* 218.

Chapter Fifteen: Lawyers' Lawyer

1. Harbaugh, *Lawyer's Lawyer: The Life of John W. Davis,* 253.

2. Davis, "Reminiscences by John W. Davis," 162.

3. Harbaugh, *Lawyer's Lawyer: The Life of John W. Davis,* 321.

4. Ibid, 354–5.

5. J. P. Morgan & Co. partners to John W. Davis, June 12, 1933.

6. Ibid., 249.
7. Davis, *Party Government in the United States*, 39.
8. Harbaugh, *Lawyer's Lawyer: The Life of John W. Davis*, 271.
9. Ibid., 273.
10. *New York Times*, October 12, 1928.
11. Harbaugh, *Lawyer's Lawyer: The Life of John W. Davis*, 339.
12. Letter from John W. Davis to Walter Lippmann, June 24, 1935.
13. *New York Times*, October 30, 1932.
14. *New York Times*, March 5, 1933.
15. Schwartz, "The Political Career of John W. Davis," 90.
16. Ibid., 93.
17. *New York Times*, July 11, 1934.
18. Harbaugh, *Lawyer's Lawyer: The Life of John W. Davis*, 265.
19. Davis, "Reminiscences by John W. Davis," 167.
20. Schwartz, "The Political Career of John W. Davis," 109.
21. *New York Times*, October 21, 1936.
22. Harbaugh, *Lawyer's Lawyer: The Life of John W. Davis*, 355.
23. Shales, *The Forgotten Man*, 11.
24. "Davis: 'The Country Lawyer,'" *W&L Alumni Magazine*, April, 1973.
25. Harbaugh, *Lawyer's Lawyer: The Life of John W. Davis*, 267.
26. Davis, "Reminiscences by John W. Davis," 93.
27. Harbaugh, *Lawyer's Lawyer: The Life of John W. Davis*, 464.
28. *New York Herald Tribune*, May 13, 1952.
29. Ibid.
30. Harbaugh, *Lawyer's Lawyer: The Life of John W. Davis*, 482.
31. Ibid., 492.
32. Ibid., 493.
33. *Time*, December 22, 1952.
34. Harbaugh, *Lawyer's Lawyer: The Life of John W. Davis*, 495.
35. Ibid., 514.
36. Alexander Bickel, *The Least Dangerous Branch* (Praeger Publishers, 2002), 42.
37. Harbaugh, *Lawyer's Lawyer: The Life of John W. Davis*, 518.
38. *New York Times*, April 13, 1953.
39. *New York Times*, April 13 and 14, 1953.
40. Harbaugh, *Lawyer's Lawyer: The Life of John W. Davis*, 526.
41. *New York Times*, March 26, 1955.
42. *Washington Post*, March 27, 1955.

Chapter Sixteen: American Sphinx

1. Sobel, *Coolidge: An American Enigma*, 368.

2. Coolidge, *The Autobiography of Calvin Coolidge*, 241.

3. Sobel, *Coolidge: An American Enigma*, 373.

4. Shales, *The Forgotten Man*, 38.

5. Cannadine, *Mellon: An American Life*, 280.

6. Sobel, *Coolidge: An American Enigma*, 384.

7. *New York Times*, December 5, 1928.

8. Sobel, *Coolidge: An American Enigma*, 389.

9. White, *A Puritan in Babylon: The Story of Calvin Coolidge*, 415.

10. Ibid., 416.

11. Greenberg, *Calvin Coolidge*, 145.

12. *New York Times*, March 3, 1929.

13. *Washington Post*, March 5, 1929.

14. *The Quotable Calvin Coolidge*, 166.

15. *Washington Post*, March 5, 1929.

16. Coolidge, *The Autobiography of Calvin Coolidge*, 243.

17. White, *A Puritan in Babylon: The Story of Calvin Coolidge*, 438.

18. Sobel, *Coolidge: An American Enigma*, 412.

19. White, *A Puritan in Babylon: The Story of Calvin Coolidge*, 440.

20. *New York Times*, January 6, 1933.

21. Ibid.

22. Henry L. Mencken, *A Carnival of Buncombe* (Johns Hopkins, 1956), 61.

INDEX

NOTE: *Italic* page numbers indicate photographs and cartoons.

(